THE ALIEN WITHIN

THE ALIEN WITHIN

Representations of the Exotic in
Twentieth-Century Japanese Literature

Leith Morton

University of Hawai'i Press
HONOLULU

Library of Congress Cataloging-in-Publication Data
Morton, Leith.
    The alien within : representations of the exotic in
twentieth-century Japanese literature / Leith Morton.
        p. cm.
    Includes bibliographical references and index.
    ISBN 978-0-8248-3292-6 (hard cover : alk. paper)
1. Japanese literature—20th century—History and criticism.
I. Title.
    PL726.8.M65 2009
    895.6'091—dc22
                                                2008040722

University of Hawaiʻi Press books are printed on acid-free
paper and meet the guidelines for permanence and durability
of the Council on Library Resources.

Designed by the University of Hawaiʻi Press Production Department

Printed by The Maple-Vail Book Manufacturing Group

CONTENTS

PREFACE

I have to thank a number of people without whose support and assistance this book would not have been written. A number of the chapters began life as papers read at symposia and scholarly conferences held at universities in Australia, North America, Japan, and Europe. In particular, in Australia I wish to thank colleagues at the universities of Sydney, Newcastle, and Queensland; Monash University; and the Australian National University. In addition I want to thank the staff at the National Library of Australia, where I read an early version of Chapter 8 to a 2003 conference on Japan and Australia.

In Europe I should also like to thank colleagues for providing venues where I was able to read early versions of certain chapters: at the University of Leeds, London University, and the Open University in Britain; the University of Bologna in Italy; Leiden University in the Netherlands; and Trier University in Germany. Also, the members of the Académie du Midi in France have helped in more ways than I can mention, especially by providing a most hospitable environment for the various symposia held at Alet-les-Bains in which to try out my ideas. In Canada, the University of Alberta at Edmonton provided an early venue for some of my work on Yosano Akiko. In the United States, conferences organized by the Association for Japanese Literary Studies founded by Sekine Eiji held at Purdue University and the University of Colorado at Boulder also provided a congenial environment for the development of my research on Yosano Akiko. Michael Brownstein's collegial invitation to visit the University of Notre Dame in Indiana also helped to hone my ideas about Yosano Akiko. I wish to thank colleagues at the International Research Center for Japanese Studies (Nichibunken) in Kyoto, whose bimonthly symposia have been of enormous assistance in helping me sharpen my focus and broaden my knowledge. And I owe a special debt of thanks to my colleagues at the Tokyo Institute of

Technology (Tokyo Kōgyō Daigaku) who have helped in numerous ways. Also in Japan, I should like to thank colleagues in Okinawa and Tokyo (at Hōsei and Waseda Universities in particular) for their support for my research on Ōshiro Tatsuhiro, and also Ōshiro Tatsuhiro himself, who has shown me the utmost kindness. To all the staff in these institutions who have been most generous with their time and resources and also for the financial and other support provided, I offer my deepest gratitude.

Some individuals have played more prominent roles than others in helping me to research this book over the last decade, and to these people I must express my most sincere thanks. In alphabetical order, I thank Hamashita Masahiro, Hattori Takakazu, Hokama Shuzen, Iguchi Tokio, Inoue Ken, Katsukata-Inafuku Keiko, Nakahodo Masanori, Sasaki Ken'ichi, and especially Suzuki Sadami. Also in Japan, I have to express my deep gratitude to my colleague Roger Pulvers at the Tokyo Institute of Technology, who has helped me in ways too numerous to mention.

Outside Japan, I wish particularly to thank, in Australia: Yasuko and Barry Claremont, Hugh Clarke, Alison Broinowski, Garvin Perram (for his friendship and support), Catherine Runcie, Matsui Sakuko, and last but certainly not least, Alison Tokita. In North America I thank: Janice Brown, Michael Brownstein, Charles Ess, Faye Kleeman, Bill LaFleur, Michael Marra, Earl Miner (lately deceased), Mike Molasky, Tom Rimer, Laurel Rodd, Raj Singh, and Stephen Snyder. And in Europe my gratitude to: Steve Dodds, Drew Gerstle, Rachael Hutchinson (then at Leeds University), Grazia Marchianó, Yves Millet, Hans-Georg Möller, Karl-Heinz Pohl, Finn Riedel, Sonja Servomaa (lately deceased), Stanca Scholz-Cionca, Robert Wilkinson, Mark Williams, and Günter Wohlfart.

I also want to thank especially my commissioning editor at the University of Hawai'i Press, Pamela Kelley, for her continuing and unwavering support (this is the second book of mine she has edited); also I am grateful to the two anonymous readers at the University of Hawai'i Press, whose suggestions much improved the manuscript. I also owe a large vote of thanks to Margaret Black, my proof editor at the University of Hawai'i Press, for the many improvements she has made to the book. My family has always provided staunch backup, and this time is no exception—special thanks to my wife, Sachiko, who has put up with much in assisting and supporting me.

Early versions of Chapters 1, 6, and 7 were published previously in vols. 30 (1998), 35 (2003), and 36–37 (2004–2005) of *The Journal of the Oriental Society of Australia;* I would like to express my thanks for permission to republish. Also, an early version of Chapter 2 appeared previously in *The Renewal of Song,* published by Seagull Books, Calcutta, in 2000. I would like to thank the publisher for permission to republish. A part version of Chapter 3 appeared in *New Essays in Comparative Aesthetics* (2007), edited by Robert Wilkinson; my thanks go to Robert for the opportunity to publish. Unless stated otherwise, all translations are my own.

INTRODUCTION

Much of what is said here
must be said twice,
a reminder that no one
Takes an immediate interest in the pain of others
——Billy Collins

My mother was Dutch
My father a Jew
And that is why I
Am so different from you.
——Stevie Smith

On a recent visit to the Shibuya ward office, or Shibuya city (these days Tokyo wards are often renaming themselves as cities), to renew my Japanese work visa, I noticed that the *gaikokujin tōroku* area had changed its English sign from "alien registration" to "foreigners [sic] registration." The registration area was still hidden away in a kind of alcove not easily visible from the main counter area. This shift in translation does not affect the vast majority of Japanese citizens, who know the titles of government services only in Japanese, but it does, perhaps, reflect a deeper understanding of the meanings attached to the English words "alien" and "foreigner." Movies like the *Alien* series featuring Sigourney Weaver—the title has been translated into Japanese phonetically as *Eirian*—have given people some understanding of the negative connotations evoked by the notion of the alien. The idea of "alien" as embracing a core meaning of nonhuman—a complex of associations that summons up the image of something deeply repulsive to one's own humanity—may nevertheless linger even in the notion of "foreign," as it has traditionally been understood by most Japanese. This connotation became especially embedded in the antiforeign propaganda disseminated by the Tokugawa government, aimed principally at Christianity, during the so-called era of "seclusion" *(sakoku)* that lasted from the seventeenth to the middle of the nineteenth century.[1]

Gerald Figal has written of the arrival of Westerners in mid-nineteenth-century Japan as follows: "Since Perry's arrival in 1853, the increased news, presence, and fear of foreigners—especially among xenophobic commoners—created conditions that were ripe for the strategic use of *bakemono* (monsters) to exploit a general fear of strangers."[2] Fear of the foreigner is a recurring theme in the cultural history of many nations besides Japan, but given Japan's relative isolation from other cultures during the Tokugawa era, the theme takes on a certain significance that may be absent elsewhere or at least more attenuated. While most Japanese from the Tokugawa period into the early years of the Meiji regime viewed foreigners with some trepidation, some intellectuals and artists displayed an intense interest in the exotic and the foreign, as is well documented by historians like George Sansom.[3] This interest persisted well into the twentieth century and has been linked by cultural historians such as Miriam Silverberg to the emerging Japanese empire, a multicultural empire where the foreign was, in a way, brought home.[4] From the Meiji period onwards, the absorption into Japan proper of foreign territories—the Ryūkyūs, Taiwan, Manchuria, and Korea to name the most prominent—meant that the foreign and the exotic signified not only the West but also something that was both Japanese and not Japanese, Asian certainly, with affinities to Japanese culture, yet still foreign and exotic, ripe for exploration and exploitation. And this is precisely what Japanese artists and writers did, with increasing gusto, as their literary adventures took them inside Japan as well as outside.

This book focuses more on the inside than the outside; that is, I am concerned with how modern Japanese writers discovered the foreign, the exotic, or even the alien within themselves, in some cases within their own bodies, in other cases within their own literary traditions. This study also treats the question of how the foreign has been absorbed into the Japanese literary sensibility, whether by translation, as in the case of translating Shakespeare, or by direct observation, in the form of travel diaries.

It is possible to argue that the distinctly twentieth-century literary obsession of Japanese writers with interior states, and the relativizing of the self against the Other in the production of literary texts, owes its impetus in some sense to the massive expansion of the Japanese empire, which brought Japan into wide-ranging and extensive contact with the alien for the first time in its history.[5] The impact of foreigners on Meiji Japan had been confined to a small number of foreign settlements, and contact with a tiny number of the elite rather than with ordinary people, unlike what happened during the expansion of Japanese settlement on the Asian continent in the first decades of the twentieth century. A number of historians have suggested that Japanese imperialism and culture are linked, and a number of literary critics—perhaps most prominently Komori Yōichi—have attempted to find connections between modern Japanese literature and Japanese imperialism.[6]

Yet literary texts are notoriously resistant to such interpretations, based as most of them are on the premise that the world of the text or the people described there are lies, beautiful lies in many instances, but fiction nonetheless. The suspension of disbelief that characterizes the reading of fiction not only acts to forestall or suspend judgment about the factual veracity (although not verisimilitude) of the text, but also, in some texts, the consideration of ethical norms. This is not to say that ethical criticism of literature is rare or unwarranted but that it is a much more complicated matter than simply taking a position about the content, broadly interpreted, of texts.[7] The use of rhetorical and stylistic strategies like irony, ubiquitous in much twentieth-century Japanese writing, also makes the hermeneutic act an exceedingly difficult one, since many, if not most literary texts, undercut or problematize the normative values enacted in those very same texts.[8] That is why literary commentators have often resorted to reading the text as a performative act, capable of many twists and turns depending upon the precise nature of the interaction between the reader and text. The language of the novel or poem has come under intense scrutiny by such distinguished literary critics as Maeda Ai and Kamei Hideo, both recently translated into English, who take great pains to tease out the slight, subtle, but immensely important significance of shifts in narrative mode, tone, register, and so forth.[9] This study has learned from these critics, and much of its analysis is a form of close reading inspired by such scholarship as well as by the work of like-minded Western critics.

In addition, a number of researchers have already touched upon the particular theme of the foreigner in literature, and their scholarship has helped in various ways. In 1988 Kinya Tsuruta edited a pioneering collection of essays entitled *The Walls Within: Images of Westerners in Japan and Images of the Japanese Abroad.* The first half discusses images of Westerners in modern Japanese fiction and poetry, with essays by distinguished specialists in Japanese literature such as Yoshiko Yokochi Samuel, Ted Goosen, Steve Rabson, and Tsuruta himself.[10] Other scholars of modern Japanese literature in the West, including Atsuko Sakaki and Indra Levy, have also touched upon the theme in passing, often focusing on the treatment of Asians from Japan's overseas empire. Rachael Hutchinson and Mark Williams have edited a recent volume of essays (one of my essays is included) on the topic of "the Other in Japanese literature," and their viewpoint and mine are not dissimilar.[11] Susan Napier's important 1996 book entitled *The Fantastic in Modern Japanese Literature*, which includes a chapter on "the alien in modern Japanese fantasy," has served as a particular source of inspiration for this volume. Napier's analysis of Izumi Kyōka and Tanizaki Jun'ichirō was of much use in formulating the ideas of the gothic in Chapter 4.[12]

Many scholars writing in Japanese have also dealt with aspects of the foreign and exotic, and I have drawn upon this when appropriate. Undoubtedly there are studies I have overlooked, but it is important to note that my approach differs significantly in several respects from much of the writing in English referred to above. My journey in this volume does not confine itself to images of Westerners or to depictions of Asia as the Other. Instead, I range further and investigate how Japanese writers internalized the exotic through the adoption of modernist techniques and subject matter. By analyzing, for example, the modern Japanese version of gothic literature, I attempt to arrive at a deeper understanding of several early twentieth-century novelists whose fiction was pivotal in securing the dominance of modernist modes of expression in Japanese writing. I also treat such themes as the portrayal of Okinawa in postwar literature. Okinawa is usually depicted by mainstream writers as an exotic, tropical enclave lodged uncomfortably within the body of Japanese literature, but I examine the literature created by Okinawans themselves, and even examine how a poet like Yosano Akiko could sense the alien within herself in her scarifying vision of the process of childbirth. Thus the scope of this book is more diffuse and larger in theme than is true of much English-language scholarship. It has some affinities with European scholarship, especially with such authors as the novelist and scholar Marina Warner. Despite the fact that I do not quote from her books in this volume, I have read and reread a number of her works in order to gain an understanding of how to "read the alien" within texts that may not appear to deal overtly with the topic. Among Warner's many works that explore the alien within ourselves, her justly acclaimed *No Go the Bogeyman* (1998), on the bogeyman in European culture, simultaneously delighted and frightened me, and encouraged me to try my hand at something similar in this book, albeit on a much smaller scale, and on the topic of the exotic rather than the horrific.

Current scholarship, whether historical, literary, or ethnological, can only hint at the difficulty of conceptualizing the notion of the "foreign" or "alien" as it has existed within the Japanese consciousness throughout history. Much needs to be investigated and analyzed before any definitive account can emerge, and even then such a study would be definitive only for the era in which it is written since human perspectives inevitably change over time. This study does not intend to explore Japanese consciousness in a systematic way; rather, the book is a series of case studies into how the notion of the alien has intruded into twentieth-century Japanese literature. It is much less ambitious, for example, than the writings of Japanese poet and ethnologist Yanagita Kunio, who devoted much of his life to exploring these questions and whose work has also served as a source of encouragement.[13] The case studies here are based upon readings of literary works that display representations of the alien or exotic—such phenomena being interpreted in an extremely wide-ranging way. I discuss both fiction and poetry, and nonfiction (but not, I argue, nonliterature) as well, and I cover the whole of the twentieth century, plus a little of the nineteenth and twenty-first centuries, with attention being devoted more to certain eras than others. I dedicate two chapters to certain writers because I believe that their achievements have not been sufficiently recognized in English-language scholarship.

My selections of authors and works are necessarily limited and subjective; a much larger group of modern Japanese writers could be subjected to quite similar analysis. Therefore this book in no way seeks to present a group of "representative" writers on the exotic, as such a study would encompass many volumes, especially if writers who mainly concentrate on travel narratives were the chief focus. The scope of this book is both broader and less narrowly focused than a study concentrating exclusively on travel narratives or fiction set outside Japan. It attempts instead to illuminate aspects of the exotic or alien in the work of certain authors that has not hitherto been explored in any detail. I also seek to draw attention to the notion of the alien or Other as a subject of some significance in modern Japanese writing. This will permit a deeper comprehension of related topics like the evolution of literary modernism and the creation of a female voice in literature.

Why have I selected these particular authors for examination? I have chosen some because I am closely acquainted with their work, having previously published on a number of them, because of the importance of their writing for the modern Japanese canon, and because to date there has been very little discussion of some of them in English-language scholarship. This is especially the case with the Okinawan novelist Ōshiro Tatsuhiro, who is well known in Japan but relatively unknown outside the country. Also, Okinawa is a fascinating example of the exotic, the alien within Japan proper, and its literature is particularly valuable as a case study of the degree to which the exotic has been absorbed into mainstream Japanese writing. I have also included important authors, particularly those writing Japanese gothic, who have already been extensively discussed by scholars writing in English because their writings are central to the theme of the exotic. I hope that my exploration will stimulate other studies on this topic that will treat many other important writers not included here.

Translation is not only essential to the representation of the alien in literature, but also to my argument throughout the book. As a consequence, I have, with very few exceptions, translated the quotations from the texts I discuss, even though fine translations already exist for many of these texts. I consider translation as a core element in the representation of the alien in literature, but not necessarily in the conventional sense. Rather, I have interpreted translation broadly to mean the process by which diverse phenomena can be "translated" into meaningful patterns, such as the way Yosano Akiko translates the experience of childbirth. Nonetheless, Chapter 1, with its examination of Tsubouchi Shōyō's translations into Japanese of William Shakespeare, is concerned with translation in the more conventional sense. The chapter also deals with the issue of translation in general and with its contribution to literary history.

The second chapter examines the poetic revolution accomplished chiefly by Yosano Akiko: the modernization of traditional Japanese verse through the rewriting in language and content of *waka*, the mainstream form of Japanese poetry for millennia or more. Akiko achieved this by adapting elements of versification that originated in translations and imitations of Western-style free verse. Thus in her poetry Akiko "naturalized" the alien by incorporating foreign verse structures (poetic figures as well as themes and narrative modes) into the most traditional of Japanese genres of poetry.

Chapter 3 takes the narrative into the second decade of the twentieth century to investigate the poetry and prose Akiko wrote about childbirth. This was an equally revolutionary theme in its day since childbirth was a taboo topic in literature, the prejudice against birth being closely related to the systematic oppression of women practiced by the Japanese state. Thus Akiko's writing not only struck a blow for the contemporary movement for women's emancipation but also helped to redefine female subjectivity for women themselves. The symbol of the new conception of womanhood that she created in her work was motherhood: the literal incorporation of the alien into the maternal body. This image was a potent expression of the fundamental alienation suffered by Japanese women, and not only in their roles as mothers. Chapters 2 and 3 reflect the supreme importance of Yosano Akiko as an author who became the most widely read woman writer of twentieth-century Japan, but whose historic significance is still barely understood in the West.

Chapter 4 is the first of two chapters on the Japanese version of gothic. The gothic movement in Europe began in the eighteenth century and in the eyes of some is still going strong today.[14] The territory of the gothic—a wild, exotic landscape populated by ghosts, demons, and unreasoning fear—is the territory of the unconscious. Japanese gothic authors were among the first to explore this territory in literature and thus the first to create a vital stage in the evolution of modernism in Japan. Chapter 4 treats Izumi Kyōka and Tanizaki: two writers emblematic of gothic concerns. Both authors have been well translated into English, for their fiction is regarded as among the finest written by Japanese novelists in the twentieth century.

Chapter 5 continues the discussion of Japanese gothic by examining various works of fiction by Arishima Takeo, a contemporary of both Kyōka and Tanizaki. Arishima's distinctive style has long been recognized as possessing elements of melodramatic excess, which also mark gothic fiction. This chapter seeks to deepen understanding of what Arishima was trying to achieve with this heightened mode of writing and attempts to link his style to the themes of his works, which, like much gothic writing, possess a political dimension critical of imperial Japan.

Chapter 6 moves from imperial Japan to post-imperial Japan, going from the first few decades to the last few decades of the tumultuous twentieth century and the fiction of Ōshiro Tatsuhiro, who is possibly the best-known contemporary Okinawan novelist. One reason Ōshiro became established as an author in the postwar era is because of the particular history of Okinawa, which was returned to Japan from American control only in 1972. Ōshiro's work incorporates a number of agendas. One is clearly to create an Okinawan vision of selfhood and identity that is not merely the fateful Other to mainland Japanese culture, but to locate the Okinawan experience within a larger conception of the Japanese self. As part of this endeavor, Ōshiro seeks to establish an Okinawan identity separate from but related to the mainland as part of his design to create a new vision of Japan, perhaps a "multicultural" Japan? The chapter analyses a story written in the 1990s that describes a phenomenon that is uniquely Okinawan—the *yuta*, or female shamans, who abound in Okinawa today. The *yuta*, as an exotic Other for citizens of contemporary Okinawa, are pivotal to the sense of an Okinawan identity different from the traditional mainland Japanese identity.

Chapter 7 examines a long historical novel that depicts a related phenomenon, *noro*, female shamans who played an important historical role in the establishment of the independent Ryūkyū kingdom in the fifteenth century. The novel deals with a famous *noro* and her romance with the Ryūkyū king and the consequences this had for history. The novel also examines the role played by *noro*, who are practitioners of uncanny arts and are objects of fear and awe for ordinary Okinawans. Ōshiro again probes the nature of the exotic, the uncanny, in an attempt to define the identity not merely of the Okinawan people but also of the historic Ryūkyū state.

The last chapter, Chapter 8, is a study of Murakami Haruki, the most famous, best read, and most widely translated novelist of contemporary Japan. The chapter analyzes Murakami's book about the 2000 Sydney Olympics, which was published a year after the event. Murakami's travel diary is located within the long tradition in Japan of this genre of writing, and, in addition, it is read as an example of how contemporary Japanese literature portrays the foreign. The view of Australia and Australians that Murakami expounds in the diary can be contrasted with earlier representations of foreigners by writers like Tanizaki Jun'ichirō. One glance at Tanizaki's depiction of the White Russian family in his masterpiece, *Sasameyuki* (The Makioka sisters, 1943–1948), reveals that Tanizaki portrays this family in a comic vein, utilizing stereotyping to persuade the reader to adopt a sympathetic view.[15] Murakami's book, on the other hand, largely avoids stereotyping in its representation of foreigners.

The Epilogue reflects upon issues raised in the volume as a whole and makes some generalizations about the significance of the alien or exotic as a subject in literature, specifically in the case of modern Japanese literature.

Japan as a nation has had a series of striking encounters with foreigners that have been represented in the literature of modern Japan: from the "opening" of Japan by Perry, through the rise of modern imperial Japan, to the establishment of Japanese control over a number of overseas territories, to the Second World War and its aftermath. This study seeks to go beyond description and analysis of such works to probe how notions of the alien and exotic have been "naturalized" into Japanese writing over the past century or so. It thus stakes out a territory different from previous English-language scholarship on modern Japanese literature and expands considerably the terrain mapped out by the few pioneer studies mentioned earlier. Much room remains for further analysis and exegesis on this theme, and I hope that this volume will stimulate further research and analysis.

CHAPTER 1

TRANSLATING THE ALIEN

Tsubouchi Shōyō and Shakespeare

Perfecting my cold dream
Of a place out of time,
A palace of porcelain
—Derek Mahon

If what we call "objective reality" is a series of more or less persuasive descriptions proposed by various languages, translation is the most fundamental and philosophical of all activities. To translate then is not only to experience the difference that makes each language distinct, but equally to draw close to the mystery of the relationship between word and thing, letter and spirit, self and the world. To translate is to awake and find oneself in the universal house of mirrors.
—Charles Simic

One of the most significant events in the history of modern Japan occurred in 1854 when Commodore Matthew Perry arrived in Edo accompanied by a powerful naval fleet with the express mission of opening Japan to the West. The last in a long line of Western attempts to prise open Japan to Western trade and commerce, it can easily be surmised from the well-armed vessels under Perry's command that he was determined to achieve this objective, and as later history has demonstrated, he succeeded beyond the wildest dreams of most citizens of the West at the time. Thus the "alien" was manifested in tangible form for one of the few times in Japanese history: in a very real sense the alien was within, both within the body politic, which was provoked by Perry into a series of far-reaching political changes, as well as within the physical reality of Japan itself. Contact with the West exposed Japan to the foreign in its purest form, that is, to the Other that was Western culture. A flood of translations from

Western languages followed the arrival of Perry and the other foreign envoys, which consisted mainly of political and technical works written by such authors as John Stuart Mill, Jeremy Bentham, Herbert Spencer, and Samuel Smiles.[1]

John Mertz has identified 1878 as the year when "a breakthrough" occurred in Japanese-language translations of Western works.[2] Unlike the books published in the years immediately following Perry's arrival, the translations published in this and succeeding years were often literary works and offered readers, Mertz argues, "the sweet pill of civilization . . . the lure of Western flavors."[3] Prominent among the works translated in 1878, for example, were novels like Jules Verne's *Around the World in Eighty Days* and Edward Bulwer-Lytton's *Ernest Maltravers* and *Alice*. Jonathon Zwicker also remarks that "from the 1870s into the 1890s, the [Japanese] market for translations is almost entirely dominated by British and French novels. . . . [I]n the 1890s the market fractures. There continues to be an almost unending stream of spy and detective novels, of sentiment, melodrama and adventure fiction but these are soon joined by the Romantics, Shakespeare, the great Russian novelists—Dostoyevsky, Tolstoy, Turgenev."[4]

For Japanese at that time the most powerful expression of the Western tradition was found in British civilization, the culture of the dominant imperialist state of the day. So it is no accident that many of the authors translated were British. The most famous English author of the time, probably of all time, was William Shakespeare, and, as Zwicker notes, Shakespeare was among the first authors to be translated into Japanese. The history of Japanese translations of Shakespeare will be discussed later, as a prelude to a detailed assessment of the translations of Tsubouchi Shōyō (1859–1935), Japan's greatest and in many ways most influential translator of the Bard. But first it is necessary to make some preliminary remarks on Shakespeare translation in general, especially as this applies to Asia, and specifically Japan, since Shakespeare is arguably more alien to Asian indigenous traditions than European. For instance, the "German Shakespeare" has taken on an existence independent of the English original, though apparently just as significant for German culture.[5] Just how the alien dramatist became Japanese, a process paralleled in the European absorption of Shakespeare, is therefore the subject of this chapter.

Shakespeare, Japan, and Tsubouchi Shōyō

In James Brandon's influential 1997 article "Some Shakespeare(s) in Some Asia(s)," the author proposes a threefold division of Shakespeare adaptations.

He is here writing primarily of stage adaptations, not Shakespeare as text. The first category Brandon calls the "canonical Shakespeare—an 'elite' or 'high culture Shakespeare.'"[6] In the case of Japan, Brandon argues that this tradition "deliberately sought out Shakespeare . . . as part of [a] quest to overcome feudal thought in [Japanese] society and to modernise [Japanese] culture."[7] This can be read as an attempt to incorporate the alien while still preserving the reality of the alien in some sense as foreign, something different from Japanese traditions, although the object is to reform these traditions. The aim of the translations made in this tradition, observes Brandon, is to "preserve the 'authentic' voice of Shakespeare in a vernacular language."[8] Authenticity thus provides for a crucial separation of the foreign from the domestic. Brandon sums up his conceptualization of the canonical Shakespeare as expressing "the single view of the world that is European, specifically English. . . ."[9] In contrast to this tradition, Brandon defines the next of his two traditions as "localised Shakespeare," where Shakespeare "draws authority from local vernacular theatrical traditions . . . rooted in the desires of popular audiences"; in other words "low-culture" Shakespeare.[10] The low-culture Shakespeare does attempt to naturalize the alien, to truly bring the foreign into the domestic realm to the degree that the distinction is blurred almost completely. Brandon's final tradition of Shakespeare he calls the "intercultural Shakespeare"—a "'post-colonial' post-modern phenomenon of the past 40 years."[11]

The last category is potentially the most interesting as it represents the reclaiming of the exotic, namely, Shakespeare as alien, not as art so domesticated it ceases to have any sense of cultural difference or alterity altogether. As can be seen from the versions of Shakespeare created by present-day directors Suzuki Tadashi and Ninagawa Yukio, versions Brandon identifies as intercultural, such a translation/reading/performance of Shakespeare is a dialogue, where the alien culture is allowed to become even more alien by being transformed into a new reading of Japanese culture itself. Theorists of the effects of translation on culture like Tejaswini Niranjana see these intercultural versions as inscribed within a "colonial discourse" which "contain[s] and control[s]," as that has historically been the case with much of Asia.[12] Following Homi Bhabha, Niranjana allows hybridity to emerge as a source of "proliferating differences" from the process of translation and thus to point to a "new practice of translation."[13] While fully cognizant of the differences between colonized Asian states such as those discussed by Niranjana and colonizing states like Japan, it may be possible to argue that, in theory at least, hybridity represents a kind of equivalence to the intercultural Shakespeare.

Writing from the perspective of literature that dramatizes or enacts hybridity (such as Salman Rushdie's novel *The Satanic Verses*), Bhabha himself notes that "cultural translation desacralizes the transparent assumptions of cultural supremacy, and in that very act, demands a contextual specificity, a historical differentiation *within* minority positions." [14] Bhabha's view of translation derives from Walter Benjamin's famous 1923 essay on the subject (translated by Harry Zohn as "The Task of the Translator") and emphasizes the process of "foreignizing" translations or, in the context of this book, creating an intercultural Shakespeare. [15] Here one can find an argument that positively advocates the radical rewritings of the text found in the contemporary theater of Ninagawa because these rewritings desacralize the colonialist aura surrounding Shakespeare. However, the "Japanizing" of Shakespeare occurred at the same time that Japan was reinventing itself as a colonial power along the lines of the West, a fact which creates an entirely new context for the connections between hybridity and colonialism.

Brandon is primarily addressing the issue of how Shakespeare is performed in theater. Other than examining and comparing actual performances, a focus on translation is the easiest way to assess differences in cultural perspective. This chapter places strong stress on translation as a means to discuss issues of cultural difference and, therefore, is concerned chiefly with Shakespeare as a textual phenomenon. This is not to argue that a clear separation can be made between theater as written text and as performance—the two are intimately related. However, when discussing cultural adaptations that have occurred over a century or more, written text is a more accessible and workable basis for discussion and analysis than secondhand accounts of performances.

Dennis Kennedy notes that, unlike the case of India, Shakespeare in Japan was not preceded by English models of culture and behavior; rather, "what was most notable about Shakespeare . . . was his utter novelty." [16] Kennedy argues that the Japanese Shakespeare is seen "as part of the *shingeki* enterprise"—an indigenous reformist genre of modern theater that began in Japan in the late nineteenth century. [17] He remarks that in 1994 there were thirty-three productions or adaptations of Shakespeare being performed in Tokyo, more than in London, but that they were seen as part of the *shingeki* tradition. Commenting on such modern Japanese interpreters of Shakespeare as Ninagawa Yukio, Kennedy describes Ninagawa's vision of the Bard as a "dislocating interculturalism ... [that] exists both in and out of the country of its origin." [18]

As numerous commentators have observed, in Japan the intercultural Shakespeare has become so dominant that this version of Shakespeare has been exported back to the West. Suzuki Tadashi and Ninagawa are the most famous exponents of the intercultural Shakespeare in contemporary Japan, and both directors have performed their versions of Shakespeare abroad. [19] Both men are familiar with the English director Peter Brook's particular theatrical style and especially his famous versions of Shakespeare at the Royal Shakespeare Company in the 1960s and 1970s, and so, in a sense, Brook's own "intercultural Shakespeare" has been taken a further step in Japan. [20] This step extends the trope of hybridity beyond Bhabha's formulation, which focuses on postcolonial expressions of culture, to move towards what George Steiner describes as the "final stage" of the process of translation (or the process of cultural absorption of the Other)—"compensation" or "restitution" where translation "recompenses in that it can provide a persistence and geographical-cultural range of survival which it would otherwise lack." [21]

I will here specifically discuss Tsubouchi Shōyō's achievements as a translator of Shakespeare, rather than his contributions to Shakespeare in performance. [22] I will also reconsider Brandon's notion of the canonical Shakespeare, into which tradition he places Shōyō without any hesitation whatsoever. I will focus particularly on *Julius Caesar* and *Hamlet*. Relating to these choices, it is interesting to note that by 1978 there were some thirty-six translations of *Hamlet* into Japanese, and since then the number may well have doubled. [23]

Tsubouchi Shōyō was born in Ōta, a small town in present-day Gifu Prefecture. He was the son of a samurai who was a minor official of the Owari domain. During his youth he frequently attended the Kabuki theater in the nearby city of Nagoya. While an adolescent, he studied English at various academies and in 1876 was selected as one of eight students from the prefecture to study at the Kaisei Gakkō, the forerunner of Tokyo University. In 1878 Shōyō was formally enrolled in Tokyo University, where he studied literature and law. Shōyō had first studied Shakespeare when he was sixteen under the guidance of an American teacher named H. Latham. At university, Shōyō renewed his acquaintance with Shakespeare as part of his English studies. [24] He was introduced to various famous Shakespeare plays, including *The Merchant of Venice* and *Macbeth*, by an American professor called William A. Houghton. [25]

In 1883 Shōyō graduated from Tokyo University and found work as an English instructor at the Tokyo Senmon Gakkō (later renamed Waseda University). By 1887 he had become known as a novelist and a theoretician of aesthetics.[26] His fame was such that he was appointed to a visiting position as a writer for the Yomiuri newspaper. But in 1889 he decided to abandon fiction, instead concentrating on translation and drama.[27] He translated Zola and Thackeray among others, but his true love was Shakespeare. His first Shakespeare translation was *Julius Caesar,* published in 1884 under the title *Jiyū no tachi nagori no kireaji* (The sharp edge of freedom's sword), which we will examine more closely below.

Shōyō lectured on Shakespeare to his students at Waseda after assisting in the establishment of a department of literature there. In 1898 he also established a private study group to read Shakespeare at his home. In 1896 he was appointed head teacher at the Waseda Middle School, and in 1899 he was awarded a doctorate of letters. However, in 1903 he resigned from his post to become a full-time writer. In 1907 Shōyō was awarded a lifetime annuity from Waseda University, and through various editorships and commissions arising from the university, he never severed his links to it.[28]

Shōyō's literary achievements are so manifold and numerous that they are impossible to list here.[29] He wrote many original dramas for the Japanese stage, of which the best known are probably *Shinkyoku urashima* (The new Urashima, 1904) and *En no gyōja* (En the ascetic, 1917).[30] He also published critical works on the theater including the well-known *Shin gakugeki ron* (A new approach to musical drama, 1904), which introduced Richard Wagner's philosophy of opera to Japan. However, more and more Shakespeare came to occupy center stage among his activities. From 1909 onwards, Shōyō published translations of roughly one or two Shakespeare plays a year.[31] In his brief 1997 biography of Shōyō, J. Scott Miller mentions that Shōyō declined an invitation to become president of Waseda University in 1918 because he wished to concentrate on translating Shakespeare.[32] In January 1926 Shōyō published an article announcing his decision to abandon all his other literary activities in order to finish the first complete translation into Japanese of Shakespeare's works. Two graduates of Tokyo University, Tozawa Koya (1873–1955) and Asano Hyōkyo (1874–1937), had already attempted something similar but after completing ten plays between 1905 and 1909, they discontinued their work.[33] Between 1926 and 1928 Shōyō translated seventeen Shakespeare plays into Japanese. Thus in 1928, at

the age of seventy, Shōyō had finally completed the monumental task of translating the entire works of Shakespeare into Japanese.[34]

By this time Shōyō had grown dissatisfied with his earlier translations, which
he considered too old-fashioned in expression. So in order to make his earlier translations conform to those done later, Shōyō reworked all his earlier
translations from 1933 onwards, signing a contract with a publisher in May
1934 to produce his *Shinshū Shēkusupiya zenshū* (Revised collected works of
Shakespeare). From November that year, starting with *Hamlet* and *Measure for
Measure,* he produced a new revision every two months. Some of these were
performed on stage, as earlier versions had been. Shōyō's Japanese biographer—Ōmura Hiroyoshi—claims that these new versions were actually rewritings of the plays in the colloquial, and not merely revisions.[35] By January 1935
the revised translations were completed, and the very next month Shōyō died
at the age of 78. Three months after his death, the new revised Shakespeare was
published in forty volumes.[36]

The Nature of Translation

It is instructive, when considering issues of translation and of how the alien
may be absorbed and recreated in the process of cultural adaptation, to consider
Steiner's much acclaimed study *After Babel: Aspects of Language and Translation*
(1975). Steiner affirms that there is no "universal axiomatic or externally verifi-
able 'method'" with respect to translation.[37] He proposes a three-stage model
for translation. First, Steiner argues the case for "the hermeneutic motion,"
which in practice means that "each act of comprehension must appropriate
another entity."[38] He quotes Saint Jerome: "[W]e 'break' a code: decipherment
is dissective, leaving the shell smashed and the vital layers stripped," or, as he
puts it later, the "translator invades, extracts, and brings home."[39] Next, Steiner
proposes an "incorporative" movement, which can assimilate or naturalize, or
sometimes dislocate and relocate, a text when it becomes part of another culture.
Perhaps this parallels the German experience of Shakespeare, for as Friedrich
Schlegel noted in 1812, German translations of Shakespeare had transformed
the native tongue and national consciousness.[40] The last stage of Steiner's model
is the creation (or as he terms it, "enactment") of reciprocity, where the "work
translated is enhanced," a stage mentioned earlier in reference to the intercultural Shakespeare.[41]

Steiner's model is offered as an anatomy of the act of translation itself, and it has undoubted similarities to Brandon's categorizations of Shakespeare adaptations or translations. In one sense the model generalizes or abstracts Brandon's threefold division, seeing all three categories of adaptation as variations on the same process, a kind of "naturalization." Brandon emphasizes the political or ideological motive in the case of Japan—Shakespeare, he contends, is used as a tool to advance modernization. There is a curious kind of decolonializing logic to this move, since early Japanese translators of Shakespeare were using one of the most distinguished literary products of one of the most rapacious of the nineteenth-century colonizers as a tactic in an anticolonial, reformist campaign to modernize the country in order to protect Japan against the predations of the very same colonial powers. Such an assertion is drawing a very long bow, but the connection between Shakespeare and colonization has been a rich source of debate over recent decades.[42]

Brandon's categories also incorporate a kind of "reverse orientalism" or, to put it more simply, "orientalism," as Nishihara Daisuke argues in the case of the author Tanizaki Jun'ichirō.[43] Nishihara proposes a variation on Edward Said's famous concept to argue that Tanizaki incorporated aspects of the Western colonial representation of the "Orient" in his own representations of both the West and Asia qua Japan in his writings.[44] That Brandon is arguing an analogous case is apparent in his first category, that of expressing "the single view of the world that is European." However, Shōyō's earliest versions of Shakespeare were almost unrecognizable as translations insofar as diction and style were concerned—Shōyō adapted them so successfully into a Japanese frame of reference, into the poetics of Japanese literature, that they could be seen as inaugurating a new kind of Japanese theater. And, in a sense, this is precisely what happened. The sense of the exotic, the alien, almost completely disappears in Shōyō's first attempt at translating Shakespeare. Shōyō was a pioneer of *shingeki,* the "new theater," which was new by virtue of the fact that it was based on overseas, imported models; however, the language of the theater and its acting conventions relied heavily on indigenous models (principally Kabuki) for its successful debut in Japan. This was inevitable, of course—the only "non-adapted" Shakespeare that one could imagine in Japan as commercial theater would be produced by the expatriate British community and performed for that same community. And even then, every such a production would still be in one sense "adapted" because audience expectations, not to mention the theater itself and its environs, would be considerably different from what prevailed in England.

One of the most intriguing notions Steiner puts forward is the "bringing home" of some work of literature—"extracted" from the source language to be brought home in the target language. This is not a simple indigenization, as Steiner reveals:

> The delineation of "resistant difficulty," "otherness" of the original, plays against "elective affinity," against immediate grasp and domestication. In perfunctory translation these two currents diverge. There is no shaping tension between them, and paraphrase attempts to mask the gap. Good translation, on the contrary, can be defined as that in which the dialectic of impenetrability and ingress, of intractable alienness and felt "at-homeness" remains unresolved, but expressive. Out of the tension of resistance and affinity, a tension directly proportional to the proximity of the two languages and historical communities, grows the elucidative strangeness of the great translation. The strangeness is elucidative because we come to recognize it, to "know it again," as our own.[45]

The "at-homeness" discloses another form of alterity, or "strangeness" to use Steiner's term; the alien survives as an alien in a hybridized form because that is the very nature of translation, of adapting foreign cultures to one's own.

One source for this notion occurs in the many writings of Martin Heidegger, which Steiner frequently alludes to. As Heidegger wrote in 1950: "To discuss language, to place it, means to bring to its place of being not so much language as ourselves: our own gathering into the appropriation."[46] Heidegger's view of translation arises from his particular brand of hermeneutics. Hans-Georg Gadamer, the foremost theoretician of hermeneutic philosophy in the twentieth century, summarizes Heidegger's understanding or formulation of the hermeneutic circle thus:

> The circle, then, is not formal in nature. It is neither subjective nor objective, but describes understanding as the interplay of the movement of tradition, and movement of the interpreter. The anticipation that governs our understanding of a text is not an act of subjectivity, but proceeds from the commonality that binds us to the tradition. But this commonality is constantly being formed in our relation to tradition. Tradition is not simply a permanent precondition;

rather, we produce it ourselves inasmuch as we understand, participate in the evolutions of tradition and hence further determine it ourselves.[47]

This is a most useful shorthand description of the process by which Shōyō adapted Shakespeare using his own literary and theatrical traditions—both indigenous and deriving from Western translations—and by doing so added to that tradition that he was in the process of reinventing. This is a version of hybridity that is both creative and re-creative: revivifying the alien by inventing an entirely new tradition of drama.

Steiner adopts a positive view of the possibility of translation and retains the right to use evaluative or normative criteria in his judgments of individual translations. However, Lawrence Venuti has challenged this view in his influential history of translation titled *The Translator's Invisibility,* published in 1995. There he writes:

Both foreign text and translation are derivative: both consist of diverse linguistic and cultural materials that neither the foreign writer nor the translator originates, and that destabilize the work of signification, inevitably exceeding and possibly conflicting with their intentions. As a result, a foreign text is the site of many different semantic possibilities that are fixed only provisionally in any one translation, on the basis of varying cultural assumptions and interpretive choices, in specific social situations, in different historical periods. Meaning is a plural and contingent relation, not an unchanging unified essence, and therefore a translation cannot be judged according to mathematics-based concepts of semantic equivalence or one-to-one correspondence. Appeals to the foreign text cannot finally adjudicate between competing translations in the absence of linguistic error because canons of accuracy in translation, notions of "fidelity" and "freedom," are historically determined categories. Even the notion of "linguistic error" is subject to variation, since mistranslations, especially in literary texts, can be not merely intelligible but significant in the target-language culture. The viability of a translation is established by its relationship to the cultural and social conditions under which it is produced and read.

This relationship points to the violence that resides in the very purpose and activity of translation: the reconstitution of the foreign text in accordance with values, beliefs and representations that preexist it in the target language, always configured in hierarchies of dominance and marginality, always determining the production, circulation, and reception of texts. Translation is the forcible replacement of the linguistic and cultural difference of the foreign text with a text that will be intelligible to the target-language reader. This difference can never be entirely removed, of course, but it necessarily suffers a reduction and exclusion of possibilities—and an exorbitant gain of other possibilities specific to the translating language. Whatever difference the translation conveys is now imprinted by the target-language culture, assimilated to its positions of intelligibility, its canons and taboos, its codes and ideologies. The aim of translation is to bring back a cultural other as the same, the recognizable, even the familiar; and this aim always risks a wholesale domestication of the foreign text, often in highly self-conscious projects, where translation serves an appropriation of foreign cultures for domestic agendas, cultural, economic, political. Translation can be considered the communication of a foreign text, but it is always a communication limited by its address to a specific reading audience.[48]

If the proposition that translation "is the forcible replacement of the linguistic and cultural difference of the foreign text" is taken to its logical conclusion, then Venuti's comments appear to point towards the notion of incommensurability, both of translation and of cultural communication generally. Yet many theorists and writers deny that different cultural phenomena cannot be communicated or translated.[49] A recent study by Zhang Longxi of the affinities between Chinese and Western literature commences with a chapter entitled "the fallacy of cultural incommensurability"—and Venuti himself advocates as "highly desirable" the strategy of a "foreignizing translation," as proposed by Friedrich Schleiermacher in 1813.[50] Such a translation "signifies the difference of the foreign-text, yet only by disrupting the cultural codes that prevail in the target language."[51] Here Venuti comes very close to Steiner's formulation of alterity and, to close the circle, also to the intercultural versions of Shakespeare cited earlier. A foreignizing translation also can be seen as a hybrid proceeding in exactly the same kind of direction Shōyō followed in his translations of Shakespeare.

To what degree was Shōyō consciously aware of this process of hybridity? Did Shōyō formulate his own theory of Shakespeare translation? Was Shakespeare to remain an exotic import, or did Shōyō see the act of translation as rendering the alien not alien, as domesticating the foreign? The answers to these questions lie primarily in his actual translations, extracts from which we shall examine. In addition, Shōyō's own writings on translation are obviously pivotal in any preliminary attempt to arrive at an understanding of his view of the act of translation, particularly as it applied to Shakespeare.

Shōyō and Translation

Shōyō wrote various prefaces to his versions of Shakespeare over the years. One of the most interesting and certainly the earliest is the preface to his 1884 translation of *Julius Caesar,* discussed in more detail below. Shōyō notes in this preface to his first translation of a full-length Shakespeare play:

> The style [of my translation] is different from the original. However, I deliberately translated it into *inpontai* [Jōruri style] for the sake of my countrymen. If you compare it to the original, there may be many errors so I ask for your understanding. I translated passages from the original into a Jōruri style where it was easy to do so. I translated dialogues that are easy to understand exactly as in the original, trying as much as possible not to lose the meaning of the original, but this version is not meant to be performed in the theater by Japanese actors. . . . I used the characters' names as they appear in the original but only for the ease of understanding. . . .[52]

It is clear that Shōyō did not intend this first translation for purposes of performance but, rather, to introduce Meiji audiences to Shakespeare's drama. Also, it is noticeable that Shōyō chooses to use a mixed translation style by incorporating the traditional diction of Jōruri theater: in a sense, he is reproducing the archaic patina of Shakespeare's own English as it was perceived by the Victorian audience, although Jōruri puppet drama was still a living form of theater for Meiji audiences, however old-fashioned the language.

In an article entitled "Hon'yaku subeki gaikokubungaku" (Foreign literature that demands translation, 1891), much cited by specialists as one of the earliest and most significant expressions of Shōyō's view of translation, Shōyō wrote that literature can be divided into three categories: intellectual *(chi),* emotional *(jō),* and logical *(i).*[53] Citing Mill and Spenser as examples of intellectual literature, and Shelley and Byron as examples of emotional literature, Shōyō observed, "Intellectual literature is difficult to translate, while emotional literature is easy to translate." Shōyō also cites such Western authorities on translation as Samuel Johnson and John Dryden to the effect that meaning is more important when translating than word-by-word renderings. He also agreed with the writers Mori Ōgai (1862–1922) and Miki Takeji (1867–1908) that literal translation was unsuitable for belles lettres.[54] It appears that Shōyō never outlined a full-blown theory of translation, but in this article he clearly indicated his preference (unsurprisingly, for a creative writer such as himself) for translations that capture the spirit of the original: he wants it "brought home," to use Steiner's phrase.

Shōyō wrote several articles that deal with the problem of how to translate Shakespeare. One of the earliest pieces Shōyō wrote on this was his "Nihon de enzuru *Hamuretto*" (Performing *Hamlet* in Japan), which was probably composed around 1907. Shōyō begins by stating the problem:

> If one is to translate *Hamlet* into Japanese, what style should one choose? Should *Hamlet* be *translated* into the style of *sewa mono* theater, which takes domestic social themes drawn mostly from the social milieu of the Edo period—as the Hongō and Shintōza troupes do? This would mean translating into the everyday diction of Meiji speech. Or should we choose the translation tone used in the so-called Shiken style, the fake narrative mode? Or, if we restrict ourselves to historical dramas, in order to create the illusion of the past—for translations set in the European feudal age—do we add vocabulary derived from our own feudal period? To suggest images of antiquity, do we take care to use our own "Kojiki" style of diction? Further, when we come to stage the drama, how should the text be interpreted? Must we conform to the readings of Western scholars and critics, or take as our prime model the example of past performances or the performance modes used by well-known contemporary actors? Provided that we do not misunderstand the intentions of the playwright, can we offer a new interpretation based on the unique perspective of the Japanese?[55]

Shōyō continues to find flaws in all the possible translation styles listed above. He mentions criticism of his own recent translation of *The Merchant of Venice,* which argued that Shōyō was mistaken to have used old or archaic Japanese to translate Shakespeare, in this case Japanese from the Edo period of the eighteenth and nineteenth centuries. This criticism came from troupes that used the contemporary language to perform Shakespeare. Shōyō argues that 70 percent of Shakespeare's language is poetry, composed for its aural eloquence, and it is even more rhythmical than the Japanese 7/5 rhythm of classical verse; thus, he maintains, it would be wrong to translate it into the ordinary prose used currently. Shakespeare's great strength as a dramatist is that he blends poetic language with prose, mixing register and rhythms. Shōyō observes that he attempted to imitate this in his translation, but not by copying the language of the dramatists Chikamatsu Monzaemon (1653–1724) or Kawatake Mokuami (1816–1893) as Shakespeare was immeasurably superior in his command of language to his Japanese contemporaries.[56] Consequently, Shōyō's translation of *Hamlet* is more akin to the classicism of the Noh theater than the "romanticism of Chikamatsu." This is a kind of counterfeit Noh, but in the vital parts Shōyō shifted to Kyōgen farce-style diction, with touches of the vernacular.[57]

Shōyō goes on to refer to a translation of *Hamlet* that he has just been working on—presumably the version that was eventually published approximately two years later in December 1909. I will examine the actual translation shortly, but there is no doubt that, in general, Shōyō's comments are a true and accurate reflection of the translation itself. Also, it is noticeable that at this stage of his career, Shōyō was following the principle of being "at home" with Shakespeare by adapting Shakespeare to existing theatrical forms and diction like Noh and Kyōgen. It is equally evident that Shōyō believed that he was being faithful to the spirit of the original and, further, that he was at least to a degree inventing a new kind of Japanese—however much it owed to archaic usages found in traditional theater—in order to translate Shakespeare.

In 1910 Shōyō put pen (or brush) to paper once again on the subject of translating Shakespeare. In an essay entitled "Shaōgeki no hon'yaku ni tsuite" (On translating Shakespeare's drama), Shōyō repeated many of the points he had made in the 1907 essay, namely, that translating Shakespeare means to pay particular attention to the poetry found in the original, and not merely the poetry, but also to the sonorous, rhythmical prose. Shōyō comments:

> I will attempt a provisional translation in Japanese in a free style. There is no doubt that the iambic meter of Shakespeare and his colleagues is quite common in English poetry, and it corresponds, more or less, to our country's 7/5 rhythm, so it is not incorrect to say that to render Shakespeare into a style mixing high and low registers *(gazoku)*—that mode of writing starting from Chikamatsu and continuing to the writer Kyokutei Bakin [1767–1848]—does not entirely miss the mark . . . but to say that, by and large, Chikamatsu's diction fits the bill causes an immediate problem in that Shakespeare's vocabulary is much larger than Chikamatsu's, and his tone is much loftier. So it is difficult to translate Shakespeare using Chikamatsu's style as the sole model. We must insert several heterogeneous elements. Sometimes we can borrow vocabulary from Kabuki; on other occa-

sions we must levy assistance from the diction of tale literature *(monogatari)*, Noh, Kyōgen, and early modern fiction. . . . Recently, circumstances persuaded me to translate *Hamlet . . .* , but I wasn't able to accomplish this to my satisfaction. It was easy to convey the meaning, to express the breathing [of the actors] on stage, but the tone, the flavor, the aroma, the color—these qualities that defy description are exceedingly difficult to put into Japanese. My text grows too long and turns into paraphrase, only the meaning is conveyed, and the taste becomes that of Japanese cuisine, Shakespeare's brevity turns into verbosity.[58]

Shōyō then lists the twelve rules he has arrived at in attempting to revise his translation. These rules are important because they comprise his anatomy of translation until 1910; to be precise, it is a translation manual for Shakespeare. Some of the most important rules are:

1. The style must be closer to free prose than to 7/5 rhythms, closer to the colloquial style of Kyōgen than to the trite verbal gymnastics of Kabuki.
2. Providing the requirements of harmony are met, the language should not depend upon one era; it is best to mix vocabulary, old and new, freely—elegant words, vulgar words, translationese, and neologisms.
4. It is important to pay attention to the balance between prose and verse; when translating, maintain a neutral tone using a colloquial style (domestic drama) and an elevated, classical style (period drama). (It's not necessary to translate the intricacies exactly as in the original.)
5. In cases where it is not necessary, do not add expressions like "however" and "consequently"; also, even if the text is simple, do not lose the length and echo of the original; avoid translation style.
7. Concrete words should be translated as concretely as possible, Latin words (depending on the situation) should be translated first as Sino-Japanese *(kanbun)* or into elegant language; puns, euphemisms, slang, dialect, etc., should be translated into the appropriate Japanese.[59]
9. Proverbs, aphorisms, adages, and the like should be translated into simple expressions.
10. It is best to avoid the use of words that have associations related to Japanese or Chinese legends and traditions.[60]

Later in the article Shōyō argues that rather than translate into contemporary Japanese, a mixture of Romanticism and Naturalism works best. The impulse to domesticate the foreign appears to be dominant here, to render Shakespeare in some sense as a Japanese dramatist, albeit not an exact equivalent of any one mode of Japanese drama, but rather a mix of genres. We should keep in mind that this was Shōyō's point of view in 1910 when he first embarked on Shakespeare translation in earnest—it would not be surprising if his view of translation changed over time. Nevertheless, as a clear statement, a program even, of translation strategies for putting Shakespeare into Japanese, it is an account of some importance, and it demonstrates just how deeply Shōyō considered this issue. This statement also emphasizes how, at this stage of his career, Shōyō was chiefly concerned with "naturalizing" the text so that it seems to read as if it were "at home" in Japanese, as his admonitions against using "translationese" demonstrate. The exotic becomes merely another version of the familiar.

In April 1916 Shōyō penned another article on the same topic: "Shaōgeki no hon'yaku ni taisuru watashi no taido no hensen" (Changes in my attitude towards translating Shakespeare), which signals a distinct shift in his translation strategy. Shōyō begins by briefly recounting the history of Shakespeare translation in Japan. He explains that originally his chief motive in studying Shakespeare was for the purpose of reforming Japanese theater (engeki kairyō), but this shifted to an emphasis on Shakespeare in performance. Shōyō began to translate Shakespeare specifically for the purpose of performing Shakespeare on stage in Japan, and so it was only natural for his translations to be based on Kabuki and Jōruri diction in 7/5 meter.

When he was thus "held captive in the kokubun (literary) tradition," someone suggested that he abandon his practice of annotating Shakespeare through explanation and instead follow Lafcadio Hearn's advice to translate Shakespeare into "vulgar" (that is, ordinary) language in the genbun itchi style of colloquial expression advocated by several leading novelists.[61] Shōyō could not accept this advice when he translated his ten-volume set of Shakespeare masterpieces; he preferred to imitate the original by employing a mixed style blending elegant literary expressions with more colloquial diction. However, "colloquial" meant the colloquial found in Kyōgen or Edo theater. As a result, his versions were often criticized as difficult for audiences to understand and, further, as having the distinct aroma of Kyōgen and Kabuki about them. Shōyō himself grew dissatisfied with this style and decided to reduce the amount of literary Japanese in his translations and make the colloquial closer to contemporary speech. As examples of this new style, Shōyō lists the translations that appeared in his "Shakespeare Masterpiece" series, which began prior to and concluded after this shift in his translating technique.[62] His change of attitude resulted in translations that were much more successful in performance. But Shōyō is careful to note that his version of colloquial Japanese is not the same as found in contemporary novels. In his translations Shōyō does not approve of contemporary usage that marks social status clearly, since Japanese society in 1916 is quite different from that depicted in the plays. He describes his translation style as *shinshiki no kōgotai*—a new type or mode of the colloquial.[63] He also comments that it is easy to translate into such a style.[64]

This article marks an important watershed in Shōyō's career as a translator. The shift to a much more colloquial style—albeit one that is still artificial and designed for the stage, not an exact imitation of contemporary spoken Japanese—indicates a determination to see Shakespeare performed before as large an audience as possible. It also signals a shift away from Shakespeare as text to Shakespeare as performance. This does not mean that Shōyō abandoned the original. On the contrary, throughout the article cited above, Shōyō continually mentions how Shakespeare's text is capable of being brought "home" to Japanese audiences in such a way that the original intent is preserved intact. The mechanics of this process will be examined presently but that Shōyō still conceived of his project as translating Shakespeare, not paraphrasing him, not creating free adaptations that obscure his foreign origins, cannot be doubted.

A number of essays on Shakespeare that Shōyō had written previously were included in a volume entitled *Shēkusupiya kenkyū shiori* (A handbook of Shakespeare studies) that was first published in 1928 but that Shōyō added to variously until a final revised version was published in 1935. Chap. 18 of this volume is entitled "Jibun no hon'yaku ni tsuite" (On my translations) and includes several remarks of interest, including a piece entitled "Kōgo to gendaigo" (Colloquial and contemporary Japanese), first published in 1933. This short note amplifies and elaborates upon the distinction Shōyō had made in his 1916 article between colloquial diction—his preferred mode of Shakespearian translation—and everyday speech. Shōyō argues that everyday speech is essentially slang, cliché, and shorthand expressions. He disapproves of "proletarian" language slipping into bourgeois speech and argues that Ophelia and Juliet sound like prostitutes (café waitresses) if such language is used. Similarly, he contends, Hamlet's mother or Lady Macbeth would sound like brothel madams.[65] His point is that everyday speech uses a limited number of words—mostly slang. Shakespeare in translation demands a much wider range of vocabulary than that supplied by everyday speech, or contemporary novels, magazines, or newspapers for that matter. This does not prevent such language being used in translation, but Shakespeare cannot be limited to such a tiny spectrum of Japanese usage. The translator should have available all the lexical resources that Japanese can offer—elegant language, archaic diction, dialect, argot, slang—whatever is necessary.[66]

Early in this chapter, Shōyō repeats the statement he made in 1916 that his translations of Shakespeare can be divided into different stages, but his tone is even harsher in his condemnation of his earliest translations, which he derides as mere literal cribs. These remarks reveal the enormous distance Shōyō had traveled as a translator and also disclose the motivation behind his numerous revisions and reworking of older translations. The shift from a translation style that preserves the mantle of the exotic, retaining alien features in its syntax by using a heterogeneous, sometimes archaic mix from different Japanese theatrical traditions, to a style that eliminates the exotic in favor of contemporary colloquial Japanese was not a simple, linear process, as can be seen from the different versions Shōyō produced over time.

Translation Practice: *Julius Caesar*

As an example of Shōyō's actual translation practice, I will begin by examining his earliest translation of Shakespeare, a version of *Julius Caesar*, by focusing on selected passages. But first, it may be useful to glance briefly at Shakespeare studies in Japan at this time in order to ascertain the historical context and to discover who Shōyō's predecessors were. As a variation on Brandon's typology, the critic Kawatake Toshio has posited a three-stage process of Shakespeare adaptation in Japan. The first stage Kawatake describes as "enlightenment" Shakespeare, where the Bard is rendered into either Kabuki or modes of late Edo literature. The second stage is "translation," where such authors as Tsubouchi actually translate Shakespeare into Japanese and the original English text is paramount. Kawatake notes that the first stage centers on theatrical productions, whereas the second stage can be mainly classified as a textual enterprise, although in time it also evolved into theater. In the second stage Shakespearean productions were eventually limited to large-scale commercial theatre *(shingeki)* or productions from abroad—the Bard had little impact on the indigenous modes of realistic, experimental theater developing within Japan. The third stage extends into the present and encompasses the new interpretations of Shakespeare referred to earlier.[67]

If we commence with the "enlightenment" Shakespeare, there was an extract from *Hamlet* in Nakamura Keiu or Masanao's (1832–1891) translation of Samuel Smiles' *Self Help* (1859), published under the title *Saikoku risshihen* (Western success stories) in 1870–1871. The complete text is now available in various Japanese collections. This is apparently the first appearance of Shakespeare in Japanese, although scenes from various Jōruri dramas have been interpreted as reflecting Shakespeare's influence, notably, Chikamatsu Monzaemon's (1653–1724) *Shaka nyorai tanjōe* (The Buddha's birthday ceremony, 1694), where one scene is claimed to resemble *The Merchant of Venice* and Chikamatsu Hanji's (1725–1783) *Imoseyama onna teikin* (The Imoseyama female analects, 1771), where a scene apparently resembles *Romeo and Juliet*.[68] Onomura Yōko suggests that the dramatist Tsuruya Nanboku IV's (1755–1829) Kabuki play *Kokoro no nazo toketa iroito* (The riddles of the heart unraveled in colored threads, 1810) may have been influenced by *Romeo and Juliet*.[69] Shōyō noted that in 1874 an English artist named Charles Wirgman (1835–1891) produced a version of Hamlet's "To be or not to be" soliloquy in mistake-ridden, eccentrically romanized Japanese, which appeared in the *Yokohama Punch* newspaper.[70] This translation is best seen as a parody of Shakespeare, as Kawatake Toshio has noted in his exhaustive analysis of the subject in his volume *Nihon no Hamuretto* (Hamlet in Japan) published in 1972.[71] In 1875 the writer Kanagaki Robun (1829–1894) published his *Seiyō kabuki Hamuretto* (Hamlet: A Western Kabuki) in the *Hiragana eiri shinbun* (Illustrated hiragana newspaper).[72] Prompted by the attempted assassination of the politician Itagaki Taisuke in 1882, a translation of *Julius Caesar* was serialized in the *Rikken seitō* newspaper in 1883. It was written by the English scholar Kawashima Keizō (1859–1935) under the title *Ōshū gikyoku juriasu shiizaru no geki* (A Western drama: The tragedy of Julius Caesar), and the work was republished in May 1886 under the title *Shēkusupia gikyoku rōma seisuikan* (Shakespeare's drama: A mirror of Roman vicissitudes).[73] A little later that year Kawashima's faithful and complete translation of *Romeo and Juliet* was published under the title of *Romyō Juri: Gikyoku shunjō ukiyo no yume* (The drama of Romeo and Juliet: The dream of the world of spring passion).[74]

In 1877 a version of *The Merchant of Venice* was rendered into Japanese and published in a contemporary journal under the title of *Muneniku no kishō* (The strange court case of breast-flesh). Its author was unknown, although speculation has centered on Fujita Mokichi (1852–1892), a well-known translator of Shakespeare.[75] The characters' names were all changed to Japanese names—Shylock became Yokubari Genpachi (Stubborn Tightfist), and Portia became Kiyoka (Pure Fragrance)—and the settings were transferred to Japan as well.[76] In 1879 the Kabuki dramatist Kawatake Mokuami (1816–1893) wrote a manuscript version of some scenes from the same play, but they were never performed.[77] This version was followed by Inoue Tsutomu's *Jinniku shichiire saiban* (The flesh-pawning trial, 1883), a translation of the *Merchant of Venice* chapter in Charles Lamb's *Tales from Shakespeare*. Here "Shylock" was rendered phonetically into Japanese as "Sairoku" and "Portia" became "Poruchia."[78] Inoue's translation was rewritten by the novelist Udagawa Bunkai (1848–1930) for serialization in the Osaka Asahi newspaper in 1885, and this text was immediately adopted as a Kabuki play for an experiment in Katsu Genzō's theater-improvement campaign; it proved to be a tremendous success. The Kabuki title was *Sakura doki zeni no yo no naka* (A time of cherry blossoms: A world of money), and the Nakamura Sōjūrō company performed the play in at least twelve separate productions in Osaka and Tokyo between 1885 and 1908.[79] Shylock became Masuya Gohei (Merchant Gohei) and Portia was called Tamae (Eternal Jewel).[80]

Kawatake Toshio notes that a Jōruri, or puppet theater, manuscript containing a partial version of *Hamlet* entitled *Hamuretto Seiyō Jōruri reigen kōshi no adauchi* (Hamlet: Western Jōruri, The revenge of the psychic prince) was made by the translator Toyama Masakazu (1848–1900) around 1881, but this did not become widely available until after Toyama's death.[81] Parts of this were revised and later published in the collection *Shintaishi shō* (A collection of poetry in the new style, 1882), which will be discussed later.[82]

Kawato Michiaki notes that over fifty books on Shakespeare (including translations) were published during the forty-five years of the Meiji era alone, the most on any single Western author, and when added to articles, translations, and the like published in newspapers and magazines the total number of publications would exceed a hundred.[83] By and large, Japanese adaptations of Shakespeare in the Meiji era can be described as falling into the second category proposed by Brandon—that of "localised Shakespeare"—where the audience may well not recognize that the plays are translations and described events and characters set outside Japan, or into Steiner's category of an "incorporative" movement.

Shōyō is, according to Brandon, the quintessential example of a translator who falls into the category of creating a "canonical Shakespeare," as his aim was to convey faithfully the foreignness of the originals. Does this statement represent Shōyō's own view of translation? Even if it can be argued that this was a position that he held at some time during his career as a translator, it certainly does not represent the position that he held at the beginning of his career, or, to be precise, the position that he maintained before 1916, as seen from his statements to that effect. The question remains: is this statement true of Shōyō's own practice as a translator? An examination of selected passages from the sequence of *Julius Caesar* translations that Shōyō created will help to establish the truth of the matter.

According to the literary historian Itō Sei, Shōyō's first attempt at translating *Julius Caesar* occurred in 1881. Itō writes that although Shōyō conceived the project in that year, he did not complete his translation until January 1883. His original publisher fell through and so the translation, under the title of *The Sharp Edge of Freedom's Sword*, did not actually appear until May 1884. This account is confirmed in the evidence Shōyō himself provides in his essays. The price was one yen for the volume, which, at the time, was rather expensive. It sold few copies but received high praise from contemporary reviewers.[84] In 1913 Shōyō published a slightly revised version of *Julius Caesar* as part of his ongoing project to translate two or so Shakespeare dramas every year. When Shōyō came to translate the play once more in 1933, he made further alterations. I will examine the various versions by back-translating one famous scene from the play into English.

Here, from *The Riverside Shakespeare*, are the first five lines of Caesar's speech to Brutus in Act III, Scene I, of the drama. This speech takes place just before Brutus stabs and kills Caesar.

> I could be well mov'd, if I were as you;
> If I could pray to move, prayers would move me;
> But I am constant as the northern star,
> Of whose true-fix'd and resting quality
> There is no fellow in the firmament.[85]

Shōyō's 1884 renders these lines in Japanese as follows:

Kono Shiizaru ga o mi no gotoku, hitome mo hajizu hiretsu ni mo, hiza o ori kōbe o sage, inu neko dōyō kobi o kenjite, hito ni tangan nasu yō naru, hikutsu no shōne o idaki oraba, o mi no negai mo kikiiru beki ga, yo ga kokoro wa daibanjaku, kano hokkyoku no hoshi naranedomo.[86]

The translation back into English reads:

If, like yourself, this Caesar is not ashamed of the glances of others, and contemptuously prays on his knees, bows his head, toadies to others like a cat or a dog, embracing a servile temperament as if beseeching others, then he would listen to your demands; but my heart is an unmoving rock, like the northern star.

Shōyō's 1913 revised version of the scene reads:

Jibun ga kimi no yō na ningen de attara, tōzen kokoro o ugodasu demo arō, mata hito o ugokasu tame ni aete inoru yō na otoko de attara, inorarete kokoro o ugokasudemo arō. Ga, jibun wa kesshite ugokan, seiza fudō o tokushitsu ni oite, hekirakuchū ni mata to rui no nai hokkyokusei no gotoku ni.[87]

Here is the back-translation:

If I were a man like you, then naturally my heart would be moved, and if I were a man who dared to pray in order to move people's hearts, then, being the object of prayer, my heart would be moved. But I will never be moved, in my steadfast and unmoving nature, I am like the peerless northern star in the firmament above.

Here is Shōyō's rendering in 1933:

Jibun ga anta no yō na otoko de attara, sō negawarerya tōzen kokoro o ugokasu demo arō, mata hito o ugokasu tame ni inoru koto no dekiru otoko de attara, inorarete kokoro o ugokashi mo suru darō ga, jibun wa ugokanai, kakko fudō o tokushitsu to suru koto ni oite, hekirakuchū ni mata to tagui no nai hokkyokusei no gotoku ni.[88]

The back-translation reads:

If I were a man like you, and if I were implored in that way, then naturally my heart would be moved. If I were a man who could pray to move the hearts of others, then, being the object of prayer, my heart would be moved, but it is not moved. It is my nature to be steadfast and unmoving, like the peerless northern star in the firmament above.

It is clear that the 1913 and 1933 versions are very similar and are indeed translations of Shakespeare's original text, but the 1884 version can at best be described as a free or loose rendering; perhaps a poetic adaptation would be a more apt description. It is interesting to see that this is what Shōyō defines as "Jōruri style," the term he used in his preface to the translation. It is now possible to confirm Shōyō's own account of the composition of the translation, as described in the essays quoted earlier. The 1884 version is written in 7/5 rhythm, whereas the 1913 and 1933 versions are composed in modern colloquial prose. Worth noting is that the 1933 version is longer than the 1913 revised version—clearly Shōyō was attempting to create a translation even more transparent to the original; indeed in places it reads as a painstakingly literal version, again confirming the account he gave in his 1916 article. The differences in the Japanese are greater than revealed by the English back-translations, but they still pale beside the 1884 version, which is so different that it could be by a different translator altogether.

As many commentators have noted, Shōyō was a devotee of Kabuki when he was young, and there is no doubt that the 1884 adaptation reads like the typical diction of a Jōruri or Kabuki drama. In that sense the 1884 version indigenizes Shakespeare's text for its contemporary audience and therefore falls into Brandon's second category of "localized Shakespeare." Further the differences between the three versions are striking, demonstrating unambiguously that the 1913 and 1933 "revisions" are far more than simple textual changes but represent, as his biographer Ōmura has stated of the 1933 version, a complete rewriting. This also confirms the veracity of the change of attitude that Shōyō himself described in the 1916 essay. These comments make generalizations about the complete translations, but in my view the passages are representative of the plays in their entirety.

Nakamura Kan in his 1986 book on Shōyō argues that the 1884 adaptation was much more than a translation. He notes that Shōyō amplified and embellished certain passages in order to advance ideas on literature and aesthetics, first expressed in his pioneering treatise on Western aesthetics, *Shōsetsu shinzui* (The essence of the novel, 1885–1886), and also to explain features of the original text that Japanese readers would have found alien and therefore would not have understood.[89] In addition, Nakamura makes a larger claim for the 1884 translation: contending that Shōyō expanded on the original text—turning the character of Brutus into a hero fighting for liberty and civil rights, for example—in order to express support for the *jiyūminken undō,* the contemporary political movement for democracy.[90] The proofs he cites for these claims arise from the insertion of such phrases as *kokka no tame jiyū no tame ni* (for the sake of the nation for the sake of liberty) that do not occur in the original play.[91] Nakamura refers to these examples as part of his thesis that Shōyō's translations were profoundly political, part of Shōyō's advocacy of the notion of *ninjō*, human sentiments or passion, an expansion of the idea of what constitutes the human, whether as political agent or as something larger, a notion that challenged the traditional polity built upon a subordination of the individual to the emperor or state. The alien, democratized human that appears in Western thought at this time is thus brought home, homogenized, as it were, so as to create a Japanese equivalent.

Indra Levy has argued recently that Shōyō's emphasis was on translation rather than adaptation, but as seen from the analysis above, Shōyō's translation practice was quite complex and did involve elements of adaptation.[92] Levy contrasts the different models championed by the next generation of theater reformers, who looked to Naturalism for inspiration. As she remarks, "At the heart of this divergence over theatrical models was a fundamental disagreement over the proper relationship between the exotic Western text, the Japanese reader-writer and the Japanese body itself. Briefly stated, Shōyō sought to fuse Western and Japanese conventions in a way that would simply refine the content of the Japanese theater, rather than marking a radical departure from it."[93] This is true as far as it goes, but Levy is writing primarily of Shōyō's theatrical practice around 1911 rather than the translations he revised later in his career, as exemplified by the versions of *Julius Caesar* dating from 1913 and 1933. In those translations Shōyō clearly sought to construct a more colloquial version of Shakespeare. Moreover, Levy's emphasis is upon performance rather than text, as demonstrated by her analysis of Shōyō's instructions to his actors to forget English acting conventions in favor of Kabuki-based performance style.[94]

The distinguished playwright Kinoshita Junji (b. 1914) comments that the fifty years separating the first and last translations of *Julius Caesar* reveal great differences in style but argues that both versions make equally serious claims to be used in performance. Both versions represent the spoken Japanese of contemporary Japanese theater.[95] This is an intriguing remark, as Shōyō himself cited the Jōruri style of the translation in his preface to his first version of the play as evidence that it was not written in the colloquial. Furthermore, in the preface Shōyō clearly stated that the play "was not meant to be performed by Japanese actors"; as he later remarked, it belonged to the realm of *kokubun*, or literature, rather than as drama meant to be performed. If I have not misread Kinoshita, it may be that he is making a comment about the nature of the colloquial as it was used in stage drama.

Translation Practice: *Hamlet*

Hamlet was the first of Shakespeare's plays to appear in Japanese translation, even if it was only in part. However, the interpretations or part-versions of *Hamlet* that appeared in 1870 and 1875 are not recognized as translations in the normal sense of the word. The first published translation—here meaning not an adaptation that obscures the foreign origin of the work but a rendering of the original text into Japanese that is recognizable as deriving from the original—occurred in 1882, although only one scene was translated. Yatabe Ryōkichi (1852–1899) was a young botanist who had returned to Japan in 1882 after studying in the United States. He was an associate of Inoue Tetsujirō (1855–1944), a philosopher who was soon to become a professor at Tokyo University. Yatabe had prepared a version of one scene from *Hamlet,* which he showed to Inoue.[96] This scene is the famous soliloquy uttered by Hamlet in Act III, Scene I:

> To be, or not to be: that is the question.
> Whether 'tis nobler in the mind to suffer
> The slings and arrows of outrageous fortune,
> Or to take arms against a sea of troubles,
> And by opposing end them? To die, to sleep,—[97]

Yatabe's manuscript reads:

> *Nagaraubeki ka tadashi mata*   *Nagaraubeki ni arazaru ka?*
> *Koko ga shian no shidokoro zo*   *Unmei ika ni tsutanaki mo*
> *Kore ni taeru ga masurao ka?*   *Mata, sawa arade umi yori mo*
> *Fukaki ikon ni tamukōte*   *Kore o harasu ga mononofu ka?*

Inoue praised this translation, which was put into 7/5 rhythm and was written in the *chōka* (long poem) style, a variety of verse popular in classical times, yet the translation was neither a *waka* nor *haiku,* the two major classical genres of poetry—it was a new style entirely.[98]

The back-translation reads:

Is it better to live long or again	Not to live long?
This is where I should deliberate	No matter how unfortunate my fate is
A better man would endure this	Or rather than enduring
A warrior would face it and wreak	A revenge deeper than the sea

The following day, according to Itō Sei, the psychologist Toyama Masakazu came to see Inoue. Toyama, like Yatabe, had also studied in the United States, and he had also prepared a manuscript translation of the same soliloquy. According to Kawatake Toshio, this was the revised version of the earlier translation of *Hamlet* prepared by Toyama.[99] Toyama's revised translation reads.

Shinuru ga mashi ka ikuru	
ga mashi ka	*Shian o suru wa koko zo kashi*
Tsutanaki un no nasake naku	*Uki me karaki me kasanaru mo*
Taeshinobu ga otoko zo yo	*Mata mo omoeba sawa arade*
Ichi sono koto ni futatsu naki	*Tsuyu no tama no o uchikirite?*[100]

The back-translation of Toyama reads:

Is it better to live or die?	This is where I should deliberate
Wretched in my unfortunate fate	My suffering and sorrows increase
To be a man is to bear this	Then, again, on second thought, this may not be the case
Having only one, not two lives	As transient as dew, should I cut my life short for the sake of revenge?

Toyama's first version of this passage was put into prose, so the change to a 7/5 poetic meter, as Kawatake Toshio suggests, was probably prompted by Yatabe's selection of the same verse meter.[101] Inoue described this kind of verse-translation, which his two companions competed to produce for him, as "new-style" verse *(shintaishi)*, since it had not existed in Japan before.[102] A few months later the collected translations of the three scholars were published in the epoch-making volume *A Collection of Poems in the New Style,* which included, in addition to the two translations of Hamlet's soliloquy, versions of verses by Longfellow, Charles Kingsley (1819–1875), Tennyson, and Thomas

Gray (1716–1771), as well as original poetry composed in the same new style.[103] This mode of poetry became the template for the development of Japanese verse in the twentieth century; and thus, in one sense, Shakespeare may be called the father of modern Japanese poetry.

Robert Morrell, comparing Yatabe's and Toyama's versions of this scene to the revised translation done by Shōyō in 1928, notes that "the quality of the latter [that is, Shōyō's version] is apparent even to the foreign student of Japanese."[104] Morrell's 1928 version presumably refers to Shōyō's first complete translation of Hamlet, which appeared in 1909 as the first volume of the *Shaō kessakusen*, or *Selected Masterpieces of Shakespeare* (later *Shaō zenshū*, edited and translated by Shōyō), mentioned earlier as the "Shakespeare Masterpiece" series. The earliest complete translation of *Hamlet* had appeared in 1905, four years before Shōyō's rendering.[105] Shōyō had tried his hand at part-versions of *Hamlet*, namely, in 1885, when he published a translation of a few scenes from the play in a journal, and again in 1896, when he published a long part-translation in the *Waseda Journal*.[106] Kawatake Toshio, in his detailed study of Shōyō's translation style, notes that each translation moves further towards the colloquial and away from the old-fashioned Jōruri diction that marks Shōyō's earliest renderings of Shakespeare. He comments that it is clear Shōyō began his career as a translator of Shakespeare by first rendering the Bard into literature and then later into theater.[107] Kawatake believes that Shōyō was never able to fully commit himself to a totally colloquial translation style—he wavered between his love for the premodern theatrical style of Kabuki performance and a more modern naturalistic mode for his versions of Shakespeare.[108]

In 1933 the revised version of the play was published as the first volume of the Shinshū, or "new edition" *Shakespeare Collected Works* (edited and translated by Shōyō), which was issued between 1933 and 1935. Here is Shōyō's 1909 version of this same famous soliloquy:

Nagarauru ka? Nagaraenu? Sore ga gimon ja . . . zanninna unmei no yadama o, hitasura taeshinōde oru ga daijōbu no kokorozashi ka? Aruiwa umi nasu kannan o mukae utte, tatakōte ne o tatsu ga daijōbu ka? Shi wa . . . nemuri . . . ni suginu.[109]

Translated back into English, the scene reads:

To live or not to live? That is the question . . .

Shall an honorable man endure the arrows and bullets of cruel fate, or does he have the will to meet the adverse seas and, by fighting, end it completely. Death is no more than sleep.

Next follows Shōyō's 1933 revised version:

Yo ni aru, yo ni aranu, sore ga gimon ja. Zanninna unmei no ya ya ishinage o, hitasura taeshinonde oru ga danshi no hon'i ka, aruiwa umi nasu kannan o mukaeutte, tatakōte ne o tatsu ga daijōbu no kokorozashi ka? Shi wa . . . nem-uri . . . ni suginu.[110]

Translated back into English, the scene reads:

To be in the world or not to be in the world? That is the question . . .
    Is it a man's desire to endure the arrows and slings of cruel fate, or does he have the will to meet the adverse seas and, by fighting, end it completely. Death is no more than sleep.

Shōyō's first version is as literal as it is possible to be (and much more effective and poetic than the literal English conveys) and still retain an element of poetic or theatrical diction, unlike the earlier versions by other translators, which are quite free. The earlier two versions are closer to poetry than both of Shōyō's translations, which are manifestly a more declamatory mode of speech. Shōyō's later version is slightly more colloquial than his earlier translation. The differences really arise only in the choice of vocabulary: a few minor changes from the first version, such as the use of *ishinage* (slings) rather than *yadama* (arrows and bullets) and *danshi* (man) rather than *daijōbu* (honorable man). These changes accord with Shōyō's remarks on this translation in his 1907 article, which provide an excellent context for understanding exactly what effects he was striving for, especially the comment that he was attempting something closer to the classicism of the Noh theater than the romanticism of Chikamatsu. Overall, the changes in the second version make it slightly closer to the original than the first translation.

    None of the versions could be described as colloquial Japanese since all retain some flavor of the classical idiom. We can compare Shōyō's renderings to the much more colloquial translation of *Hamlet* of critic and scholar Nojima Hidekatsu (b. 1930), published in 2001, where, for instance, Nojima translates the first few lines of Hamlet's soliloquy as "*Ikiru ka, shinu ka, sore wa mon-*

dai da./Dochira ga rippana ikikata ka. . . ." This is as plain and contemporary a Japanese translation as one is likely to find and makes completely apparent the old-fashioned and elegant character of Shōyō's diction.[111] But it is useful to remember the dramatist Kinoshita Junji's comment that when hearing Shōyō's version of *Hamlet* as a schoolboy, he found nothing unnatural or stilted about it. Nor presumably did the other patrons of the Little Tsukiji Theater where it was first performed well over half a century ago.[112] Indeed, Kinoshita notes that no contemporary critic described Shōyō's diction as old-fashioned; for the audience of the day, that *was* theatrical dialogue. It is important to note that this comment refers specifically to *Hamlet* and not *Julius Caesar;* this may help explain Kinoshita's rather puzzling comments cited earlier.

Nakamura Kan traces Hamlet's famous soliloquy through the several versions of Shōyō's translations and concludes: "By translating *Hamlet* and retranslating *Hamlet,* Shōyō digested Hamlet's soliloquy and made it his own."[113] The point of Nakamura's remark is that Hamlet's question represented a profound restatement of the political relationship between citizens and the state and that Shōyō's continued engagement with this issue through his translations of *Hamlet* led directly to the adoption of a similar political stance among the leading writers of the day.[114] The alien notion of self expressed in this soliloquy had become, by the time of Shōyō's death, the accepted position for a majority of Japanese.

On the matter of the colloquial—and this issue bears directly on Brandon's categorizations of "canonical" and "localized" versions of Shakespeare—a comparison between Shōyō's first version of *Hamlet* in 1909 and the final revised version of 1933 will reveal just how many alterations Shōyō was prepared to make in his last years to accord with changing theatrical fashions.

Here I examine Hamlet's remarks to Ophelia, which occur shortly after his famous soliloquy, in the same Act III, Scene I, of *Hamlet.* In answer to Ophelia's question: "Could beauty, my lord, have better commerce than with honesty?" Hamlet replies:

HAMLET: Aye, truly, for the power of beauty will sooner transform honesty from what it is to a bawd than the force of honesty can translate beauty into his likeness. This was sometime a paradox, but now the time gives it proof. I did love you once.

OPHELIA: Indeed, my lord, you made me believe so.[115]

Shōyō's 1909 version reads:

HAMLET: *Kemonai koto. Naze to oshare, misao o otosu bi no chikara wa bi o hikiaguru misao no chikara no ikusōbai ja. Kore ga furikutsu to omowareta koro mo atta ga, ima wa sore ga yo no tsune ja. Izen wa sonata o ba itoshii to omōte ita.*
OPHELIA: *Jitsu, warawa mo sō to ba shi omōte orimashita.*[116]

Back-translated this reads:

HAMLET: There is not the slightest doubt. Why do you say so? Because the power of beauty to bring chastity to a fall is a thousand times stronger than the power of chastity to raise up beauty. Once this was to be thought to be illogical, but now it is the way of the world. I once felt that you were my beloved.
OPHELIA: I did think this too.

Now, the rewritten 1933 version:

HAMLET: *Kemonai koto. Naze to iiyare, misao o tsuiraku sasuru bi no chikara wa bi o hikiaguru misao no chikara no ikusō bai ja. Sore ga fugōri to omowareta koro mo atta ga, ima wa sore ga atarimae ja. Izen wa sonata o itoshii to omōte ita.*
OPHELIA: *Shinjitsu, warawa mo sono yō ni zonjite orimashita.*[117]

There is no point in back-translating the 1933 version as it is almost identical with the 1909 version, except for two or three slight changes in vocabulary. Here is evidence that confirms the truth of Shōyō's remarks in his 1933 piece to the effect that the entire resources of the Japanese language should be brought to bear on translating Shakespeare: Shōyō deliberately retained some of the archaic diction included in the 1909 version in the later revision. Of course, without a detailed, complete examination of the 1909 and 1933 versions—impossible to do justice to in a single chapter—it cannot be assumed that this operates uniformly throughout the two translations, although my impression on a first reading indicates that this is the case.

Tsubouchi Shikō, Shōyō's nephew and heir, believes that this passage is still old-fashioned in its diction and also a little difficult to understand, but he feels that the general mood is conveyed.[118] Nevertheless, there is no doubt that this is a translation, not a version so "naturalized" that it is unrecognizable as Shakespeare, and a not unpoetic one at that.

Conclusion

What conclusions can be drawn from comparisons of these versions of Shakespeare that Shōyō created? One conclusion suggests itself immediately: Brandon's categories need to be loosened, as clearly his first and second categories overlap somewhat in Shōyō's versions, albeit more in the earlier translations than the revised 1933–1935 versions. The categories overlap because Shōyō was, above all, a man of the theater. This became especially apparent after a re-evaluation of the translating process and the earlier Shakespeare translations that he undertook around 1916. After this time he constructed his translations with an ear for the performance of the plays rather than an eye to the text. It can be argued that the rhetorical dimension of stage Japanese as expressed in Shōyō's translations, which, as one might expect, have echoes from such other indigenous theatrical traditions as Noh and Kabuki, contain elements that to the modern audience seem old-fashioned and quaint. Shōyō dealt specifically with these objections in such pieces as the 1933 essay, where he argued that the colloquial in performance is by no means identical with the language of everyday Japanese.

On the other hand, it may be argued that such a patina of antiquity is closer to the reception that modern audiences give to Shakespeare's antique English diction. Kinoshita Junji has argued that Shōyō's own plays use more old-fashioned diction than his Shakespeare translations. He claims that this is because of the influence of Shakespeare's English, which naturally inclines Shōyō to use modern Japanese, for he describes Shakespeare's English as *kindai Eigo,* or modern English.[119] Harry Levin uses the term "Early New English" to describe Shakespeare's idiom and notes that it is further away from contemporary English than the distance between A. W. Schlegel's translations of Shakespeare into German more than 150 years ago and current German.[120] It seems strange to non-Japanese to see Shakespeare's English as an argument to support Shōyō's use of modern Japanese as his preferred idiom for translation. Perhaps the greater difference between the literary Japanese of the seventeenth century and now compared with their English equivalents provides the impetus for Kinoshita's argument.

One point worth repeating is Kinoshita's reaction as a young student to Shōyō's Japanese, which he did not perceive as archaic or old-fashioned. Written Japanese has changed remarkably over the course of the twentieth century, far more so than English. So the much vaunted "Jōruri style" of Shōyō's early versions may indeed be closer to the vernacular than is generally thought to be the case, especially after an examination of Shōyō's original plays written in a similar style, which presumably had to appeal to contemporary audiences in order to succeed as commercial theater. Peter Milward argues that Kinoshita's own translations of Shakespeare—he is referring specifically to Kinoshita's version of *Othello*—lose much of the vividness of the original, as he notes "the concern for modern colloquial Japanese often leads to banalities of expression which contrast strangely with the usually dignified setting of Shakespearian drama." [121] He also finds that Shōyō's mixed style succeeds in avoiding the inadequacies of modern colloquial Japanese because of "his careful selection of words and dignified style." [122]

In any event, a number of commentators—but most notably Shōyō's adopted nephew and official heir, Tsubouchi Shikō—have stressed how hard Shōyō worked to produce translated texts that could be performed in the theater. The orality, that is, the rhetorical structure of the text, can at times persuade listeners with both its archaic and colloquial elements, as such features are typical of the language of performance, which is not the language of everyday speech, no matter how cleverly it might be made to appear otherwise, as Shōyō has repeatedly argued. The "actability" of Shōyō's translations thus persuades the audience to accept his language as "natural," despite whatever distance it may have from everyday speech. In this respect Steiner's remarks about bringing home the text to the degree that the work "is enhanced" ring true. On the other hand, the question of whether Shōyō created a new tradition of Shakespeare translation, as Gadamer's description of the "hermeneutic circle" may imply, cannot be resolved without further study. Kawatake Toshio noted that the modern author Dazai Osamu (1909–1948) in his play-like novel *Shin hamuretto* (The new Hamlet, 1948) parodied Shōyō's translations of *Hamlet*—evidence that Shōyō's versions had achieved canonical status by the mid-twentieth century. [123]

Nakamura Kan's study of Shōyō reveals the political dimension of translation, even when the subject matter of translation is theater. [124] Shakespeare was a writer whose plays engaged directly with politics, so it is no surprise that Shōyō could expand upon the political elements in them. But, as Nakamura demonstrates, Shōyō found in Shakespeare more than mere slogans: he discovered a new view of what it is to be human, and this viewpoint was realized directly in Shakespeare's characterizations. In Shōyō's translations as performed on the Japanese stage, audiences could literally see and hear a new mode of expressing their humanity that was alien to Japanese tradition; they could experience it in a vastly more powerful way than was available in political tracts. Nakamura finds that this new notion of selfhood effected a major change in the literary expression of self and also had important political implications.

Shōyō's lifelong engagement with Shakespeare demonstrates how strongly Shakespeare's plays were perceived as performance art. This feature of the Japanese reception of Shakespeare is perhaps common to other Asian societies as well. The fact that English is a foreign language for virtually all of Asia is the key element in seeing Shakespeare more as a dramatist than a poet. The alien, paradoxically, is less so when it is a visual rather than a textual phenomenon.

The complexity of translating the alien is a more convoluted exercise that can be outlined here. The culture that Shakespeare represents or even embodies is, to use Peter Milward's words, "remote and alien," even for the contemporary Japanese audience, let alone when Japanese first encountered Shakespeare over a hundred years ago.[125] But the encounter with the alien is an integral element in the formation of culture itself. Emily Apter's first thesis on translation is "Nothing is translatable"; this develops into her eighth thesis, "Translation is an oedipal assault on the mother tongue." Surely Shakespeare is the apotheosis of such a thesis. Her next thesis is: "Translation is the traumatic loss of native language," which perhaps we may read as gesturing towards the process that actually occurred in Japan of a complete rewriting of indigenous traditions of literature under the assault of Western literature via translation.[126] But her nineteenth thesis reads: "Translation is the system-subject," which leads her to her final contradictory yet triumphant thesis: "Everything is translatable."[127] Shōyō's translations are now almost unreadable for Japanese students, who need modern colloquial translations of Japanese texts that were written a mere century ago, and which are seen as heralding the birth of the modern in literature. In this sense the alien that was once domesticated or, more properly, refigured in a different form not as alien as the original undoubtedly is, becomes alien once again to an audience from a different age and needs refiguring and retranslating all over again, as Apter implies, in a never-ending loop.

CHAPTER 2

NATURALIZING THE ALIEN

Yosano Akiko's Revolution in Verse

Of course you might say why not invent new names new languages
but that cannot be done. It takes a tremendous amount of inner
necessity to invent even one word, one can invent imitating movements and emotions in sounds, and in the poetical language of some
languages you have that . . . but this has really nothing to do with
language. Language as a real thing is not imitation either of sounds
or colors or emotions it is an intellectual recreation and there is no
possible doubt about it and it is going to go on being that as long as
humanity is anything.

—Gertrude Stein

You just have to choose, making sure all the choices are wrong, and
the sky then of your own privacy caves in on you, collapses, is com-
fortable as sleep. In that distant forest nothing can live separate, and
it's a dream. A difficulty. For one. For one exchanging one neutral
memory for another.

—John Ashbery

In the late nineteenth century one of the last bastions of Japanese tradition,
the *waka,* the dominant genre of traditional Japanese poetry and a mode of
writing that constituted the mainstream of Japanese literature from ancient
times, was breached by the irruption of Western poetry and poetics. Western
poetry was seen as alien to the spirit of traditional Japanese verse, which has
been thought at various times to embody the very essence of what it means
to be Japanese. It was viewed from at least the seventeenth century as having
a spiritual dimension that could not be reproduced in foreign languages.[1] It
was brandished by conservatives, throughout Japanese history, as something

irreducibly Japanese that was cast in opposition to foreign modes of verse, principally Chinese, although these were also exploited by Japanese poets.[2] The poet Yosano Akiko (1878–1942), together with her husband, Hiroshi, and other poets including Hiroshi's teacher Ochiai Naobumi (1861–1903), made the first historic attempt at reforming or renovating *waka*. In Akiko's case, she accomplished this as much by importing ideas drawn from translations of Western verse as from other sources: in other words Akiko attempted to naturalize the alien tradition of Western poetry in her efforts to remake and revitalize the native verse tradition. Conservatives could imagine nothing more shocking, and Akiko's poetry did indeed outrage conservative poetry circles.[3] So it is only appropriate to begin with an account of what constituted traditional Japanese *waka* in the period immediately preceding Akiko's verse revolution.

New-style Poetry versus Old-style Poetry

In 1919, some eighteen years after the twenty-three-year-old Yosano Akiko had published *Midaregami* (Tangled hair, June 1901), the single most celebrated volume of poetry written by a Japanese woman in the twentieth century, T. S. Eliot published his influential essay "Tradition and the Individual Talent." Akiko's critical writings on poetry make no particular reference to this essay, but if she had read it, she would have found much with which to agree. Eliot's concluding remark, about poetry being an escape from emotion and personality may or may not have struck a sympathetic chord, but the need for the poet to believe in the past would certainly have gained Akiko's agreement.

Eliot criticizes the tendency to praise a poet's individuality, especially regarding the respects in which the poet differs from his predecessors. But approaching the poet without this prejudice, he notes, "we shall often find that not only the best, but the most individual parts of his work may be those in which the dead poets . . . assert their immortality most vigorously."[4] Eliot further refines this notion by adding, "No poet, no artist of any art, has his complete meaning alone. His significance, his appreciation is the appreciation of his relation to the dead poets and artists."[5] Eliot then links the sense of an appreciation of the past to the development of the young writer by asserting, "What happens is a continual surrender of [the artist] as he is at the moment to something which is more valuable. The progress of an artist is a continual self-sacrifice, a continual extinction of personality."[6]

It cannot necessarily be said that Eliot follows his own dictum; for many readers would perceive far more of the personality of the avant-garde artist Eliot in the *The Waste Land* (1922), for instance, than the poetic heritage of Dante or John Webster. However, in Japan at the turn of the century, as in many other places, the force of tradition on the present was an issue much debated. And it was nowhere more hotly debated than in discussions about *waka,* the traditional poetry of Japan.

Indeed, Eliot's point of view was already enshrined in the principles and practices of traditional *waka* poets. These principles are condemned in the following quotation from Ochiai Naobumi's 1903 lecture "Kadan no ichi" (A first lecture on poetry). Naobumi was a *waka* poet determined to reform poetry, to create a new poetry for a new age: "If we examine the poems of the 'old school' as to their materials, expression, diction and thought, we shall find that they are all imitated from the poets of former times, and there is nothing novel or interesting about them." [7]

Two examples of *kyū-ha,* or "old-style" *waka,* follow. The first is by the poet Inoue Fumio (1800–1871), who belonged to the Edo school of poetry, one of the three dominant *waka* coteries of the day. Poetry of this time was marked by beautiful language that often focused on a lovely scene. The Edo school modeled itself on the poetry of the past, inspired by the *waka* of Kamo no Mabuchi (1697–1769). But there is nothing personal or innovative about the poetry: it merely repeated the rhythms of a well-tried melody. [8] Inoue's *waka* reads:

Otomego ga	In the shape of
Monohajishitaru	A maiden
Omokage ni	Shy and awkward
Nioi idetaru	Many-petaled cherry blossoms
Yaezakura kana	Open to fragrance [9]

The second *waka* is by the Kyoto poet Irie Tamemori (1868–1936). Irie belonged to the Dōjō poetry circle, which was associated with a traditional style of *waka* composed by courtiers. [10] Irie's poem reads:

Isozaki ni	Against the rocky cape
Yosuru nami yori	The waves lap
Miesomete	Approaching visibility
Honobono shiramu	A glimmering whiteness
Haru no unabara	The spring sea [11]

The scholar-poet Ōta Seikyū (1909–1996) describes these two poems as old-fashioned because the traditional language is tired and hackneyed.[12] New-style *waka* attempted to introduce contemporary language and a contemporary sensibility into poetry, as can be seen from Ochiai Naobumi's verse, which follows. It should be noted that the diction of Ochiai's *waka* is intentionally incongruous, with formulaic phrases from the *waka* tradition mixing with more modern vocabulary.

Otomego ga	The maiden
Ushio ami nishi	Bathing in the sea
Tōasa ni	In the shallow waters
Ukiwa no gotoki	Like a float
Tsuki no ukabinu	The moon has bobbed up [13]

However, it was Ochiai's disciple, Yosano Hiroshi (1873–1935), who proposed the more radical reforms and wrote the more revolutionary verse. Better known at this time under the pen-name Tekkan, Akiko's future husband and poet-mentor was the first to attempt to introduce a new sensibility into the *waka* tradition, one which originated in ideas of modernity that arose outside Japan, although he saw this as a process of reform or renovation.[14] As the leader of the literary world at that time, the novelist Mori Ōgai (1862–1922) stated in his preface to Tekkan's largest collection of poems, *Aigikoe* (Love poems, 1910): "Exactly who has raised up this 'new-style' poetry? The only person who can answer 'Me' is Yosano."[15] A sample of Tekkan's verse is the following, from his collection *Murasaki* (Purple, April 1901). It preceded *Tangled Hair* by only a few months. The other person mentioned in the poem, it goes without saying, is Akiko.

Koi to iu mo	We have not yet exhausted
Imada tsukusazu	This thing called love
Hito to ware to	Myself and one other
Atarashiku shinu	Have made new
Hinomoto no uta	The poetry of Japan [16]

On 3 November 1899 Tekkan codified in pamphlet form the rules of his new poetry society, the Tokyo Shinshisha, and on the first of April the following year a simplified version of these rules was published in the first issue of a magazine called *Myōjō* (Morning star), which Tekkan had founded to popularize his views and promote his tastes in poetry.[17] The rules stress the role of the indi-

vidual in discussing literature and criticizing art and state that Tekkan's society is devoted to "Kokushi kenkyū," the study of national poetry. Tekkan goes on to emphasize the leadership of the reform *waka* poets *(shinpa waka)* and *shintaishi* poets in the development of his new poetry society.[18] It is important to note that Tekkan generally uses the word *shi* rather than *waka* to refer to poetry, both in the name of the society and in the critical pronouncements that proceeded from it. As he used it, the word *shi* meant the new-style verse that was emerging from translations of the Western poetry discussed in Chapter 1.

On the very first page of the initial issue of *Myōjō,* a journal with which Akiko quickly became intimately associated, there appeared an abridged translation by the scholar Umezawa Waken (1871–1931) of an article on *waka* by W. G. Aston (1841–1911), whose *History of Japanese Literature* had been published the previous year. Aston is scathing about *waka,* about which he makes statements like the following that appeared in Umezawa's translation: "In short, *waka* are merely epigrams, limited to the lyric, only the first step in the expression of emotion."[19] Tekkan's reformist zeal as well as his polemical agenda is evident in his placing such a piece virtually beside the masthead. Distinguished writers of new-style poetry, like Susukida Kyūkin (1877–1945) and Shimazaki Tōson (1872–1943), are featured in this first issue, as is an article by the scholar and poet Utsumi Getsujo (1872–1935), placed prominently on page 7, extolling the virtues of Goethe's masterpiece of romantic angst, *Die Leiden des Jungen Werthers* (The sorrows of young Werther, 1774). In one sense the strategic placing of such poets and articles constitutes an ideological agenda that was to result, not too long after, in Tekkan's virtually dissolving the differences between *shi* and *waka* (or *tanka* as the genre soon came to be known).[20] He announced that the new poetry was to be known simply as *shintaishi:* "Our poetry should be called 'new-style verse' irrespective of whether it is long or short [*chōtan ni ron naku*]." This manifesto was published in the seventh issue of *Myōjō,* which appeared in October 1900. In the preceding September issue, another manifesto had proclaimed: "We will publish poetry about our own egos [*jiga no shi*]. This will not imitate the poetry of the past but will be our poetry, or rather, the poetry we have created individually."[21]

On page 28 of the September issue sixteen *tanka* appeared under the name of Hō Akiko, a young author who had only recently made her debut in the world of new-style *waka.* Hō was Akiko's maiden name—several months were to pass before Akiko and Tekkan married—and her *waka* in many ways demonstrated the truth of Tekkan's claims about poetry. It is important to note that prior to writing poetry in the new-style that Tekkan advocated, Akiko had published twenty "old-style" *waka*.[22] The fact that later she acknowledged only the poetry written from the time she began to publish in the journal *Yoshiashigusa,* explicitly (and falsely) denying any contact with "old-style" *waka* poets, is clear evidence of her total adherence to Tekkan's *waka* revolution.[23]

The first of three poems that I translate from this group of sixteen *tanka* was later published in Akiko's first collection of poetry, *Tangled Hair,* in August 1901. Although this collection, and the verse revolution inaugurated by it, forms our principal subject of investigation, I want to investigate certain other poems that Akiko published at the time that were not, for various reasons, included in *Tangled Hair*.[24] The leading Japanese commentator on Akiko, Itsumi Kumi, argues that the following poem is written purely as a product of Akiko's imagination on hearing that Tekkan had fallen ill.[25]

Yamimaseru	Around your fevered neck
Unaji ni hosoki	I place
Kaina makite	My slender arms
Netsu ni kawakeru	Upon your fevered lips
Mikuchi wo suwan	I kiss you [26]

The next two poems, unlike this first one, were not included in *Tangled Hair,* yet they are equally expressive of the heat generated by Akiko's fiery passion for Tekkan.

Chishio mina	This young woman
Nasake ni moyuru	Her blood-tide burning
Wakaki ko ni	With emotion
Kurui shine yo to	Does your poem instruct her
Tamō miuta ka	To madly die? [27]

And:

Shirazu to te	You do not know this
Tsumi ni ya wa aranu	But are not your words
Koigatari	Of love too cruel?
Kimi ni yamu ko no	Beside the one who is
Katawara ni shite	Sick with love for you [28]

These poems seem to epitomize, to literally embody, Tekkan's injunctions about ego and individuality. They seem to directly contradict, even scorn, Eliot's admonitions about the poet's continual extinction of personality, of a modest and restrained effacement of the self. But did Akiko spring unborn, without progenitors, into this world as a poet? Did Akiko, like Wallace Stevens, hold herself aloof from influence?[29] Or was she "caught up in a dialectical relationship (transference, repetition, error, communication) with . . . [other] poets," as Harold Bloom, in his famous study *The Anxiety of Influence* (1973), so confidently asserts is the fate of all poets.[30] To discover the answers to these questions, it is necessary to examine Akiko's first attempts at poetry, and the environment in which these poems were composed.

Experiments in Verse

Tekkan's injunction that each poet write about his ego appears to be contradicted by Bloom's observation that "we need to stop thinking of any poet as an autonomous ego," and here, Bloom seems to share some of Eliot's presumptions concerning tradition.[31] It is instructive, therefore, to find that Akiko's first published verses in *Yoshiashigusa* were not directly beholden to the *waka* tradition, because they were *shintaishi*. So the question changes: what relationship existed between these verses and the new *shintaishi* tradition?

The first poem Akiko published after abandoning the "old-style" *waka* genre, which she had taken up as a result of her early apprenticeship with the Sakai Shikishima Poetry Association—her old-style *waka* are seen by virtually all critics to be of little aesthetic value—was the *shintaishi* "Shungetsu" (Spring moon), which appeared in *Yoshiashigusa,* the house journal of the Kansai Seinen Bungakukai (Kansai Youth Literary Association).[32] This work was the first of two poems, both *shintaishi,* both published in the same journal, which preceded any of Akiko's attempts at new-style *tanka.* "Spring Moon" is a short poem written in a regular 7/5 meter and was published on 11 February 1899, when Akiko was twenty.

Wakarete nagaki kimi to ware	Long separated, you and I,
Koyoi aimishi ureshisa wo	Drinking unceasingly of the sweet wine
Kumite mo tsukinu umazake ni	Of the joy of meeting you tonight
Usukurenai no someideshi	Blushing pale crimson
Kimi ga katahō ni bin no ke no	On your cheek a lock of hair

Haru kaze yuruku soyogu kana.	Brushed by the soft spring breezes.
Tanoshikarazuya kono yūbe	How happy we are this evening!
Haru wa yūbe no usugumo ni	Between the wisps of spring cloud this night
Futari no koi mo satoru kana	We came to know of our mutual love
Oboro ni niou tsuki no moto	Under the moon's soft fragrance
Kimi kokoro naki hohoemi ni	To your innocent smile
Wakaki inochi ya sasagu beki.	Should I chance my youthful fate? [33]

If Akiko has a precursor here, then who would it be? Most Japanese critics point to the major *shintaishi* poet of the Meiji era, Shimazaki Tōson, as the most likely candidate. Tōson wrote four volumes of poetry before he abandoned verse for fiction, of which the first was *Wakanashū* (Seedlings), published in 1897, two years before "Spring Moon." Echoes of Tōson's *Seedlings* have been found in various lines from Akiko's verse. Her fifth and sixth lines, *"Kimi ga katahō ni bin no ke no / Haru kaze yuruku soyogu kana"* (On your cheek a lock of hair / Brushed by the soft spring breezes), bear a striking resemblance to Tōson's *"Bin no ke wo fuku kawa kaze yo"* (River breezes brushing against your tresses), as Morishima Yukie notes.[34] These lines are found in Tōson's famous poem "Okume," which is the first in a sequence of six poems, all monologues spoken by women, that Tōson later titled "Rokunin no Shojo" (Six maidens). Okume's declarations of love shocked many readers of the day and clearly influenced some of Akiko's *tanka* in *Tangled Hair*, as well as her *shintaishi*. Stanza 7 of the poem reads:

Koi wa wagami no yashiro nite	Love is my shrine
Kimi wa yashiro no kami nare ba	And you are its god
Kimi no tsukue no ue nara de	Where should I consecrate my heart
Nani ni inochi wo sasage mashi	If not to your altar? [35]

The last stanza is even more passionate:

Kokoro nomi ka wa te mo ashi mo	My heart, my hands, my arms
Wagami wa subete honoo nari	Every part of my body is aflame.
Omoi midarete ā koi no	And dying of love, ah
Chisuji no kami no nami ni	I let the thousand strands of my hair be
nagaruru	carried by the waves [36]

In this poem Tōson uses Christian imagery, familiar to him from his youthful infatuation with the religion, to liken a woman's passion to a sacrifice to a deity. These images of love both exotic, and, from certain Christian perspectives, near blasphemous, infused the *shintaishi* with a life and daring that had entirely disappeared from traditional poetry, even though most commentators regarded such passion as belonging almost totally to the realm of fantasy, and not as a reflection of real experience.[37] This was the first example of "modernized" Japanese verse, a mode of expression prompted by translations of Western poetry, to gain a large readership. As a result of Tōson's influence, the alien mode of poetic discourse known as *shintaishi* was imported into the tradition of Japanese poetry and became "naturalized." It is this model that Akiko was eventually to follow.

In her poem "Spring Moon" Akiko is more realistic, less rhetorically extravagant, as she poses a question in the last line: should her protagonist commit herself to her beloved on the basis of a smile? Such a dilemma, such rhetoric, clearly draws on the older tradition of *waka* poetry dealing with love from a woman's perspective and written mainly by women. This tradition is described by Sarah Strong as one of "waiting."[38]

In the *shintaishi* that followed, called "Waga oi" (My nephew), which was published in *Yoshiashigusa* in May 1899, Akiko takes the part of an older woman, an aunt, warning her nephew about the dangers of love. In the second sequence of the poem (lines 14 to 26), Akiko writes:

> Your aunt has fallen because of love
> Having forgotten all the wise advice
> > I wander alone over the pastures and parched fields
> Do not fall in love, sad love
> > Butterflies dozing in the flower-garden
> Where flower upon flower blossom in their thousands
> > Dream this happy dream!

Then the last three lines:

> Like the forever-ivy's forever
> Is there any way we can remain children?
> > In the image of God.[39]

The lament in this poem is again traditional, of women unlucky in love, and seems to owe little to the new tradition established by Tōson and others. The realism of the aunt's voice stands in stark contrast to the eroticized passion of Tōson. However, in the third of these early *shintaishi*, the tone changes. This third poem is called "Ato no mi" (My after-body) and was published in *Yoshia-shigusa* in November 1899. The poem has a number of notable features:

My body after living
      What will become of it? You wonder
         My tender love smiles
            I will become a flowering tree

Then will you become a lovely cherry-tree?
      In the morning sunlight when I gaze at this heavy-scented tree
         No other form could
            Better capture your heart

An exquisite moment of dream blossoms into full flood
      Passes into yesterday
         Today no one comes from afar
            So I can see deep into your heart

Then will you not become a mandarin tree
      Mandarins leaning over the eaves?
         The far-reaching fragrance
            Spreads even into the most tranquil of huts
               So sweet is your heart-fragrance

My fragrance drifts to a dreaming pillow
      Asleep, he is remembering an old love
         Shall I see the tears of lament
            So bereft of love that his spirit had vanished

Then are you not a maple deep in the mountains?
      Am I wrong to trust in you
         Your passion burning
            A thousand shades of crimson?

How empty your words! How absurd!
　　I am not an autumn maple!
　　　　In the heart of the goddess of autumn dwells
　　　　　　The failure of color

In this fickle human world,
　　Flourishing trees are hateful!
　　　　I do not wish for the pines' one thousand years
　　　　　　Yet I envy their steadfast color

Near the pure waters of the rock crevice
　　Where the muse reigns
　　　　Shall you and I
　　　　　　Become great pines, our branches intertwined?

We will make cool shadows for
　　Summer travelers in the mountains
　　　　When fair maidens
　　　　　　Lament love's obstacles

We will engulf the sadness of this fickle world
　　If there are evenings when young poets under the trees
　　　　Sing of love
　　　　　　We will join their pure harmonies [40]

The first thing worth remarking is the fact that the chief narrator in this dialogue between lovers is male, answering in a teasing way the question of his beloved as to what tree she will become after death. It was an established tradition for male poets, especially those belonging to the new *shi* tradition, to take female personae, but the reverse was quite rare. Another noteworthy feature is the realistic detail of the dialogue. The various alternatives the lovers explore in their rhetorical search for the appropriate troping to describe their love encompass not merely erotic love, but the obstacles and difficulties of real-life love, as well as the mutual support offered by conjugal love. Here Akiko plays upon, and in a sense "modernizes," the older tradition of *sōmonka*, or exchange poetry. However, in this case it is *shintaishi* rather than *waka* that are modernized. "Ato no mi" changes radically the patterning of earlier exchange poems, which were not constructed on assumptions of equality between the two erotic or romantic agents, as Akiko's poem is.[41] In this way Akiko's poem creates the possibility of reading the earlier tradition in a fashion quite different from what readers at the time were accustomed to. Does Akiko's "misreading" of the tradition—a notion that arises in Bloom's notion of creative misprision—"hold," to use Bloom's terminology, the older tradition "open"?[42] Does it, in fact, radically change it?

The answer must be in the negative, for Akiko's *shintaishi* is simply not strong enough to sustain such weight. To revivify or recreate the older *waka* tradition, Akiko needed diction that owed far less to that tradition than "My After-body," which borrows heavily from the language of *waka*. For that, she had to turn to Tōson, and other precursors, in a more deliberately self-conscious way than her *shintaishi* revealed or, perhaps, the genre itself permitted.

In the April 1899 issue of *Yoshiashigusa*, two months after Akiko's first *shintaishi* was published, a poem called "Koi no kami" (The god of love) appeared. The author of the poem was Kawai Suimei (1874–1965), a leading poet from Sakai, the city where Akiko lived and where her literary talents were nurtured by virtue of her membership in the Shikishima poetic circle. The title strikes one immediately—the combination of *kami* and *koi* was to become a staple trope of Akiko's *tanka* in *Tangled Hair*, and other stylistic features anticipate Akiko's later use of them. The third stanza reads:

Me wo hirake koi wa tada	Open your eyes! Love is
Kiyoku arubeshi tsumi no tame ni	Purity itself. The consequences of sin
Koi wa kegaruru iro narazu	Do not result in any color that can stain love [43]

The use of the word *tsumi* referring overtly to erotic love, and implicitly to adulterous love, contains nuances that become basic to the use of the word in *Tangled Hair*. The word takes on similar overtones in Tōson's poem "Betsuri" (Parting) in *Seedlings*. Moreover, in Tōson's last volume of poetry, *Rakubaishū* (Fallen plum collection, 1901), there is a long poem titled "Tsumi," which tells of the plight of a man who falls in love with a married woman.[44] The word *tsumi* itself is first found in the eighth-century *Man'yōshū*, Japan's earliest collection of poetry, however, its association with adultery would appear, if not to originate, then to be much reinforced in the new *shintaishi* tradition. The following poem from the *Man'yōshū* (Book 4, No. 712) illustrates the classical notion of *tsumi*.

Umasake wo	Is it the sin of
Miwa no hafuri ga	Touching the cedar
Iwau sugi	Blessed by the priests of Miwa,
Tefureshi tsumi ka	Miwa of sweet wine,
Kimi ni aigataki	That stops me from seeing you? [45]
(The maiden Ōme of Taniwa)	

Further proof that the new tradition of *shintaishi* added overtly Christian overtones, in respect of the association with sex and guilt, to the word *tsumi* is found in the following poem by Yosano Tekkan's mentor, Ochiai Naobumi. It was published around 1899–1900 in the magazine *Kokubungaku* (National literature).

Tsumi to iu	I believe
Hanzai saji to	I have not committed
Omou mi ni	Any sins at all in my body
Moshi tsumiareba	If I am sinful
Kami yusushimase	Please God forgive me. [46]

Love and sin are frequently yoked together in Akiko's verse, the following poems from *Tangled Hair* provide a perfect illustration.

Yasenitare	Wasted though I may be
Kaina moru chizo	The blood surges through my arms
Nao wakaki	How youthful I am!
Tsumi wo naku ko to	Do not look upon me, God
Kami yo mimasu na	As a child weeping over her sins! [47]

And:

Mune no shimizu	The pure water of my breast
Afurete tsui ni	Overflows and then
Nigorikeri	Turns to mud

> *Kimi mo tsumi no ko*   You are a child of sin
> *Ware mo tsumi no ko*   And so am I [48]

In the view of the scholar-poet Baba Akiko, these poems, and others like them, demonstrate how new and revolutionary Akiko's verse appeared to the readers of the day. The meaning expressed by the word *kami* (god) here has no precedent in the *waka* tradition; it clearly originates in the West. [49] Rather than referring to the Greek gods, however, I believe that the combination of the words "God" and *tsumi* (sin) connotes a play on Christian ideas, which became well established in the new poetic vocabulary of *shintaishi*. [50]

Another poem utilizing the word *kami* that is equally defiant of *waka* conventions, yet which clearly owes much to the new *shintaishi* tradition, is the following verse.

> *Midaregokochi*   Feelings all a-tangle
> *Madoi gokochi zo*   I have lost my way
> *Shikiri naru*   I cannot hide my breasts
> *Yuri fumu kami ni*   From the god who tramples
> *Chichi ōiaezu*   The lilies in all their glory [51]

Yosano Tekkan commented on this poem a month after its publication, noting that it reads visually, like a painting of a Western nude. [52] This remark suggests not only how important the vocabulary of Western poetry was for *Tangled Hair,* but it also evokes the visual vocabulary of Western art, especially Art Nouveau, which is, in many ways, the iconographic equivalent of Akiko's literary troping, as Haga Tōru has shown. [53]

The fifth and sixth stanzas of Kawai Suimei's poem, cited earlier, further emphasize the metonymic link between *kami* and *koi* in a way that is reminiscent of Akiko's later expansion of these two interlinked notions.

> *Ya yo kajin wa okiidete*   Oh, poet awake!
> *Koi wa kami nari tokoshie ni*   Love is an eternal god
> *Kami wa imasu to sakebu beshi*   You should cry aloud that god exists!
>
> *Yo wa odorokan utagawan*   The world will be shocked and doubt you
> *Yoshi odoroku mo utagau mo*   You say that you are the messenger of god
> *Kami no tsukai to nanori na ba*   Their shock and doubt do not matter [54]

Only four poems in *Tangled Hair* combine the words *koi* and *kami*. All utilize troping similar to Kawai's in the *shintaishi* quoted above. The following *tanka* by Akiko, more than the other three verses, not only gestures to the modern idiom of love created by Kawai, Tōson, and the other *shintaishi* poets, but also reaches back to the *Man'yōshū* with its personification of *sumire* (violet). Akiko and Tekkan often composed poems with violets suggestive of images of love.[55]

Kike na kami	O my lord! Listen!
Koi wa sumire no	Love is the exultant voice
Murasaki ni	Of violets
Yūbe no haru no	Purple
Santan no koe	In the spring evening[56]

Another Kansai poet whom many critics find an influential precursor in diction, as well as semantic intent, is the poet Susukida Kyūkin (1877–1945). Akiko herself wrote in the afterword to the Iwanami Bunko edition of her poetry:

I began composing poetry in 1900 about the time I was twenty. Tōson's new poetry was published in magazines, and various individual volumes by him also appeared. Susukida Kyūkin's fresh, new poetry also made an appearance, but after Tōson . . . in terms of expression [I owe much to] Kyūkin's use of language.[57]

Kyūkin's first book of verse was *Botekishū* (Evening flute), published in November 1899. This book broke all records that had been held for poetry published in Osaka. According to various accounts, all 5,000 copies of the volume's initial print run sold out in record time.[58] The most daring poem in this volume was a long *shintaishi* consisting of 105 four-line verses in regular meter called "Ama ga beni" (The nun's rouge). Verses using diction that was to become Akiko's trademark in *Tangled Hair* include the following; first, verse 3:

Somo onnago wo tatoureba,	To what shall I compare that girl?
Shitodome kuguru kumihimo ka,	A braid through an eyelet?
Sugata hosoku mo, waga koi no,	Her form is slender, my love
Koki kurenai ni moyuru kana.	Burning darkly crimson[59]

The last line, especially, resembles possibly the most sensual *tanka* in *Tangled Hair*, which was later deleted from the collection because of the threat of censorship.

Chibusa osae	Clasping my hands to my breasts
Shimpi no tobari	The curtain of mystery
Soto kerinu	I gently kicked aside
Koko naru hana no	How crimson is my flower
Kurenai zo koki	And how dark! [60]

Next, verse 15 from "The Nun's Rouge":

Shibashi kokage ni, chisu tokishi	For some time in the shady arbor, I recalled
Jitsu aru koro wo shinobishi mo,	Those days I spent in study in the real world
Chibusa sawarite waga mune no	But touching my breasts, I grew
Chikara aru chi ni ki wa tachinu.	Excited at the power of the blood beating in my chest [61]

As well as echoing the previous *tanka*, Kyūkin's verse brings to mind the following *tanka* from *Tangled Hair*:

Haru mijikashi	Spring is brief
Nani ni fumetsu no	Who can live forever?
Inochi zo to	I let his hands
Chikara aru chi wo	Explore
Te ni sagurasenu	My firm breasts [62]

Finally, we have verse 71 from "The Nun's Rouge":

Kano yawahada ni te wo furete,	If you touch her soft skin
Soko no izumi wo sagurimiba,	And seek out the fountain below,
Ten no konzu ka?, karaki naru	Is it heavenly nectar? Behold
Otoko no shiranu shumi wo min.	A delight withered men know not. [63]

This verse borders on the pornographic, but commentator Yano Hōjin finds it the direct source of Akiko's acclaimed poem about her own soft skin, or at least, the skin of the female narrator, which still puzzles readers as to whether the poet actually referred to a specific person or not. [64]

Yawa hada no	Beneath my soft skin
Atsuki chishio ni	A hot surge of blood

Fure mo mide	You have never felt
Sabishikarazu ya	Are you not lonely?
Michi wo toku kimi	You who teach the way[65]

Do these adaptations by Akiko of motifs and diction from the modern *shintaishi* tradition amount to a continual surrender of the artist, an extinction of the personality, as Eliot advocated? This question may seem facetious, as the tradition was almost wholly new, and was still in the process of being made. However, the point here is that while most of the precursors quoted above have faded into literary obscurity, Akiko's verse lives on and even now inspires imitators and imitations. To take up Bloom's theory once again, Akiko has not merely misprisioned her predecessors but has imprisoned them in the rhetorical structures created by her own verse, most notably in *Tangled Hair*.

The shift from *shintaishi* to *tanka* meant that Akiko drew upon the older *waka* tradition much more as a source, though by no means an unmediated or untroubled one, for her poetry. But, as we have seen, this did not prevent her from adapting the new tradition of the *shintaishi* into her *tanka*. The chief reason for the shift, and for its success, was to create a narrative structure for her poetry, a narrative built around the notion of love based upon an episodic patterning. In a sense both Kyūkin and Suimei, not to mention Tōson, construct similar narratives in their *shintaishi*. Their voices derive chiefly from monologues, but Akiko's voices in *Tangled Hair* derive from dialogues.

Akiko had already explored the monologue form in her *shintaishi* but chose not to indulge in the erotic fantasies that occur in her *tanka* precisely because of this very form. The relative modernity of the genre, the rare perspective that Akiko brought to *shintaishi* as a woman poet, combined to produce *shintaishi* that, in their realism, were in clear contrast to the effusive outpourings of Tōson, Kyūkin, and company. When she attempted to create a dialogue, as in "My After-body," she immediately produced a work closer in spirit to her later *tanka* narrative. But only after she had joined with Yosano Tekkan and Yamakawa Tomiko (1879–1909) in a complex series of exchange poems in *Myōjō*, *Kansai bungaku* (the successor to *Yoshiashigusa*), and even in private correspondence, was she able to produce *shintaishi* that approached the dialogic form she achieved in *Tangled Hair*, although she quickly abandoned this form for the *tanka* narrative.[66]

The chief influence on this dialogic structure were her poet-collaborators Yosano Tekkan and Yamakawa Tomiko, and it is Akiko's interaction with them, and especially with Tekkan, the man who became her husband and who was also the editor of *Tangled Hair,* that determined the semantic field in which the narrative unfolds.

Naturalizing the Alien

Assuming that the influence of the *shintaishi* tradition was decisive in the formation of the *Tangled Hair tanka,* most of which were written and published prior to their incorporation into the carefully conceived structure of the book itself, can we then assume that the millennia-long tradition of *waka* poetry played only a small part in shaping the final form that these *tanka* took, when (in many cases) they were rethought and rewritten for the book? This question goes to the heart of Eliot's understanding of the role that tradition plays in creating an individual talent. For Eliot, the poet continues to develop a "consciousness of the past"; while creating his own oeuvre, the poet in some sense becomes subsumed into it.[67] Bloom's figuration of the same process highlights conflict with the precursor poets—in Bloom's terminology this process of thesis, antithesis, and synthesis is referred to as daemonization, askesis, and apophrades. So it does not speak of a sublimation—this is my reading of Eliot; it is not Eliot's term—but more of a purgation and then a reconstitution of the original in the poet's work in such a striking way as to recreate any precursors.[68] My reading of Akiko's work in *Tangled Hair* coincides more with Bloom's articulation of the problem than Eliot's.

Akiko "made new" the Japanese *waka* tradition, as Tekkan claimed in the famous *tanka* translated earlier, which appeared in *Purple,* his "precursor" volume to Akiko's *Tangled Hair.* Her intervention into the sacred space of the *waka* tradition took the shape of a very real rupture with the past, but then the poetic project of both Akiko and Tekkan was itself the product of the rupture in this space brought about by the poetry traditions of the West. Akiko's attempt to renovate the tradition by a daring recreation of it—naturalizing something irreducibly alien to this tradition—resulted in something unique in the development of Japanese poetics.

Did the poetry Akiko produced bring about a thoroughgoing renovation of the *waka/tanka* tradition? The question is difficult to answer at this point in time. The different direction taken by major poets such as Masaoka Shiki (1867–1902) and his successors, such as Saitō Mokichi (1882–1953), was overwhelming in its long-term impact. As a result, in the view of the scholar-poet Ōoka

Makoto, the *tanka* tradition since Akiko has shown little evidence of traveling the path she opened.[69] However, some modern *tanka* poets like Nakajō Fumiko (1922–1954) and Tawara Machi (b. 1962) have been compared to Akiko, and it is generally acknowledged that Akiko's verse has been a major influence on modern *shi,* or free-verse poetry, especially poetry written by women.[70]

But this is to proceed to a conclusion without examining the evidence, and without charting the course of the process of renovation and recreation. An examination of Bloom's dialectic at work within *Tangled Hair* could start with several motifs and trace these motifs back to their precursors. We have already done this to a limited degree with the analysis of imagery common to Akiko and the *shintaishi* tradition. It is important, however, to begin at the beginning, by tracing motifs, both traditional and new, in the very first *tanka* included in *Tangled Hair,* the poem that acts, so to speak, as the opening sentence of the narrative.

Yo no chō ni	Now amid the stars
Sasameki tsukishi	In the bedchamber of night
Hoshi no ima wo	We have exhausted our sweet murmurings
Gekai no hito no	While those in the world below
Bin no hotsure yo	Their tresses are all a-tangle[71]

My reading of this poem follows the interpretation given by Itsumi Kumi in her 1996 annotated edition of *Tangled Hair;* namely, that the grammar of the text dictates that the poem be built around a clear contrast between the first clause, ending in *ima wo* (now) and the final clause, ending in *hotsure yo* (all a-tangle). A sharp juxtaposition is obtained between lovers in the stars, whose passion is fulfilled, and those on earth, whose passion is in disarray. The poem thus provides a fitting opening to this complex, polyphonous poem-narrative by painting a portrait of the fate that awaits earthly lovers. The contrast between the fantasy ideal of the stars and the troubled reality of the earth also shapes one of the underlying patterns found throughout the collection.[72]

Itsumi's reading is based on the grammatical and semantic weight she places upon *ima* rather than *hoshi* (stars) as the subject of the opening clause. But Tekkan in his comments on this poem in *Myōjō* in October 1901 interprets it in a very different way: stressing "stars," he identifies this word as the grammatical subject and argues that the word is singular and refers to "I," the female narrator/persona who is fallen to the earth. The expression *hoshi no ko* (children of the stars) was commonly used in the exchange verse of Akiko, Tomiko, and Tekkan as an ambiguous poetic metonym standing for lost love, ecstatic love, and a complex of personal relationships between the three poets, as well as expressing various other connotations.[73] Tekkan uses this exact expression in his rewording of the poem.[74]

Tekkan's view is supported by Ueda Bin (1874–1916), a distinguished poet and translator who was one of the earliest commentators on *Tangled Hair*. However, Itsumi's interpretation has its adherents also, with the reading itself probably originating in the poet-critic Hiraide Shū's (1878–1914) comments on the poem in his famous study *Shinpa waka hyōron* (A critical study of new-style *waka*), which appeared in October 1901, a few months after the publication of *Tangled Hair*.[75]

Itsumi's view in her 1996 annotated edition differs in some respects from that expressed in her 1978 annotated edition. The earlier book reads the poem in a biographical light, seeing the verse as pointing to Akiko and Tekkan's relationship at the time.[76] In this view Akiko portrays herself as struggling with the anguish of a powerful love, while Tekkan is sanctified as a deity, the sacred object of her love. The only reference Itsumi identifies as being related to the classical tradition of *waka* is the word *chō*, which she argues is an abbreviation of *chōdai*, a Heian term for a kind of bedchamber.

In an exciting study of this poem first published in 1983, the critic Isoda Kōichi comes to some startling conclusions. Isoda observes that the traditional usage of the word *chō* indicates a standing screen used around bedding in Heian times. He notes Hiraide Shū's view of it as a bedchamber but finds most intriguing the annotation by Yasukawa Yukiko in 1956 where *chō* is read as *tobari* (curtain).[77] No such usage occurs anywhere in the classical *waka* canon. Where could such a reading originate?

The only answer Isoda could find was the Western tradition of verse. He cites a hymn that appeared in 1878 where the phrase *yo no tobari* (curtain of the night) occurs, a clear importation from the West, argues Isoda. Further, in an early translation of Shakespeare's *Romeo and Juliet*, the trope makes its appearance in the line "spread thy close curtain, love-performing night," where *tobari* again translates as "curtain." Isoda's conclusive evidence is in an article entitled "Eishi hyōshaku" (Commentary on English poetry) by the novelist and translator Tozawa Koya (1873–1955), published in the second issue of *Myōjō* in May 1900, where the word "curtain" from Tennyson's "Mariana" (1830) is glossed as *tobari*.[78]

Isoda does not stop at *tobari,* however. He asks where does the line "While those in the world below / Their hair all a-tangle" originate? For Isoda this line immediately brings to mind Dante Gabriel Rossetti's (1828–1882) famous poem "The Blessed Damozel" (1850). The first link he finds is the *tanka* Akiko published in the eighth issue of *Myōjō* in November 1900.

Rosecchi no	The young aunt
Shi ni nomi nareshi	Who is only familiar
Wakaki oba ni	With Rossetti's verse
Katare to semuru	Is pressed to tell stories
Shita kirisuzume	A sparrow whose tongue has been cut[79]

The sparrow refers to a traditional folktale of a wicked old woman who cuts off sparrows' tongues out of spite, but in the context of this poem it signifies a new Meiji woman more familiar with Western verse than with the tales of her own country; thus the comparison with a tongueless sparrow is unflattering. For Isoda the verse confirms Akiko's familiarity with Rossetti. Beginning in the September 1900 issue of *Myōjō,* published two months prior to this *tanka,* Tozawa Koya had begun analyzing "The Blessed Damozel" in his "Commentary on English Poetry." This analysis and his translation of Rossetti continued until July 1901, the month before *Tangled Hair* was published.

Tozawa reads Rossetti's poem as a vision of heaven that is central to Western art; he singles out the notion of religious love, and its apotheosis in heaven, and also the notion of sin as the most difficult areas for Japanese readers to comprehend. Tozawa quotes and translates the following lines from the poem to explain some of these ideas.

> The blessed Damozel leaned out
> 　From the gold bar of Heaven;
> Her eyes were deeper than the depth
> 　Of waters, stilled at even;
> She had three lilies in her hand,
> 　And the stars in her hair were seven[80]

Tozawa contrasts this vision of "Heaven" with the "earth," which he translated as *gekai* earlier. This juxtaposition, Isoda argues, is imported directly into Akiko's poem. Rossetti's poem portrays the heavenly maiden's hair tumbling to earth ("her hair / Fell all about my face") as signifying her love for the man on earth, which is transformed into the conceit of the locks of the maiden. This, in turn, signals the fall to earth of Akiko's maiden, who has tasted of the joys of heaven. The "tresses are all a-tangle" image is a powerful reminder of the torment that passion can cause. Isoda reasons that *Tangled Hair* played a vital role in linking the Japanese and Western poetic traditions, and so in a sense Akiko initiated a new tradition for poets who came after her.[81] But, as we saw earlier, the *shintaishi* tradition, from which Akiko borrowed heavily, was already an amalgam of traditional *waka* motifs and Western poetic conceits. Scholars like Kimata Satoshi have demonstrated how much of Shimazaki Tōson's poetic vocabulary, for instance, is borrowed from classical *waka* poets like Fujiwara no Teika (1162–1241).[82] Tōson drew on a large range of sources, both Western and Japanese for his language, which he then transformed into an innovative and fresh poetics. This became the backbone of the *shintaishi* revolution and accomplished the task of "bringing home" the alien, to use Steiner's notion.[83]

Edwin Cranston's rendering of the opening poem from *Tangled Hair* seems to cleave closely to Isoda's interpretation. I prefer Itsumi's 1996 reading of the poem for the reasons she gives, including grammatical coherence, but I am in general agreement with Isoda's approach. As Cranston's fine translation better reflects Isoda's argument, it is reproduced here.

Yoru no chō ni	In sweet whisperings
Sasamekitsukishi	'Neath the curtain of the night
Hoshi no ima o	She, a star, would love—
Gekai no hito no	Now fallen to the world below,
Bin no hotsure yo	A mortal with disheveled hair [84]

Isoda's argument covers a great deal more than just this first poem, investigating a large range of metonymic links to Western and *shintaishi* traditions. His views relating to the "lily" imagery, which he sees as adding a new layer of meaning from Western art and poetry onto older nuances originating in the classical Japanese tradition, are particularly apposite.[85]

In any case Isoda's study confirms that Akiko was engaged, quite overtly, in creating a rupture with the previous tradition of *waka*. This was the very essence of the new-style *waka* revolution that Ochiai and Tekkan inaugurated. No one thought it unusual that "new-style" *shi* would draw heavily upon Western sources, as the genre itself was based on translations from Western poetry. Was Akiko's purgation and reconstitution of the *waka* tradition, therefore, a mere imitation of the new legacy left by the *shintaishi* revolution? An examination of one crucial metonymic pattern, that of "tangled hair," which has a central role in the classical *waka* canon, may provide some answers.

Ōtomo Hideto's analysis of vocabulary in *Tangled Hair* tells us that the verb *midaru* (including its morphological variants), meaning to be in disarray, disheveled, tangled, occurs in eleven separate *tanka* in the collection, and eight times occurs in combination with *kami* (hair) in some form. The expression "tangled hair" occurs in four of these *tanka*.[86] The phrase *kami no midare* also occurs once. The word *kami* occurs in some thirty *tanka*, and five of these contain the word *kurokami* (black hair). The word *bin* (tresses) occurs in four separate *tanka*.[87] From this it is evident that the metaphorical patterns centering upon the core figures of "black hair," "disheveled" hair, "tangled hair," and so forth play a major role in the poetic rhetoric Akiko adopts for her collection. One of the most famous verses to form part of this pattern is the third poem in *Tangled Hair*:

Kami goshaku	If I loosened all five feet
Toki naba mizu ni	Of my hair in the waters
Yawarakaki	How soft it would be
Otome gokoro wa	My gentle maiden's heart
Himete hanataji	I keep hidden, never to betray[88]

Here the hair motif begun in the first poem is extended. Itsumi Kumi notes that the poem, by evoking the beauty of a woman's hair, conjures up the lost world of the past.[89] The implied contrast between the ease of the woman dipping her long hair in the water, which spreads out like a fan, and the lack of ease a vulnerable heart brings is, perhaps, the most striking aspect of the verse. Haga Tōru, in his elegant and celebrated study of the trope of tangled hair, first published in 1981, begins his discussion with the following haiku by Yosa no Buson (1716–1783):[90]

Makura suru	A spring stream
Haru no nagare ya	Turns into a pillow
Midaregami	Hair all-a-tangle

The link between stream and pillow derives from a Chinese model, but, as Haga observes, the poem goes far beyond mere reference to create a world of great beauty. The hair and the spring stream are one. Haga is arguing that this association of water and hair is a precursor to Akiko, that Akiko's verse, in a sense, reaches back to Buson's poem. He claims that this precise association appears to originate in Buson, although poems using such words as *kurokami* and *midaregami* are found throughout the classical *waka* tradition.[91] Haga's argument possesses great force, for in 1897, only four years prior to the publication of *Tangled Hair*, Masaoka Shiki published his famous study *Haijin Buson* (The haiku poet Buson), which led to a revival in Buson studies and to a surge of interest in Buson. Sunaga Akihiko argues that Buson's influence on Akiko was profound, indeed that Akiko's view of the classical *waka* tradition was shaped by her reading of Buson.[92]

Satake Kazuhiko claims that the following verse by Buson is the source of another *Tangled Hair* poem. Buson's haiku, based on a Chinese tale, reads:

Kara zake ya	Dried salmon:
Kin ni ono utsu	An axe breaking a *koto*
Hibiki ari	Echoes [93]

The *Tangled Hair* poem is:

Kami no sadame	God's judgment
Inochi no hibiki	Echoes my life
Tsui no wa ga yo	At my world's end
Koto ni ono utsu	Listen to the sound
Oto kikitamae	Of the axe breaking the *koto!* [94]

Buson's poem, though borrowing the metaphor from a Chinese source, simply likens the sound of breaking salt-dried salmon to the exotic Chinese image of an axe breaking a *koto* (a Japanese harp). Akiko uses the same images to convey a different tenor altogether: the sharp crack of the axe denotes the finality of God's judgment upon the speaker's life. Viewed biographically, this poem could refer to Akiko's decision to dedicate her life to love, to choose Tekkan as her lover.[95]

Satake also cites the following haiku of Buson as a source for another *Tangled Hair* poem:

Kaidō ya	An aronia flower
Oshiroi ni beni wo	Mixing by mistake
Ayamateru	Rouge with white face powder [96]

Buson's verse plays on a double conceit. First, the mistake of mixing rouge with white face powder results in a pretty gouache that resembles the aronia flower.[97] Second, the aronia flower is a traditional metonym, originating in China, for an elegant, beautiful woman; in Japan the expression had become something of a cliché.[98] Akiko uses both associations to create a traditional kind of pictorial beauty.

Kaidō ni	Under the aronia
Yō naku tokishi	Tossing away
Beni sutete	The rouge she carelessly mixed
Yū same miyaru	Gazing at the evening rains
Hitomi yo tayuki	Such languorous eyes [99]

The following *tanka* from *Tangled Hair* returns to the world of the haiku by Buson cited first, where water and hair come together:

Kumo zo aoki	Blue are the very clouds
Kishi Natsuhime ga	The summer goddess has come!
Asa no kami	In the morning
Utsukushii kana	How lovely is her hair
Mizu ni nagaruru	Floating in the water [100]

Haga Tōru links this traditional poetic metonym with fin-de-siècle art. The influence of Art Nouveau on the illustrations found on the cover of *Tangled Hair* and also in *Myōjō* by artists like Fujishima Takeji (1867–1943) is well known. The Pre-Raphaelite Brotherhood was formed in 1848 largely at the instigation of Rossetti, and the rich, florid romantic style found in the paintings of its members, such as John Everett Millais (1829–1896) and Edward Burne-Jones (1833–1898), who later became associated with Rossetti, provided a model for Japanese adherents of Art Nouveau. The trope of "tangled hair," Haga argues, features prominently in the art and literature of these writers and painters, and this played some role, either directly or indirectly, in the evolution of the same trope as the key motif in *Tangled Hair*. Millais' painting of Ophelia

(1851–1892), with her long black hair, and similar works, such as Rossetti's *Lady Lilith* (1864) and his *Astarte Syriaca* (1877), all highlight the long, languorous hair of the female subjects. As an example of how the trope had penetrated European fin-de-siècle literature, Haga cites the Belgian dramatist Maurice Maeterlinck (1862–1949)'s *Pelléas et Mélisande* (1892), which places heavy weight upon images of tangled hair.[101]

Here Akiko remakes the older *waka* tradition in the image of the 1890s, specifically, in the image of the fin-de-siècle art of the West. Buson's poem linking long, black hair and water and air dovetailed perfectly with the same metonymic associations found in Art Nouveau illustration, especially the figure of Ophelia, who was painted several times by fin-de-siècle artists. Ophelia adds death to the already spicy cocktail of water imagery and hair, a mix made all the more powerful in the light of Freudian analysis (also dating from this time), which interprets these figures in a decidedly sexual light.[102]

The *Shinkokinshū* (New collection of poems ancient and modern) is considered by such scholars as Shinma Shin'ichi and Ozaki Saeko to be one of the prime sources of the *waka* tradition that Akiko drew upon in her use of the tangled hair motif.[103] Two *waka* from this collection (compiled in the thirteenth century) are often cited as typical of those from which Akiko borrowed.

Kaze kayou	A breeze wakes me.
Nezame no sode no	My sleeve is fragrant
Hana no ka ni	With the scent of cherry blossoms,
Kaoru makura no	The same fragrance perfumes my pillow
Haru no yo no yume	With dreams of a spring evening.[104]

(The Daughter of Kōtaigōgū no Daibu Toshinari 1170?–1254)

And:

Kakiyarishi	I combed
Sono kurokami no	That black hair
Suji goto ni	Every single strand,
Uchifusu hodo wa	When I lie down
Omokage zo tatsu	Her form rises up[105]

(Fujiwara no Sadaie 1162–1241)

This last poem is commonly seen as a response to the following poem by Izumi Shikibu (976?–?):

Kurokami no	When I lie down
Midaremo shirazu	Without caring how
Uchifuseba	Tangled is my hair
Mazu kakiyarishi	I long for the one
Hito zo koishiki	Who combed it first [106]

Akiko wrote commentaries on a number of Izumi Shikibu's poems in various books and articles, the first such commentary published in 1909; in 1928 she noted that she read the Japanese classics until late into the night while still a girl.[107] As a result, most scholars assume that Akiko was quite familiar with poets like Izumi Shikibu and their poems.[108] As a consequence, various attempts have been made to trace the influence of troping from *Shinkokinshū*, Izumi Shikibu, and a host of other classical poets. As Akiko probably wrote more on the *Genji Monogatari* (The tale of Genji) than any other classical work, completing a complete modern translation between 1912 and 1913, many studies have been published finding motifs from this work in virtually all of her major poetry collections, including *Tangled Hair*.[109] The simplest associations that are possible between the classical canon and *Tangled Hair* are at the level of vocabulary, and links have been made between many of the words associated with the trope of tangled hair. In addition to the poems cited above, Haga Tōru finds the following *tanka* by the woman poet Taikenmon'in Horikawa reminiscent of a number of Akiko's *Tangled Hair* verses:

Nagakaran	Your feelings may
Kokoro mo shirazu	Spill and linger long
Kurokami no	But my black hair
Midarete kesa wa	This morning is in disarray
Mono wo koso omoe	My heart despairs [110]

Despite the fact that Akiko stated that the only time the *Man'yōshū* influenced her poetry was in 1907–1908, scholars have argued that the tangled hair trope can be traced, whether directly or indirectly via the influence of later poets working from *Man'yōshū* models, back to this earliest compendium of Japanese verse.[111] I will quote two examples of *Man'yōshū* poems utilizing this trope that are favored by recent scholarship.

Nubatama no	My lacquer-black
Waga kurokami wo	Hair
Hikinurashi	I tug and tug,
Midarete sara ni	My heart in disarray
Koi wataru ka mo	I love him all the more [112]

And a poem by Mikata no Sami to his wife far away:

Takeba nure	Tied up, it comes loose
Takaneba nagaki	If you don't tie it up
Imo ga kami	Your hair is too long
Kono koro minu ni	I haven't seen you for a while
Kaki iretsuramu ka	Have you combed it back and tied it up? [113]

The hair metaphor occurs in many of the Akiko poems translated earlier, but two of the most famous examples from *Tangled Hair* that utilize this trope are the following:

Hito kaesazu	The fine air of
Kuremu no haru no	The spring evening
Yoi gokochi	Will not let my love return
Ogoto ni motasu	Leaning against the *koto*
Midare midaregami	My hair all a-tangle

Kurokami no	My black hair
Chisuji no kami no	A thousand strands of my hair
Midaregami	My hair all a-tangle
Katsu omoi midare	And my heart all a-tangle
Omoi midaruru	My heart all a-tangle [115]

It is useful to note that much of this same troping occurs in *shintaishi* poets like Tōson and Kyūkin. Shimazaki Tōson's "Six Maidens" poem-sequence, in particular, has several verses that utilize this trope. The following lines occur in the first stanza of "Okiku":

Kurokami nagaki	My black hair long
Yawarakaki	and soft
Onna gokoro wo	Who knows
tare kashiru	a maiden's heart?

The fourth stanza reads:

Midarete nagaki	Your long, tangled
bin no ke wo	strands of hair
Tsuge no ogushi ni	With a boxwood comb
kakiage yo	lift them up! [116]

A Revolution in Poetry

As can be seen from this small sampling—only a tiny tracing in fact—of one particular trope from *Tangled Hair,* the process of rupture and renovation was occurring simultaneously. A new tradition of poetry was being created at the same time that an older tradition was being recreated. Akiko's poetic intervention, then, can be seen to fit the model proposed by Bloom quite easily, but it does not make such a exact fit with that proposed by Eliot.

What does this renovation or rewriting of the older *waka* tradition signify? The obvious answer is that it is part of an explicitly ideological agenda, the agenda outlined by Yosano Tekkan when he founded the Tokyo Shinshisha. In the sixth issue of *Myōjō,* when he made his aims plain, Tekkan stated: "We read with pleasure the poetry of the past, but we will not resile from cultivating anew the ground opened up by the ancients." [117] As the poet Nagata Kazuhiro remarked, this implies a new kind of *honkadori,* or response to the poetry of the past. [118] Simply put, it means that the intricate web of allusion spun by traditional *waka* poetics is augmented by a new web of allusion and reference located in the poetic practice of the Shinshisha poets, principally, Tekkan, Akiko, and Tomiko.

Nagata argues that since it is impossible to completely explicate a verse form as brief as *tanka,* then poetic meaning must develop in two directions. *Tanka* poetry can become accessible but, in a sense, "superficial," for the semantic content is capable of being grasped by readers with no acquaintance with the authors of the poetry, or, indeed, any tradition from which it derives. Or *tanka* may develop in the opposite direction and become obscure to the point where, without a detailed knowledge of the authors of the poems, and the context in which the poems were composed and published, no real understanding is possible. Tekkan pushed the *Myōjō* poets in the latter direction. The most obscure but, paradoxically, the most powerful poetry composed from among the *Myōjō* group is Akiko's.[119]

Akiko's poetry gained its characteristic intensity and power precisely because of its highly allusive, self-referential, and obscure content. Her verse is composed in almost a private language, but, as shown above, with significant borrowings from both the new tradition of *shintaishi* and the older *waka* tradition. Akiko did not spring "unborn," without progenitors, as a poet into the world. Bloom is right concerning the futility or meaninglessness of conceptualizing a poet as an autonomous ego if we apply this generalization to the case of Yosano Akiko. However the process of rupture, renovation, rewriting, and reframing a whole tradition is an immensely complex one, which can be barely hinted at in this preliminary analysis. For Akiko was actively undermining a traditional mode of allusive reference, as Nagata claims.[120] She was, in a very real sense, a revolutionary poet, deliberately creating a rupture in a rhetorical tradition a millennium old. At the same time Akiko was recreating, rewriting this tradition as a new genre of poetics explicitly linked to Western verse and the *shintaishi* movement, which was the child of the West. In this way, by naturalizing the alien modes of expression created by translations of Western verse, Akiko opened up new possibilities for poetry, although it took many years before Japanese verse written in traditional modes was to fully absorb the conceptual foundations of Western poetics.

Furthermore, Akiko did not accomplish this alone; she was part of a collective effort to recreate *waka* as *tanka*, not merely as part of an ideological or intellectual crusade but also as an expression of a complex and changing set of personal relations, imagined and real. *Tangled Hair* gathers together in one historic moment the past, the present, and the future, both of poetry itself and of its makers.[121]

CHAPTER 3

THE DEMON WITHIN

Yosano Akiko and Motherhood

Then there is this other abyss that opens up between the body and
what had been its inside: there is the abyss between the mother and
the child. What connection is there between myself, or even more
unassumingly between my body and this internal graft and fold,
which, once the umbilical cord has been severed, is an inaccessible
other? My body and . . . him. No connection. Nothing to do with it.
. . . The child, whether he or she, is irremediably an other . . . the flash
that bedazzles me when I confront the abyss between what was mine
and is henceforth but irreparably alien. Trying to think through that
abyss: staggering vertigo. No identity holds up.
> —Julia Kristeva

you open, to give birth, to a heart
to an infinite, to the very different, dark of
the first heart, the first one
it begins to beat & to think the world again
This is my loving darkness, in which the world will be held—
dense, smooth, piled, soft—airy, aether, black—
> —Alice Notley

A reconceptualization of motherhood emerged at a decisive moment in the
history of modern Japan—the end of the first decade of the twentieth
century—through the writings of the poet Yosano Akiko on childbirth.
Akiko's verse represents the processing of a self, the poet's unique self, into
public textual form via the expression of her own experience of giving birth.
Childbirth was traditionally a taboo subject in Japanese literature because of

the element of blood-pollution, seen as ritual self-defilement by generations of Japanese.[1] Akiko's act of self-revelation could also be read as (self)-violation, shame, or guilt, but for Akiko it was one step towards a redefinition of the role of the female subject in imperial Japan. For Akiko motherhood was an encounter with an alien or, to use her own image, a demon; simultaneously it was a symbol for the new conceptualization of the woman that she inaugurated, but it was also an alien being, the very essence of the Other, who had taken root in her body.

As we saw in Chapter 2, Akiko's first book of poetry, *Tangled Hair,* gave the self of the new emancipated woman a body, indeed myriad complex bodies, a veritable host of projected or implied authors or characters: some are the classic femme fatale, others are ingenuous and beautiful young women, while still others are women tormented by their passions. All these versions of the female body create an entirely new vision of the female and her subjectivity that combine to challenge male conceptions of the female, especially those focusing upon female sexuality. In addressing Akiko's response to motherhood, the challenge is of a different kind, but no less profound, for Akiko brings her poetic powers to bear upon the female as mother, an ideal long venerated in traditional Japanese thought, especially in Neo-Confucian thinking, the dominant mode of conceptualization in the Tokugawa age that immediately preceded Akiko's era.[2]

Poetry as Being-in-Process

The domains encompassed by this chapter are primarily literary and aesthetic, so it is appropriate to begin with some preliminary remarks concerning the notion of selfhood as interpreted through the perspective provided by these domains. What aesthetic will make it possible to consider and understand exactly what Akiko accomplished? I suggest that the many parts that make up our selves be read as characters, in exactly the same way as the myriad selves produced by *Tangled Hair* are read, that is, as literary characters. This method of linking art to reading, or more precisely, personality, is not new. The critic Wayne Booth in *The Company We Keep* (1998) put the rationale thus:

> If I think of myself . . . as a character—as someone doing my best to enact the various roles "assigned me"—I discover that there are no clear boundaries between the others who are somehow both outside and inside me and the "me"

that the others are "in." As Gregory Bateson puts it, in his book *Steps to an Ecology of Mind* (1972), I am not bounded by my skin.[3]

Later, Booth elaborates on this point as he attempts to formulate an ethics of fiction and of reading.

> If . . . I am not an individual self at all, but a character, a social self, a being-in-process many of whose established dispositions or habits belong to others—some of them even to all humankind—then I need have no anxiety about finding and preserving a unique core for the various characters that in a sense have colonized me and continue to do so. I should be able to embrace the unquestioned ethical power of narratives, in order to try on for size the character roles offered to me.[4]

Finally, in this next statement Booth links the "self" of me to the "self" of art, namely, to judgment, ethical and aesthetic.

> Applying this . . . to the problem of choosing among powerful narratives gives us one kind of model for our use of many narratives to create for ourselves a flexible, growing, yet not amorphous character. Narratives . . . both depend on and implant or reinforce patterns of desire. If we do not surrender to these patterns, we cannot really be said to have "taken in" a given narrative; yet if we do surrender, we find ourselves to some degree shaped into those patterns. If we are characters-in-process, taking on and playing widely diverse roles, how can we ever say that one preferred role is superior to another? I am suggesting that we do that roughly in the way [the philosopher Charles] Taylor says that we make our other ethical judgments: we acquire, from the stories we are told, a desire to become a different kind of desirer.[5]

I suggest that by reading Akiko's poetry, Japanese people, or indeed anyone who reads her poetry, by surrendering to the patterns of desire inscribed in them, become a different kind of desirer. Or, to put it another way, Japanese notions of self—whether aesthetic or ethical construct—changed upon encountering Akiko's book.

This approach to reading is not confined to Booth alone. The critic Wolfgang Iser in his *The Act of Reading* (1978, originally published in German in 1976) proposes a similar hermeneutic, where an author or text creates a framework of theme and horizons that create or stimulate readers' responses or (to use Booth's term) implied readers within the consciousness of the actual reader himself.[6]

Nor is this approach confined to the West. In 1957, in his first in-depth study of a single writer, an analysis of the of the poet Takamura Kōtarō (1883–1956), eminent Japanese critic Yoshimoto Takaaki (b. 1924) wrote that the artist creates the objective, outside world within the world of his linguistic expression. To quote Yoshimoto: one "makes objective description immanent within one's own autonomous self."[7] This was a first step in Yoshimoto's developing his own theory of linguistic expression, which eventually led him twenty years later to argue in *Kigeki no Kaidoku* (The interpretation of tragedy, 1979) that the self can be read or deciphered in the same way as a literary work.

The most influential and fully developed of Yoshimoto's meditations on the self and language is his magnum opus *Gengo ni Totte Bi to wa Nanika?* (What is beauty in respect of language? 1965), where in discussing 1930s Japanese experimental fiction, he made the same point more starkly:

> Slipping towards dissolution, and colliding with homogeneity, the consciousness that is self begins to find a way out by moving in the direction of turning itself as a subject into the object of literary expressions; becoming one with the mass, the self seeks in language to compensate for the dissolution of self occasioned by the reality of society.[8]

Yoshimoto is making more or less the same claim that Booth made in a more developed form two decades later. And Yoshimoto himself expressed this claim in a different form in 1979, as noted earlier.

The purpose of this excursion into the relationship between the self and language is not simply to retrieve from the past these striking and penetrating insights from the pens of Booth, Iser, and Yoshimoto; nor is it just to weave a fine thread linking meditations on the poetry of Yosano Akiko to the physical experience of childbirth—the real purpose of these quotations is to provide a justification for reading from poetry, from literature, to the self.

The Day Mountains Will Move

In September 1911 an event of profound importance occurred. The first magazine edited by women, written by women, and directed at women readers began publication in Japan. This was *Seitō* (Bluestocking).[9] In that epochal first issue, a poem by Yosano Akiko was published in a collection of verses grouped together under the title "Suzurogoto" (Trivial words), a conventional epithet applied to essays written in the old style. These verses were later broken up by the poet into twelve separate poems. The first of these was a *shintaishi* that Akiko titled "Yama no ugoku hi" (The day mountains will move):

The day has come when mountains will move.

Having said this, no one believes me,
But the mountains have only been slumbering for a time,

Long ago, they all moved, burning with fire.

Still, whether you believe this or not,
Everyone, whoever you are, believe me now,
Women who were all in a slumber
Now are awake, and are on the move.[10]

The famous feminist Hiratsuka Raichō (1886–1971) on reading this poem was so inspired that on that very same night she penned another poem, which like Akiko's verse, became one of the unofficial anthems of the women's emancipation movement in Japan, and like Akiko's her poem was included in the first issue of *Bluestocking*.[11]

The self that springs out of Akiko's poem is immediately recognizable. The aggressive, powerful tone of the stark declaration of female authority and power poses a clear challenge to men; it is easy to imagine how readers in 1911 may have reacted to this brutally compelling verse. The persona projected by the work, the character Akiko inscribed on the template waiting to colonize minds and memories, is made even more authoritative by the fact that this poetic manifesto is written in a style clearly associated with the tradition of private, feminine poetic expression.[12] The contrast between form and content makes the message stand out all the more.

In 1911 the status of women in Japan was clearly inferior to men, whether in terms of legal rights relating to suffrage (women did not win the right to vote until after World War II), inheritance, property ownership, social status, education, or expectations. Women were expected to be quiet and reserved, gentle and docile. In 1889 an anonymous correspondent in the journal *Bunmei no haha* (Mother of civilization) commented on the notion of a woman author: "If a woman should shun her 'natural calling' of mothering and housekeeping, and 'aspire to fame' [such as that brought by literature], then we will laugh at her foolishness with gusto and reprove her mistaken beliefs with a thunderous roar!"[13] Irie Haruyuki notes that even in the revisions to the Meiji Civil Code promulgated in 1898 women were forbidden to become heads of the family, and they were still denied the right to inherit property. Similarly, women had no right to sue for divorce.[14] From this it is obvious how challenging Akiko's words were for her audience. But Akiko not only created the character of a strong, female self awakening sleeping mountains of women, she broke other taboos as well, which in turn presented readers with even more challenging images of the female—both as private self and as national subject.

One taboo was Akiko's attack on the Japanese military and Japan's military tradition, which will be discussed below, but her most famous poem directly challenging the notion of a "just" war was "Kimi shinitamō koto nakare" (Little brother, do not die!), published in September 1904 in *Myōjō*. An enormous controversy arose over this poem, which continues to the present day. It has been translated into English numerous times and has generated a huge secondary literature in Japanese.[15] This poem was not a *tanka*, but a *shintaishi*, and has been widely read as a powerful antiwar polemic. The poem indirectly censures the emperor for sending off innocent boys like Akiko's brother to die at the front. As numerous commentators have pointed out, a number of other poems criticizing the Russo-Japanese war were published prior to Akiko's poem, and poems critical of the war followed it.[16] However, no other work approached Akiko's poem for the furor and controversy it created. Apart from confirming for the public Akiko's importance as a writer, the poem raised the issue of the role that women play in Japanese society. She was only twenty-six when the poem appeared, but young as she was, Akiko embraced the role of a public writer who was not afraid to comment upon subjects affecting the Japanese nation as a whole. As time passed, Akiko increasingly explored a whole range of issues—political as well as social—in essay form, and by the end of the Taishō era in 1926 she was recognized as one of the most prominent social commentators in Japan.

The Body as Self: Childbirth

The prose piece "Ubuya monogatari" (Delivery room story) was originally published in April 1909 in a newspaper but later reprinted in *Ichigū yori* (From a nook, 1911). This book comprised Akiko's first collection of essays, a historic collection in terms of its significance for the contemporary movement for woman's emancipation, and it came out only two months before her poem in *Bluestocking.* "Delivery Room Story" was important because it violated an unspoken code concerning the female body. In this essay Akiko gave the self of the new woman a body, but it was a body in childbirth, traditionally a taboo subject in writing.[17] Not simply a violation of tradition or decorum, Akiko's essay is in fact a fierce denunciation of men who refuse to grant women status as national subjects in their role as life-givers. The essay concerns the birth of Akiko's sixth child and third son, Rin, born only the month before, in March 1909.

On the evening of the Doll Festival, after giving birth to a boy, I was confined to the delivery room and forbidden writing materials or reading matter by the doctor. . . . Lying down quietly I felt as if I had gone on a journey alone, as if I had just bathed in a spa, free of cares, and thoughts normally incapable of expression rose to the surface of my mind. I jotted down a few things in secret, without the doctor knowing.

The tribulations of pregnancy, the pain of childbirth, I believe these things are totally beyond the comprehension of males. Women fall in love at the risk of their lives. But this is seldom the case for a man. If it so happens that a man does risk his life for love, he has no connection to childbirth, which puts one's life in peril, and he is of no use whatever. This is a heavy trust that all women under heaven bear: we can speak of the state, learning, or war being important, but I believe none of these duties surpasses that of women who give birth to humankind. From long ago women were given this thankless task but, while carrying out this duty in danger of their lives, in the eyes of Buddhist scriptures, morality, and the laws of the land, all written by men, women appear as deeply sinful creatures and are treated as inferior and weak. What manner of logic is this? Even allowing for some sinfulness and faults, starting with great religious leaders like Prince Shakyamuni and Jesus Christ, the achievements of women in giving birth to countless great scholars and heroes throughout history are quite magnificent.

. . . Every time my contractions started and I was struck by intense labor pains, if I tell the truth about my emotions at that time, I always felt that I hated men. Wives break out in a greasy sweat on the border between life and death and moan aloud, feeling that every bone in their body was being broken, while their husbands are of no use, of no help whatsoever. Even if all the men in the world visited me at that time, there would not be one man I could call a true friend. Isn't it the case that when our lives are in peril, that for men who cannot become our true friends, from the most ancient times it has already been determined that women are the enemy. Is their everyday love and affection a mask to betray women completely? When tormented with thoughts like this, I hate men.[18]

The self produced by Akiko in this essay is a female self almost in confrontation with the state, let alone the male sex. For Akiko the personal is the political. At the very least, the female character imprinted on the text is renegotiating the relationship between women and the state in an era when women were not permitted even to leave their own homes on political business.[19] The redefinition of the female self revealed here had an enormous impact on Akiko's contemporaries and stimulated a flood of publications on the issue of childbirth.[20]

This essay is one of several documents Akiko composed around this time that take as their subject the experience of childbirth. Another essay, entitled "Sanjoku no ki" (A record of childbirth), was first published in *Jogaku Sekai* (Woman's world), a well-known magazine, in April 1911, but was reprinted in July in *From a Nook*, the same collection in which "Delivery Room Story" appeared. *From a Nook* was one of the very few collections published by a Japanese woman between 1868 and 1912.[21] In "A Record of Childbirth," an essay about the birth of her second set of twins, when one baby was stillborn, Akiko includes some *tanka* about childbirth, again violating the unwritten code for women of her time. Following are some extracts from this essay:

During the seven or eight days before and after the birth, I wasn't able to sleep at all. Two nights before I gave birth, when I lay on my back, I felt as if something like an aeroplane had moved up from my belly to my breast; it was so difficult to breathe that I thought I would suffocate, and so, sitting straight up, groaning, I waited for the dawn to lighten my door. Compared to the time I conceived before with twins, three months after falling pregnant, the pain was completely different. Dr. Morimune noted that the baby above was positioned badly. This was the baby that I felt to be in an aeroplane shape. I had an attack of nephritis and my whole body swelled up. I was resigned to being possessed and killed by the aeroplane, and was admitted to hospital by Dr. Sakaki . . .

Otoko wo ba   Men!
Nonoshiru. Karera   I curse them all!

Ko wo umazu	They bear no children
Inochi wo kakezu	Do not risk their lives
Itoma aru ka na	How free they are!

. . . I hate Bushidō as a survival of a barbaric tradition; womanhood, which at risk to one's existence devotes itself to propagating new life, possesses eternal glory in stark contrast to this barbarian way that has tormented the emperor and the people over the past seven or eight hundred years with the violence of the military caste as its foundation. Truly I believe that the happiness of humankind will be born from womanhood. These are not the lies of a sterile woman, I write this with blood that purified the eight children who tore my womb open.

Those who caution Japanese women, following the example of the West, to avoid marriage are far too hasty. Japanese women all desire a happy marriage. They are preparing to give birth to strong and sturdy children.[22]

In this powerful essay Akiko's criticism of men reaches a crescendo. Initially her anger at men arises from her difficult conception and pregnancy, and the frank way in which she discusses the agonies of childbirth—referring by implication to one of the twins in her womb as a demon who is about to take possession of her—reveals a bluntness of diction rare in Meiji women's writing. Later her ire is expressed in a powerful poem attacking men, which then turns into an attack upon the essence of male culture as it was glorified and sanctified by Meiji society. Bushidō was primarily a Meiji invention and amounted to a deification of the martial male values traditionally associated with samurai warriors.[23] But Akiko does not stop there; she extends her critique of Bushidō to the families and class that created it: the samurai elite who founded and dominated the very state in which she was living. To posit female culture or female values not simply as a rival to the dominant male culture but as superior in terms of its contribution to the future of humankind is a gesture the likes of which had not been seen before in Meiji letters. The persona Akiko adopts here is one of national seer, embodying an alternative set of values to that of the state.[24]

Immediately following this, Akiko wrote another essay about childbirth, a prose account in diary form. This was published under the title "Sanjoku bekki" (Additional note on my confinement) in the magazine *Fujin gahō* (Women's pictorial) in May 1911 and later republished in *From a Nook*. "Sanjoku bekki" gives a graphically realistic and moving account of the travails of childbirth that demonstrates Akiko's considerable gifts as a writer. Here the persona is clearly that of Akiko herself as mother and wife, or at least the version of self that Akiko wanted the public to see. Following are extracts from this essay:

Feb. 23.

A pale light fell onto the agonizing nightmare I had been experiencing. At the same time as the clock was striking six or seven, the white color turned yellow and then orange; I was not conscious of opening or shutting my eyes. While Nurse Ogawa was cleaning the room, and until I gargled, I had thought the object covering my eyes was a cloth over my face, but it appears there was nothing there. I had also thought that I had three or four cups of milk in my stomach, but Nurse Ogawa informed me I had drunk only one small bottle. I am remembering little by little what happened before I took a strong sleeping draught last night. The pain in my body was terrible, but my awareness yesterday was incomparably clearer than today. The deputy director of the hospital, who visited me on his rounds last night, said to take the sleeping medicine if the pain was too much to bear, and having heard this, around nine o'clock I declared I would take it. I thought that it would compensate for the seven or eight days I had been without sleep.

"It's better not to take the medicine," Nurse Ogawa said.

"I understand," I replied, and, anticipating that I would be extremely tired if I did, I decided not to take the medicine, but Ogawa came to the conclusion that I really wanted to take the sleeping draught, so after half an hour she brought water and the medicine in powder form. It seems I really wanted the medicine and opened my mouth and swallowed it. I remember seeing Mrs. Enami and my housemaid Matsu and also my young secretary Kan come to my bedside for a visit. I recall nodding when I saw Mrs. Enami's face. The nightmare has continued from that point until now. Fumiko from Motozono-chō brought [my children] Shigeru and Nanase to see me. And my maid Momo also came.

"Congratulations!" said Nanase, bowing, but it seems that Momo had taught her what to do. I wasn't able to open my eyes for long, though I wanted to see Nanase's face. . . . [I]n the evening my husband came.

I said to him, "Today definitely half my body died. No, not half, more like 70 or 80 percent."

Feb. 24.

My husband came early in the morning to tell me that he was going to Kirigaya crematorium to take delivery of the ashes of my child, who had been sent there the day before. Today I was able to look up and see the verandah door, but I had a headache. My husband returned in the afternoon. He had bought some flowers from the Myōkaen greenhouse, but looking at his cheerless, lonely face my eyes filled with tears. . . .

Feb. 25.

In the evening, my headache was terrible so I asked for ice for my head. Unable to sleep, I was caught up in something, a nightmare, a painful hallucination, I don't know which. A bush warbler was singing in the drizzling rain. Everything just pressed heavily upon me.

"The harsh winter has passed. I'm really happy in the spring. I'm as happy as anything." A nurse said this to someone in the corridor. There was a funny note in her voice, and it slid into my head even more gently than the spring rain or the bush warbler's song. Last night in the room next door someone was singing hymns.

"After ten years I'm looking forward to joining the Salvation Army and working for the people." So she said.

Today a baby was admitted to a special room three rooms away. Ms. Yoshiki, the nurse who was assigned to me when I was admitted, was shifted to the baby. I was told I could eat porridge but have no appetite whatever. . . .

Feb. 26.

Irritated by the baby crying off and on in the room down the hall, I did not sleep at all last night. . . . [My son] Shigeru came with Mr. Yone from the military academy. Gold buttons. The red of his epaulettes was so bright that my tired brain started to ache. . . .

Feb. 28.

It was a hot day. I had a high temperature. I remembered the night I came here and quietly wept.

My children's voices from the entrance to the house still echo in my ears, or so I feel. Ms. Yoshiki brought my baby for me to see, cradled in her arms. I felt comforted by the baby's beautiful eyes. . . .[25]

As the quotation above makes clear—"Today definitely half my body died. No, not half, more like 70 or 80 percent"—Akiko was determined to destroy any disembodied image of childbirth that did not deal with the very real physical agonies that she herself had undergone. Her prose did away with any blood-less Neo-Confucian ideal of the mother and remade female identity into a flesh-and-blood woman who saw the developing fetus as the ultimate expression of the Other.

Watanabe Sumiko, one of Akiko's biographers, is critical of some of Akiko's utterances in these pieces, arguing that her attitude was typical of a conserva-tive point of view and exalted the status of motherhood over women who could not give birth or chose not to have children. However, Watanabe acknowledges Akiko's significance as a leading feminist whose writings had a major impact upon raising the status of women and praises the power of her writing on child-birth, especially Akiko's criticism of Buddhist misogynist attitudes.[26] The prob-lem with such a critique is that it is open to the charge of being ahistorical, rest-ing upon the values of a much later age, not that of Akiko's time. It also does not take sufficiently into account the nature of Akiko's writing itself at that juncture: her explosion of prose and poetry on childbirth was not primarily designed to be a political or ideological polemic. Akiko's engagement with feminist ideas arises out of her exploration of the female voice in literature, which is primarily an aesthetic engagement, although one that has, as a consequence, a number of political implications.[27]

In "A Record of Childbirth" Akiko included a number of *tanka* that were later collected with several other *tanka* on the same theme written in 1911 and published in newspapers. These were later included in her tenth poetry collec-tion, *Seigaiha* (Blue ocean waves), published in 1912, which consists of some 535 *tanka* in total. The title of the collection is the name of a piece of traditional Japanese music and also of a dye pattern made up of blue waves. These poems dealing with childbirth are even more emphatic in their rejection of the tradi-tional notion of the long-suffering but silent mother, and all the more confron-tational in their representation of the fetus's demonic, alien presence. It is fair to say that until the emergence of Itō Hiromi in the 1980s, no other female poet (or Japanese poet of either sex) had written with such realism and power about childbirth.[28] Following are translations of these verses; all but one are in the order in which they appear in *Blue Ocean Waves.*

The Demon Within

Fukashigi wa   More wondrous
Ten ni nijitsu no   Than two suns

Aru yori mo	The same
Waga tai ni naru	Three hearts beat
Mittsu no shinzō	In my body[29]

This poem is the first in the sequence referring to Akiko's seventh pregnancy, which resulted in the birth of her daughter Uchiko, but also in the death of Uchiko's twin, and when Akiko's own life hung in the balance for two days.[30] Here the implied self of the author seems almost without artifice. As appropriate to the first poem in a sequence on childbirth, the verse records the initial joy and wonder of the experience of childbearing as experienced by a mother who is pregnant with twins.

Kono tabi wa	This time
Inochi ayaushi	My life is in danger
Haha wo yaku	Burning mother
Kagutsuchi futari	Two fire gods
Waga tai ni iru	Dwell in my womb[31]

This second poem, in contrast, is concerned with the difficulties posed by twins. The reference to "fire gods" (kagutsuchi) not only emphasizes the physical pain involved in the pregnancy but also acts to elevate the mother's role, as the terms refers to the deities who play a central role in the foundation myth of Japan. The contrast between the carnal and sacred typifies many of Akiko's poems in this sequence.

Ikite mata	I did not think
Kaeraji to suru	I would return alive
Waga kuruma,	Riding in the car
Keijō ni niru	Looking like a scaffold
Byōin no mon	The hospital entrance[32]

The mention of a scaffold in this verse has been interpreted as referring to the so-called "incident of high treason" (taigyaku jiken). A band of activists plotted to assassinate the Emperor Meiji, partly as an expression of their opposition to the government's oppression of socialism.[33] Twelve people were condemned to death after the plot was uncovered in 1910. The leading socialist thinker, Kōtoku Shūsui (1871–1911), although not directly involved in the plot, was accused by the government of being the main conspirator. Together with eleven others he was executed in 1911. Akiko had a connection to one of the executed conspirators, a distant acquaintance of her husband, Hiroshi. Akiko was asked from prison by the socialist Kanno Suga (1881–1911), Kōtoku Shūsui's lover and the sole woman executed as part of the plot, for a copy of one of her poetry books, but Akiko did not respond, fearing that she and her husband would be caught up in the antisocialist hysteria created by the government at the time.[34] The affair resulted in the following poem, also published in this sequence.

Ubuya naru	In the delivery room
Waga makurabe ni	Beside my bed
Shiroku tatsu	Twelve white
Daigyakushū no	Coffins appear
Jūni no hitsugi	Prisoners of high treason [35]

One source of this verse is the traditional belief or superstition that ghosts come to gather at one's pillow at death. The poet and critic Hirako Kyōko notes that following the stillbirth of the second twin, and five days after her discharge from hospital, Akiko collapsed. This event, according to Hirako, reveals the terrible stress that Akiko was under and provides a context for the horrific delivery room hallucination of the twelve coffins.[36] The next poem returns to the sequence, to the theme of childbirth.

Onoga mi wo	My body
Atonaku kora ni	Devoured totally completely
Kuwaresaru	By children
Mushi ni hitoshiki	I am nothing more than a worm
Owari chikazuku	The end approaches [37]

This verse expresses the deep anguish and fear that arises during a difficult pregnancy where the mother's life is put in peril by her own fetus. The personal connection is made in this poem by use of a word for children *(kora)* that refers to twins.

Ōyuki ni	As if using
Makura suru goto	Heavy snow as a pillow
Ikinagara	Still alive

| *Iwa ni iru goto* | As if burrowing into a rock |
| *Shiroki byōshitsu* | The white hospital room [38] |

The metaphors used in this poem are somewhat extreme, if not a little odd, but powerfully convey the sense of oppression that results from being immured in a hospital room and, by implication, in one's own body by pregnancy.

Akuryō to	Without becoming
Narite kurushimi	A tormented, evil dragon
I to narite	Without bellowing
Nakazuba hito no	A wild boar's bellow
Umigataki ka na	One cannot give birth [39]

The figure of the suffering mother is graphically expressed in this poem with its extravagant metaphors of dragons and wild boars.

Oya to ko o	Strife begins
Tatakau hajime	Between mother and child
Kanashiku mo	Sad though this may be
Atarashiki yo no	It is the beginning of
Umareru hajime	The birth of a new world [40]

The stark contrast between the word "strife" *(tatakau)* and "new" *(atarashiki)* references an old maxim that creation emerges out of conflict. In this sense the poem also restates the simple truth of the cost of new life to the mother and can be read as a gentler meditation on birth and also on the metonymic implications of this event for the world. The next poem turns on a startling trope.

Hebi no ko ni	The snake child
Tai wo sakaruru	Tearing the womb in two
Hebi no haha	Of the snake mother
So wo tsumetaku mo	How cold
Toki no mitsumuru	The stare of time [41]

In the first version of this poem, published in "A Record of Childbirth," the word "time" *(toki)* is put into inverted commas. This acts to intensify the indifference of fate to the struggle of birth (at least from the mother's perspective). That sense of cold indifference is beautifully expressed in Claire Dodane's French translation of this verse: "La mére serpent / à l'utérus déchiré / par son tout petit . . ., / Combien est indifférent, / cruel, le regard du temps. . . ." [42] The poet-critic Baba Akiko describes the trope of the snake-child as "superb" and heaps praise upon the contrast provided by the use of time, claiming that the two senses, of human time and time indifferent to human needs, reveal the "pathos of life itself" as exemplified by birth. [43]

Tai no ko wa	The baby in the womb
Haha wo kamu nari	Devours mother
Kage no goto	Like a shadow
Mugon no oni no	Every time the silent
Te wo ba furu tabi	Demon shakes a fist [44]

Akiko's diction and the underlying trope of the baby turning into a demon (*oni*) was imitated a half a century later by the modern poet Soh Sakon (1925–2006) in his award-winning poetry collection *Moeru haha* (Mother burning, 1968), which envisages the poet-persona as a vengeful demon eating his mother from the inside. [45] But at last Akiko brings the mother deliverance.

Sono haha no	Breaking every bone
Hone kotogotoku	In her
Kudakaruru	Mother's body
Kashaku no naka ni	Buffeted by pain and guilt
Takiko no naku	A healthy baby's cry [46]

The last line of this verse is a transparent expression of the relief of the mother after a painful delivery. Baba Akiko argues that through the use of the word *kashaku* (pain, guilt) this poem reflects the narrator's complex reaction to the suffering of childbirth: an acceptance of the physical pain as atonement for the trauma arising out of female physiology, and, implicitly, an acknowledgement of the Christian notion that birth pains are a divine punishment for female perfidy. [47] Like many of Akiko's *tanka*, this poem makes much use of alliteration to convey the sharpness of the pain felt by the mother and also the sharp strength of the baby's cry.

Aware naru	How piteous
Hanshi no haha to	Mother half dead

Ikisezaru	Her child breathes no longer
Ko to yokotawaru	Lying down together
Usuguraki toko	In bed half in darkness [48]

In contrast to the previous poem, this verse expresses the profound sorrow resulting from a stillborn child, a direct reflection of Akiko's own experience.

Kyomu wo umu	Giving birth to nothingness
Shi wo umu kakaru	Giving birth to death
Daiji wo mo	Such terrible words
Yume to utsutsu no	I heard on the border
Sakai ni te kiku	Between dream and reality [49]

This poem echoes the previous verse in expressing the horror at having a child born dead. Baba Akiko discerns in the verse an apprehension of birth signifying the absolutes of both life and death but also the necessity of forgetting—unless the memory of childbirth fades, she contends, women would feel little inclination to undergo the experience again.[50]

Shi no umi no	Upside down
Kuromeru mizu e	Into black water
Sakashima ni	The sea of death
Otsuru waga ko no	My child falls
Shiroki maboroshi	A white phantom [51]

In this verse a new trope of water appears, a traditional trope of death due to its association with the word *mizuko*—literally meaning "water child," but used to indicate a miscarried or aborted baby. It may also refer to amniotic fluid.

Yowaki ko wa	The weak baby
Chikara oyobazu	Was without strength
Tai ni shinu	And died in the womb
Haha to tatakai	Fighting mother
Ane to tatakai	Fighting elder sister [52]

This poem, like the previous verses, refers to Akiko's own two-day struggle for life. The image of the fetus fighting for life is noteworthy here as it has few precedents in *waka* tradition.

Aware ni mo	How piteous
Haha no inochi ni	The child exchanged
Kawaru ko wo	For mother's life
Utsuwa no gotoku	Like a container
Ki no hako ni iru	Placed in a wooden box [53]

The container in this poem refers to a type of ceramic bowl that comes in a small wooden box, an allusion to the tiny body of the fetus.

San no ato	After giving birth
Kashira tsumetaku	My head cold
Chi no usete	And pale
Kōri no naka no	I am a fish
Uo to nariyuku	Packed in ice [54]

Akiko uses a striking visual metaphor for her own persona's body that follows the example of the previous poem.

Chi ni someru	With tiny,
Chiisaki morode ni	Blood-soaked hands
Shiinishi ko ga	The dead child
Nemutaki haha no	Peels the skin off
Me no kawa wo hagu	Her mother's eyes [55]

The mother's anguish is expressed in graphic, imaginative detail. Baba Akiko notes that the reality of the child's death shocks the mother—who is drifting into sleep—awake with powerful imagery that is a reminder of the shock of life itself. [56]

Ma wo okite	At intervals
Araku kokyū wo	As if scratching wildly
Suru gotoku	At a Chinese fiddle
Utsuro no tai no	My empty womb
Sara ni itaminu	Ached all the more [57]

In this poem Akiko chooses a very different trope to express the anguish of a mother of a dead child.

Mizukara wo	Ashamed of myself
Kurushimuru wo ba	Ashamed of suffering
Haji to seshi	This shame
Ware mo kurushimu	Even I have fallen into the way
Haha no narai ni	Of the suffering mother [58]

This poem may simply refer to the Japanese custom of deploring any expression of a mother's pain during childbirth, or it may be something universal, thus echoing the theme of guilt explored earlier in the sequence.

Ide waga ko	Come my child
Saiwai are to	And be joyful
Mazu arau	First of all your mother will
Haha ga mi wo saku	Wash you in new blood
Atarashiki chi ni	From her torn body [59]

This poem to the living infant signals the beginning of the final three *tanka* and introduces a new thread into the narrative.

Haha to shite	As mothers we know
Nyonin no mi wo ba	No world exists
Sakeru chi ni	Unpurified by
Kiyomaranu yo wa	Blood torn
Araji to zo omou	From female flesh [60]

In traditional Japanese culture, blood defiles, and there is no more potent a source of pollution than that which pours from the female body. The word Akiko uses for "female" in the poem carries a connotation of woman as an agent of ritual defilement. To imagine the blood of birth as purifying the world, and to extend this trope to encompass all, creates a self so powerful as to suggest divinity, but a self that is also implicated in a subtle form of political polemic.

Nagaretsutsu	As if trailing behind
Ashi no ne nado ni	Weed-roots
Yoru gotoku	Floating aimlessly
Ubuya ni hiete	I have grown cold
Otoroeshi ware	And weak in the delivery room [61]

This poem ends the sequence, an appropriate coda to this complex narrative of pregnancy, birth, death, and loss, since what remains after this powerful and world-creating, as well as world-ending, experience is the broken figure of the mother, lost in the flotsam of the future.[62] Shinma Shin'ichi describes this sequence as having left a unique mark on the history of modern Japanese *tanka*.[63]

The Poetics of Naturalism

Language is not a transparent medium; it has its own rules and conventions, and traditional Japanese poetry, with a history extending back over a millennium, is as closely enmeshed in convention as any comparable body of verse. The poems considered here and in Chapter 2 define a series of female selves—sometimes challenging, sometimes overwhelming in their power—in language that frequently verges on blunt declaration. This is quite deliberate. By 1912 Japanese poetry, indeed Japanese literature, was caught up in an aesthetic current that flowed from European Naturalism and sought to focus on the truth of the private self, rather than the public truth of society. Akiko's poetic diction was altering at this point in time under the ascendancy of Japanese Naturalism, but her poetic subjects, in their probing of the incarnate female self, were far in advance of any comparable poetic or poet in early twentieth-century Japan. It is one of those pivotal points in literary and aesthetic history, where the personal fuses with the ideological (seen as the harbinger of modernity) and where a distrust of the fictional otherworld of the imagination is born.

The impact of Japanese Naturalism on *tanka* is a complex subject that demands a far more detailed treatment than one chapter can provide, but a brief summary will allow readers to grasp something of the context that surrounded Akiko's writing at this time and in particular the background behind her conceptualization of the fetus as an alien. The period from 1910 to 1915 ushered in a revolt against the kind of bold, romantic portrayal of the self that is found in *Tangled Hair*.[64] The naturalist self was far less prone to Akiko's extravagant rhetorical flourishes, which drew upon the classical *waka* tradition for their diction and characteristic obscurity, although Naturalism shared the same obsession with the individual self as Akiko's verse. This mode of writing derives from a variety of sources. First and foremost is the notion of *shasei*, which was defined by the poet and critic Masaoka Shiki in 1900 as "portraying things just as they are."[65] Shiki was determined to free traditional genres of poetry from what he saw as unnecessary ornamentation and empty, florid clichés. As the poet and critic Tsubouchi Toshinari notes, this was a decisive move in the direction of what later became known as Literary Naturalism.[66] Shiki's reform agenda quickly picked up steam and was embraced by a large number of *tanka* poets. The literary historian Senuma Shigeki finds Shiki's successor Takahama Kyoshi (1874–1959) to have played a pivotal role in extending the notion of *shasei* to *haiku* and the novel.[67] Senuma nominates the *tanka* poet and novelist Nagatsuka Takashi (1879–1915) as the inheritor of Shiki's move to *shasei* as the vital component of *tanka*.[68] By 1916 the poet Shimaki Akahiko (1876–1926), the editor of *Araragi*, the most influential *tanka* magazine of the Taishō era, could write in that journal: "That which we call *shasei* is not the description of external phenomena, it is to grasp the single truth of the inner life. It is expression itself . . . if we believe in *shasei*, pray for *shasei*, proceed single-mindedly and have faith in *shasei*, then we will come into the inner sanctum."[69]

The shift in focus from external things to the inner self is characteristic of Japanese Naturalism as it was manifested in literature.[70] Senuma argues that the influence of Naturalism on *tanka* was crucial to the future development of the genre and resulted in the publication of a number of important poetry collections from 1910 onwards. He names Maeda Yūgure (1883–1951) and Wakayama Bokusui (1885–1928), two young *tanka* poets who were much influenced by Akiko, as representative of this trend.[71] Women *tanka* poets who were close to Akiko also came under the spell of the brand of Naturalism advocated by *Araragi*. Hara Asao (1888–1969) was an accomplished poet whose early verse was heavily influenced by Akiko's style in *Tangled Hair*. Akiko wrote in the preface to Asao's first collection, *Ruikon* (Tear traces, 1913): "In the world of verse in Japan where so many poets are too clever by half, sharply sensuous and superficially decorative, I am delighted to find a poet who composes pure lyrics like you."[72] Asao returned Akiko's compliment by writing verse like the following poem that clearly looks back to Akiko's *tanka*:

Kurokami mo	Neither my black hair
Kono morochichi mo	Nor my two breasts
Utsushimi no	No one
Hito niwa mohaya	In this world
Furezarunaramu	To touch them[73]

The spirit and diction of Akiko's verse can be apprehended in this powerful expression of loneliness. But, as the poet Michiura Motoko notes, Asao soon joined the *Araragi* poetry circle and turned to writing poetry that emphasizes realism amid the trials and tribulations of ordinary life, such as the following *tanka:* [74]

Imawashiki	A memento
Koi no katami to	Of a disastrous love affair
Chi no ue no	The cuts
Ha no kizuato ni	Above my breast
Kokoro furuinu	Still my heart trembles [75]

This poem is plainer than the prior verse and does not romanticize or idealize the implied suicide attempt on the part of the narrator. The work can be seen as closer to Akiko's verses on childbirth than to those in *Tangled Hair.* The resemblance is no accident, as Akiko was also moving in the direction of a leaner, sharper, and more pointed mode of verse composition associated with Naturalism and the *Araragi* journal, and her poems on childbirth represent the first indication of this. The poet and critic Akitsu Ei, in her history of women's *tanka* during the first decade of the twentieth century, remarks that Akiko fell under the sway of the realistic mode of writing championed by Naturalism and that *Blue Ocean Waves* was the first volume of Akiko's verse that could be described as a product of this movement. [76]

In her biography of Akiko, Watanabe Sumiko praised the quality of Akiko's verse, but argued that Akiko's writing was typical of a conservative point of view. Seven years later, in 2005, Watanabe penned a more appreciative critique of Akiko's writings on childbirth. Watanabe contrasts Akiko's portrayal of the horrifying physical pain associated with labor—with the "alien" fetus within bringing her to the point where she hates men for their relative indifference to women's suffering—to various writings on childbirth published between 1913 and 1916 by the celebrated novelist Nogami Yaeko (1885–1985). In her short story "Atarashiki inochi" (New life, 1913), Nogami describes her excruciating labor pains giving birth to her second son as a woman's joy. Nogami declared that to believe that the suffering of pregnancy and labor was a sacrifice was just "vile egotism." [77] This, argues Watanabe, was the point of view prevailing at the time when Akiko wrote her various critiques, which only serves to emphasize how revolutionary Akiko's perspective was.

Itsumi Kumi, in her revised biography of Akiko and Hiroshi, published in 2007, agrees that from about 1909 onwards, Akiko's verse and other writings were profoundly influenced by Naturalism. Itsumi sees the influence of this movement as inevitable, given the commercial pressures under which Akiko was working—if she did not follow the literary mainstream, then she risked a loss of sales.[78] She praises the essay "Delivery Room Story," highlighting Akiko's comparison of childbirth with Christ's ordeal on the cross, where Akiko writes: "it is always women who hang on the cross and create a new human world."[79] Itsumi comments that this is the voice of truth; an indication of how powerfully Akiko's literary intervention into the sacred space of childbirth revolutionized attitudes regarding childbirth for later generations. Itsumi stresses that another theme of Akiko's writings at this time is the depth and power of a mother's love—this is a traditional theme in Japanese literature, as it is in the literature of most societies, but Akiko personalizes it in a dramatic fashion in her *Zakki chō* (Miscellanea notebook), which was also published in *From a Nook*: "My heart is breaking! Breaking! Influenza has sickened three of my children! Though the cool rain falls, they are sweating so much, coughing a hacking cough in their sore throats. . . ."[80] How can one explain the startling contrast between the image of the fetus as a demon within, an alien inhabiting the poet's body, and the equally arresting image of a just-born child as "a precious jewel scooped from the bottom of the ocean"? The jewel image comes from "Delivery Room Story" and was directly preceded by the following: "During the experience of childbirth, risking life and limb, a part of my flesh was ripped from me. This is what I keenly felt."[81] The jewel metaphor is followed by the comment: "How lovely was my baby, beautiful beyond words!"[82] The paradox inherent in describing a baby as simultaneously a demon and a jewel is resolved in the fact that both experiences are, in Itsumi Kumi's words, "the voice of truth." The image of a demon itself suggests, conversely, the opposite notion: that the process of birth is also something arising from the very wellsprings of divinity: birth can be seen as an aspect of the numinous, as Akiko herself implied with the comparison of childbirth with Christ's ordeal on the cross.

Itsumi contends that by apotheosizing the female experience in this way, Akiko is constructing an argument for the equality of men and women in a society where men were seen as superior. Itsumi asserts that the process of childbirth allowed Akiko to ennoble the "way of the woman," to advocate such a way—traditionally known as *fudō*—in order to argue for women being accorded respect equal to men. By insisting upon recognition of their unique biological role and the immense suffering this entailed, Akiko made a powerful case to the society of her day for recognition of the intrinsic worth of women.[83]

Conclusion

Akiko accomplished her positioning of the self as resistant to the state (often indirectly and by implication) primarily by using poetry, as can be seen from the allusions to the 1911 executions, but she also availed herself of a variety of other literary genres to project the many selves we have met in these two chapters. This historical moment was decisive and changed the future direction of the aesthetic, intellectual, and political conversation that was taking place in Japan. Further, the various personae or versions of self that Akiko created were crucial in their significance. The role of women, the poetics of beauty, the poetics of alienation, and the shifting of gender roles are but a few of the ideas embodied and given expression in these personae. Akiko's verse represents the processing of a self, the poet's unique self, into public textual form. She did so via the expression of her own experiences of giving birth, but she also created and expanded the single self of Akiko into a much larger panoply of selves who challenged traditional taboos of self-defilement. Akiko's act of self-revelation could be read as a (self)-violation, but for Akiko this was not the case, as can be seen in *Tangled Hair,* where the female self is recreated or reprocessed into a myriad selves, a myriad personae whose presences redefine the nature of the female just as powerfully as her later verse on childbirth does. Akiko forced readers to see unborn children, one of the most revered representations of the mother-child bond, as alien beings, demons inhabiting the bodies of their mothers. By her re-creation, her reimagining of the fetus, Akiko brought about a profound change in thinking. As later historians and readers have come to acknowledge, Akiko's vision of motherhood as in some sense an expression of the alien was a major step towards the redefinition of the role of the female subject in imperial Japan.

CHAPTER 4

THE GOTHIC NOVEL

Izumi Kyōka and Tanizaki Jun'ichirō

As we enter the seventh sphere, you will discover a thin
layer of ice just beginning

To form on your limbs
Do not be alarmed, this is normal

You will experience difficulty breathing, this is normal
The breathing you experience is difficulty, this is normal
. . . .
Prepare executions and transfusions
Put on your latest gear
　　　—Michael Palmer

Runs falls rises stumbles on from darkness into darkness
and the darkness thicketed with shapes of terror
and the hunters pursuing and the hounds pursuing
and the night cold and the night long and the river
to cross and the jack-muh lanterns beckoning beckoning
and blackness ahead and when shall I reach that somewhere
morning and keep on going and never turn back and keep on going
　　　—Robert Hayden

The gothic mode of fiction began in Europe, specifically in England, in the eighteenth century. However, the gothic as a mode of fantasy has persisted until the present day, and it has now spread beyond the novel to encompass several other art forms, most notably, in recent times, the cinema. The characteristics of Gothic fiction in the eighteenth century were the motifs of wrongful imprisonment—the classic plot is an innocent immured for years in a castle or abbey—madness, death, and evil spirits or ghosts. The horrors of the French Revolution served as fertile territory for eighteenth-century English Gothic novelists to explore. Although Gothic fiction was almost always exaggerated and melodramatic, there was an element of realism in the portrayal of evil monks and wrongful imprisonment. In parts of eighteenth-century Europe, aristocrats exercised considerable control over the lives of the peasants who worked their fields. And anticlericalism can easily be traced to the excesses of the pre-Reformation medieval Christian Church. Then in the late nineteenth century, with the growth of large urban conurbations in Europe, especially London and Paris, gothic fiction underwent a revival. But this time, especially for the fin-de-siècle artistic movement, gothic stood for the territory of the unconscious. The isolated urban worker produced by the industrial revolution had generated a form of literature in which ghosts, demons, and wild, romantic landscapes were, more often than not, metaphors for the psychological stress and utopian fantasies of alienated city-dwellers. Gothic fiction, which had been often been denounced by contemporary critics but was widely popular with readers, became respectable in Europe, and many of the leading writers of the day tinkered with the genre. It was the fiction produced by these writers that was translated and consumed by Japanese readers and writers alike in ever-increasing quantities as the nineteenth century drew to a close.[1]

Gothic has been defined as a mode of romance, as an elaboration of fantasy, and in a variety of other ways. One thing that gothic writing in both Japan and the West shared was a link to the Modern movement, the turn towards a literature of the unconscious, and this aspect of Japanese gothic will also come under scrutiny in this chapter. Hence I define gothic in the broadest possible sense to cover a number of related modes of writing, and by applying the term to two practitioners of fiction in early-twentieth-century Japan, I intend to illuminate stylistic and thematic affinities common to these writers without drawing any specific historical parallels to the Western mode of gothic. My approach will be generally comparative, utilizing the notion of gothic for specific hermeneutic ends, but I will make no sustained effort to trace historical influences from the Western to the Japanese tradition, notwithstanding the fact that such cross-cultural influences certainly existed.

The Gothic Mode of Fiction

Hashimoto Yoshiichirō, in a brief history of aestheticism in modern Japanese literature, traces a tradition of the decadent (which later developed into diabolism) from late-nineteenth-century thinkers like Takayama Chogyū (1871–1902)—known as the foremost interpreter of Nietzsche to Meiji Japan—to such romantic theorists as the poets Kitamura Tōkoku (1868–1894) and Ueda Bin. Hashimoto constructs a chain of influence that results in such novelists as Nagai Kafū (1879–1959) and Tanizaki Jun'ichirō (1886–1965), who, Hashimoto argues, are the inheritors of this decadent tradition of aestheticism.[2] "Decadent aesthetics" signifies another aspect of fin-de-siècle writing common to both Japanese and European literature, namely, the concern with eroticism, with guilt or sin, and with the notion of "beauty" untrammeled by any concern with conventional morality or ethics. Darwin's *Origins of the Species* was widely read as revealing humans to be basically animals insofar as they were governed by instinct rather than reason, and, in regards to Japanese fiction, this viewpoint accelerated the portrayal of sexual passion as bestial in nature. Literature also became more openly erotic, and representations of the erotic tended to concentrate on adultery, that is, sinful eroticism, and on the perverse. In France the writers Émile Zola (1840–1902) and Guy de Maupassant (1850–1893), and later, Pierre Louÿs (1870–1925), and in England Oscar Wilde (1854–1900) and Ernest Dowson (1867–1900) are representative of this trend. Gothic influences are also present in popular literature in the work of Japanese writers like Edogawa Rampo (1894–1965), but my focus will be on a slightly earlier period, and as much as on style as on theme, so the chain of influence posited by Hashimoto will look rather different in light of this contrasting perspective.

Stephen Snyder has emphasized the enduring influence of French modernist "self-referential" fiction on Nagai Kafū's writing. This accounts to some degree for Kafū's choice of the demimonde as a setting for his mature works, and also for the characteristic structure of his narratives: the story within a story.[3] This also can account for Kafū's early embrace of the gothic mode of fiction, for, as argued earlier, French authors were crucial in the development of this genre of writing. Even Kafū's reverse "Orientalism," where he adopts, somewhat ironically, a Western gaze and looks upon Japan as exotic and backward and the West as modern is capable of being read in this way.[4] A pioneering study of narrative styles, which argues an analogous case for Izumi Kyōka (1873–1939), is Noguchi Takehiko's *Shōsetsu no nihongo* (The language of the novel, 1980).

Noguchi begins his study of the evolution of modern fiction with Iwano Hōmei (1873–1920), an author, as Noguchi himself comments, hardly read today. In Noguchi's analysis Hōmei brought about a fundamental breakthrough in fictional technique that allowed the Naturalist movement to go beyond the conventional bounds of the fiction of the time. Incidentally, it is interesting to note that Kafū is conventionally grouped with the Naturalist school. However, the writer who took Japanese fiction into a new kind of conceptual poetics altogether was Izumi Kyōka. Noguchi argues that Kyōka's use of metaphor and simile is so extravagant and fantastic that it evokes an other world, an anti-real world. Indeed Kyōka's use of metaphor exceeds conventional rhetorical modes of discourse not merely by expressing tenor by vehicle, but by going beyond such schematization altogether. "Tenor" and "vehicle" are technical terms invented by the British linguist I. A. Richards in 1936 to convey a fairly simple idea: the tenor is the subject of a metaphor, while the vehicle is the image that embodies the tenor. Noguchi further argues that in Kyōka's fiction we apprehend a separate linguistic space that has mythic overtones but derives solely from Kyōka's own tortured youth—the trauma of losing his mother at very early age. In other words Kyōka's demons—the ghosts, witch-women, and fantastic apparitions that inhabit his "separate worlds"— are real demons that lurk in his heart.[5] The same kind of analysis can and has been applied to the gothic novel. Peter Brooks in his important study *The Melodramatic Imagination* (1976) has argued that the gothic novel represents a "quest for the numinous"; it reasserts the presence of forces that cannot be accounted for by the daylight self and the self-sufficient mind. The individual ego is declared the central value, and so the world collective itself shrinks, or expands (depending upon one's viewpoint), to encompass the ego itself, the inner being. Such a reading builds upon an earlier view of the gothic expressed by Leslie Fielder in his classic study *Love and Death in the American Novel* (1960).

> Implicit in the Gothic novel from the beginning is a final way of redeeming it that is precisely opposite in its implications to the device of the explained supernatural, a way of proving not that its terror is less true than it seems but more true. There *is* a place in men's lives where pictures do in fact bleed, ghosts gibber and shriek, maidens run forever through mysterious landscapes from nameless foes; that place is, of course, the world of dreams and of the repressed guilts and fears that motivate them. This world the dogmatic optimism and shallow psychology of the Age of Reason had denied; and yet this world it is the final, perhaps the essential, purpose of the Gothic romance to assert. . . .[6]

Charles Shirō Inouye has translated a number of Kyōka's stories under the rubric of *Japanese Gothic Tales,* and his definition of Kyōka's fiction as belonging to the realm of the gothic arises from the same logic as employed by Noguchi, Brooks, and Fielder, namely: "Suffering, like Poe, from the untimely death of his mother, Kyōka sought to memorialize her youthful beauty and maternal gentleness through hundreds of literary excursions into the world of the dead. . . . By projecting the image of his mother onto these gallant though often unfortunate women [Kyōka's heroines], he was able to visit and revisit deprivation in a way that allowed him to find a measure of relief from dread. . . . Given his own desire to commune with the dead . . . Kyōka wanted to believe in and write about metamorphosis at a time when the anti-figural force of modern language reform precluded the reality of ghosts and monsters."[7]

The Quest for the Numinous

Kyōka made his initial impact on the literary scene in the 1890s; his most famous early story is "Gekashitsu" (The surgery, 1895), in which a surgeon operates on his married lover, a certain Countess Kifune, who refuses an anesthetic, so determined is she to keep their relationship secret. In the end Countess Kifune plunges the surgeon's scalpel into her breast while still on the operating table.[8] Donald Keene has described "The Surgery" as "impossibly melodramatic," but the story has exercised a strong hold on the imagination of Japanese readers.[9] The exaggeration in the piece is essential to its appeal, and it is worth noting that several Japanese commentators have stressed the debt Kyōka owes in both technique and themes to the eighteenth- and nineteenth-century traditions of popular, melodramatic fiction called *sharebon* (clever books) and *kusazōshi* (popular illustrated fiction).[10] Other critics have pointed to folk stories *(minkan denshō)* as sources for Kyōka's plots.[11] Katsumoto Seiichirō has written that "Kyōka is the bastard child of the decadent literature of the end of feudalism and enlightenment writing, enchanted by the ghastly image of foreign gods," thus emphasizing how Kyōka is heir to both the Western and Japanese romantic, decadent traditions.[12] In the West, Izumi Kyōka has repeatedly been characterized as an author of "gothic" fiction. As early as 1984, Juliet Carpenter wrote an article on Kyōka describing him as a "Meiji-Era Gothic"; in 1994 Cody Poulton described Kyōka's Japan as "grotesque and Gothic," and so, more recently, did Charles Inouye.[13]

Kyōka wrote many tales of the supernatural; apparently he himself believed in ghosts, so his fiction resembles the Western gothic novel much more than do the works of some other writers, like Arishima Takeo (1878–1923), who used similar techniques. However even with Kyōka's supernatural apparitions, it is possible to apprehend a more personal landscape, a landscape of the psyche. Noguchi Takehiko has already drawn attention to this. Rosemary Jackson in her study of fantasy notes that "from Gothic fiction onwards there is a gradual transition from the marvelous to the uncanny—the history of the revival of Gothic horror is one of progressive internalization and recognition of fear as generated by the self." [14] The use of the word "uncanny" in this context is no accident, for in Freud's famous essay on "Das Unheimlich" (The uncanny), published in 1919, the uncanny is defined (in Jackson's paraphrase) as "the effect of projecting unconscious desires and fears into the environment and onto other people." [15] Freud links the experience of the uncanny to repressed complexes or primitive beliefs (specifically citing the fear of death): "an uncanny experience occurs either when infantile complexes which have been repressed are once more revived by some impression, or when primitive beliefs which have been surmounted seem once more to be confirmed." [16] Perhaps the most famous example in Kyōka's fiction of the expression of a primitive fear—of a landscape coming alive in this way, assuming the form of psychic excess, an uncanny excess clearly reflecting the narrator's innermost apprehensions—is to be found in *Kōya hijiri* (The holy man of Kōya).

First published in 1900, this novel is almost entirely narrated as a monologue by a renowned priest, Shūchō, to a traveler whom he has met by chance. The priest tells the strange story of another journey he undertook into the remote Hida mountains. In this story he loses his way in a mysterious forest and encounters bizarre, unnatural creatures before he finds refuge in a mountain cottage. The cottage is inhabited by a half-wit and a beautiful young woman. The young woman leads the priest to a stream to bathe; she washes his back, stirring sexual passions in the priest, which, however, he is able to master. The woman rebuffs several amorous animals but is surprisingly kind to the idiot. The priest leaves the following day but is plagued by desire for the woman. On his journey back, the priest meets an old man who had been at the cottage earlier. The old man tells him the woman is really a supernatural being who seduces men and turns them into beasts. Only the priest's pure nature saved him from this fate. So the priest ends his tale and takes his leave from the unnamed traveler. [17]

The story is thus a mixture of three narratives (by the traveler, the priest, and the old man) and each narrative is embedded in the other. Kyōka's use of myth and fable, clearly reworked in this story, has often been remarked upon, as has his penchant for complicated narrative structures. But, as with much of Kyōka's fiction, what has struck Japanese readers of this story more than anything else, is the language. Kyōka's language is poetic and dense, his imagery is almost cinematic in its control of pace and movement. The famous novelist Mishima Yukio (1925–1970) observed in 1969 that Kyōka steps out into the "world of dream and surrealistic linguistic experiment" while also noting that Kyōka pursues "solely the drama in the depths of his ego," again making a link between rhetorical and psychological excess.[18] Yoshida Seiichi remarked of this novel that "readers are carried off by the text and find that they cannot return."[19] Kawamura Jirō states that Kyōka's "narrative style is a method of expression designed to emphasize a separate, fantasy world which the world of the tale cuts off from everyday reality. . . . The locus of the characters lies in a different class of fantasy space from that of the everyday world."[20]

This comment could equally well be applied to fiction in general, but the notion of a fantasy space constructed from language is the element that deserves attention. One specific example from *The Holy Man of Kōya* demonstrates how Kyōka invests landscape with gothic overtones of supernatural terror, overtones that reflect inner realities as much as external. From chap. 8, where the priest journeys into the Hida mountains, he notices, after entering the dark forest, that something has fallen from the branches of the trees onto his rush hat:

Feeling as if it were a lead weight, perhaps a fruit from the tree, I tried two or three times to dislodge it, but it was stuck fast and would not come away; when I imprudently reached up to grasp it, it came into my hand cold and slippery.

I saw that it was something like a torn-open sea slug with neither eyes nor mouth, yet it was definitely a living creature. It was ghastly, and when I attempted to hurl it away, it slid down to the tips of my fingers and clung there limply. From the end of my extended fingers, blood dripped, cherry-red, beautiful; startled, I brought my fingers right before my eyes and examined them carefully, hanging onto the crook of my elbow was a mountain slug with the same shape, three inches long and half an inch wide.

I was dumbfounded. Before my very eyes, it shrunk into itself and then grew fatter and fatter as it greedily sucked my lifeblood; on the creature's slippery mud-black skin were liverish-brown stripes, like a blood-sucking warty cucumber, it was a leech! . . .

Meanwhile, the area around my neck had become itchy. When I rubbed it with my open hand, my palm slid sideways to touch the slimy back of another leech; one had also hidden itself in the folds of my sash just below my chest; I blanched and slowly looked about to find another on my shoulder.

Jumping involuntarily, my whole body shaking, I dashed away as fast as I could from under the great branches; fleeing, in a frenzy, pulling off as many leeches as I could feel on me.

It was horrifying. In my fear, I wondered if the leeches were actually growing on the branches, turning to look, uncertain of which branch on the tree I was staring back towards, the outer layer was a mass of leeches. In a state of shock, I realized that the branches to the right of me, the left, in front, everywhere I looked, were covered with leeches.

A yell of terror escaped my lips. And then to my horror, into my vision came heavy drops of rain intermingled with skinny pitch-black leeches, rain that started to fall upon me.[21]

In this passage the very elements themselves are transformed, along with the lineaments of the landscape, into horrible blood-sucking leeches. The apparition, or is it reality, is a symbolic harbinger of the danger awaiting the priest at the cottage where a demon cloaked in the guise of a woman is waiting to suck his lifeblood from him. The vampiric quality of the woman's sexual hunger is transformed into an aspect of nature itself. The language appears realistic, but as the apparition becomes even more horrifying, so the underlying gothic fantasy becomes transparent. The style appears almost rococo in its rhythms. Here can be found an almost perfect illustration of the gothic mode of expression as applied by Rosemary Jackson to Victorian fiction: "An uneasy assimilation of Gothic in many Victorian novels suggests that within the main, realistic text, there exists another non-realistic one, camouflaged and concealed, but constantly present."[22]

Underlying a sense of psychic excess is often a darker motif. In the extract from *The Holy Man of Kōya* that follows, the apocalyptic vision created by Kyōka intimates deeper apprehensions in the narrator, if not in the author. In this context Hélène Cixous' revision of Freud's notion of the uncanny seems quite apposite. Cixous argues that "the uncanny's unfamiliarity [is] not . . . merely displaced sexual anxiety, but . . . a rehearsal of an encounter with death, which is pure absence."[23] Following his encounter with the leeches, the priest muses on the horror he has just witnessed.

What will bring humankind to extinction will not be the splitting asunder of the thin crust of the earth or fire falling from the sky, nor will it be the flooding of the great oceans, but first will come the transformation of the forest of Hida province into leeches, and finally all will turn to black slugs swimming in the midst of blood and mud; that will be the coming of the next world, I mused.

The entrance to the forest held no fears at all, but as I came further inside it was as I described, and if I were to enter deeper into the interior, all the trees without exception would have rotted from the roots up and would have turned to mountain leeches; nothing could save me; my fate, it seemed, was to be murdered by evil spirits. I suddenly realized that this melange of speculation had arisen because I had come so close to the moment of death.[24]

At this point the priest-narrator achieves a kind of enlightenment. He has brought his fears out into the open. Once he has faced openly the prospect of death and realizes that his apocalyptic visions are but the product of this confrontation, then he can summon the necessary inner strength to go on. Kyōka in the next sentence writes: "I came to a resolution," a resolution to conquer his fears and proceed, but the term resolution *(kakugo)* also implies he has come to a realization of the truth. This use of the word *kakugo* incorporates its specifically Buddhist connotation of *dōri o satoru* (finding the way), because, for the priest-protagonist, this journey into the terrors of Hida forest is also a Buddhist journey towards enlightenment.[25] In this apprehension, the narrator's perception of the gothic horrors assailing him is revealed as an insight into his own psyche, a perfect demonstration of the uncanny.

Brook's concept of melodramatic excess can be seen in *The Holy Man of Kōya* to meld into a Japanese version of gothic. As noted earlier, Kyōka's themes and techniques appear to derive more from the Japanese tradition of late Edo writing than from any European antecedents, but as demonstrated here the affinities between Kyōka's writing and the European gothic novel go beyond mere similarity in genre to point to parallel concerns with representation and the uses of romantic fantasy.[26] To explore the reasons behind the common concerns of Kyōka and practitioners of late European gothic like Emily Brontë would be a major undertaking indeed, but that there are such affinities cannot be doubted.

Kyōka's fictional technique exploits ambiguity to a superb degree. It is impossible to know whether the priest is actually hallucinating much of what he describes or whether the supernatural horror he recounts is somehow a literal representation of the truth. Noguchi Takehiko argues that what Kyōka is describing is "a linguistic universe in which both tenor and vehicle interchange roles. And, as a result, the language of Kyōka's fiction performs a double semantic function, because of the principle of this interchangeability; it has a double linguistic order, simultaneously real and anti-real." [27] Noguchi is saying that in Kyōka's fiction the literal subject of literary tropes becomes confused with the analogy or image to which it is compared, or in some cases, to which the meaning is transferred. A confusion between the literal object of comparison and the object to which it is being compared is characteristic of Kyōka's fiction, argues Noguchi, and the result is that the real world *(jitsu sekai)* and the non-real world or the world of dream, the world of fantastic image, become reversed, or, in some instances, the same. Ambiguity in meaning is fundamental to Kyōka's writing because it arises from the very semantic matrix of his style. This ambiguity results in a suspension of belief that is peculiarly modern, a necessary consequence of the self-conscious explorations of the late Romantic tradition as it was absorbed into European and Japanese fiction alike.

Modern Horror

Kyōka's linkage between gothic horror and the inner phantasm of psychological dread can be seen in his later works as well. Indeed, there is no doubt that this connection held true for much of Kyōka's writing throughout his career. Twenty years after the publication of the *The Holy Man of Kōya*, Kyōka serialized a novella of about the same length called *Murasaki shōji* (The violet sliding door) in the March and April 1919 issues of *Shinshōsetsu* (New fiction). The tale has been described by the critic Higashi Masao as a "modern horror story" and can stand as a fine example of Kyōka's mastery of this genre.[28]

The novella is based on two separate sources or ideas: one is the notion of a *kōketsujō* (tie-dying textile castle): the word refers to a cultic site where devotees practice occult rituals. A famous tale concerning one such site, called there a *kōkechi no shiro* (a variation on the term *kōketsujō*), can be found in Book 11 of the prose collection *Konjaku monogatari* (Tales old and new), dating from the eleventh century. Kyōka's tale recounts a story, set in Kyoto, of a vampiric cult. The story's other source is the legend of a cult of female snake-worshippers, which is also based in Kyoto.[29] The first notion is made manifest at the end of the novella with the sentence: "This was probably a kind of cultic site," where I have translated the word *kōketsujō* as cultic site.[30] And, as demonstrated by *The Holy Man of Kōya*, the appearance in Kyōka's fiction of serpent women is ubiquitous. As Nina Cornyetz has noted, "the serpent-demoness . . . has enjoyed a long reign of terror in virtually every classical Japanese genre and . . . appears in many of Kyōka's . . . texts."[31] The serpent woman is not the only stock charac-ter from Kyōka's repertoire to appear in this tale, which is typical of the mode of fiction adopted by the mature Kyōka, but in other respects the story is a more transparently modern narrative than such earlier works as *The Holy Man of Kōya.*

As in *The Holy Man of Kōya,* the story is an embedded narrative, but the unnamed narrator is clearly meant to represent the unnamed author (who may or may not represent Kyōka), for from time to time the narrator breaks into the narrative with asides to the reader. The opening page begins with description of a man awakening in a Kyoto inn; then the narrator intrudes into the scene, speaking directly to the reader with a description of the protagonist, who is called Mimizuku, or the "owl":

> Mimizuku . . . I will call my friend by this name. Properly speaking, I should call him A or B, but there's no necessity to use something as fancy as the alphabet because he's only an ordinary man who if he got hold of the money just might be able make a sightseeing trip to the West of Japan. However, since he told me to keep this story a secret, I thought of calling him a nightingale because of his connection to the nursery rhyme that goes "Nightingales, Nightingales, fly to the capital," and I also thought I'd give the title of "Nightingale" to the story, but, in shape and appearance, no matter how you look at him, he is not a nightingale type of man. In addition to telling me that he lazed about during the day, but at night wanted to see and hear wild and wonderful things with ears pricked and eyes wide open, he stammered out his tale with his lips tightly pursed, and so I felt that oddly enough he looked like some other creature . . . that's right, he is the spitting image of an owl, and that's why I call him Mimizuku.[32]

The use of humor from the very beginning of the narrative marks the story as more modern in structure and sensibility than *The Holy Man of Kōya.* "Mod-ern" here denotes a style of narration closer to the dominant Naturalist school of writing discussed in Chapter 3: a more conscious attempt at realistic narra-tive, with verisimilitude an important element in the text.[33] However, when they are compared to *The Holy Man of Kōya,* these differences in composition and stylistic technique are a matter of degree only. Kyōka never joined the Natu-ralist clique; he even wrote an anti-Naturalist polemic in 1908 and maintained his "romantic" writing style fairly consistently over the course of his career.[34] Another feature is the relatively frequent use of realistic narrative: while the reader cannot tell at the beginning of a description whether Mimizuku is dreaming/hallucinating or actually experiencing the events described, often the narrative is a relatively straightforward account (in Kyōka's distinctive rococo style) of meals, travel, and so forth, and Mimizuku is usually described as "awakening" from his reveries. So, in effect, the reader is usually told whether the sequence is real or imaginary. Kyōka sets the story in the present—no attempt is made to create an archaic setting or to consciously evoke the past—and owing to its origin as a serial, it is divided into twenty-six short chapters of approximately the same page length.

The story begins with Mimizuku staying at an inn in Kyoto called Tamashiba and feeling ill; almost immediately he awakens from his dream of nausea and feels better, but the motif of nausea reoccurs throughout the narrative. The nausea is linked to a fishy taste and rotten smell, and scenes where Mimizuku is eating at restaurants are liberally interspersed into the text. The detailed descriptions of the famous regional cuisine of Western Japan, and its consumption, contrast with repeated references to Mimizuku's increasingly upset stomach, and this too occasionally strikes a humorous note. Mimizuku is a poor man who has been befriended by a wealthy businessman named Soya, who finances a trip for Mimizuku and a beautiful geisha called Ashie, with whom Mimizuku has become infatuated, to see the sights of Western Japan. They travel together to Nara and then to Kyoto, staying at expensive Japanese-style inns near famous temples and doing the things one does on such a journey.

However, at least half the story is narrated in a complex series of flashbacks, Soya's name is not mentioned until chap. 9, and the precise nature of the connection between the three of them does not fully emerge until chap. 12, almost halfway through the tale. Kyōka shifts the narrative perspective continuously, and the reader is never sure where the events taking place fall on the narrative timeline. The narrating voice often merges with Mimizuku's thoughts, which usually (but not always) appear in quotation marks (square brackets), and the text is studded with embedded conversations conveyed by a variety of devices including conventional punctuation, dashes, and parentheses. Kyōka demonstrates his famous command of dialects by using a broad array of Western Japanese voices in the text—usually maids—who speak several different regional dialects, but at one point he has Ashie, who should, and usually does, speak an urban Osaka dialect, conversing in the distinctive drawl of a Kyoto woman.[35]

Thus the tale is not easy to follow, and several times the narrative falls into an extravagant expansion of metaphor and simile (often focusing on color), common to much of Kyoka's fiction, which follow their own etymological logic. These usually occur in the description of clothing or Ashie's beauty—whether this is Mimizuku's musing or the words taking over the text is difficult to decide. Here is a typical, but important sample of this type of rhetoric:

> Behind the glass in the door [of the Kyoto inn] the figure of a blue woman could be seen through the sliding glass door of the old cottage hidden behind the trees. . . . No, let me describe it as a dark-ultramarine blue, the color of verdigris, a bronze mold color, resembling the blackish moss found on the bark of old trees. . . .
>
> Through the glass, sitting upright, her shoulders, neck, chest, and sash were visible: a half-figure seen through the pine and plum leaves, her color could not be compared to blue or green or aquamarine, the thought occurred to him that her sleeves and kimono were divided into ultramarine shadows. Her thin face in profile was visible from the left, her gaze being cast down at an angle, and appeared more blue than indigo; the Shimada-style of her hair was swept up into a darker shade of ultramarine. As in a shadow picture, he could clearly see her slight, wispy stray cerulean locks through the depths of the fine misty rain, amid the green of the garden like a jade pool: she was the embodiment of the dark mass of the forest covering the mountain behind.
>
> Whether seconds or minutes had passed, he couldn't tell; he stared unblinking at the silhouette of the woman and during that time not a hair on her head as much as moved.
>
> When he was able to release his gaze from her, in the dusk the electric lights of Kyoto were scattered about glimmering wetly, shadows floated in midair and the lights flickered fitfully in the pine garden.
>
> The sliding screen door of his room suddenly turned violet.
>
> The window in the cottage where the blue woman was sitting was an even darker, thicker shade of violet.[36]

In this vital passage from chap. 25 Mimizuku sees (or imagines) clearly for the first time the snake woman whom he has half-glimpsed in his imagination and half-detected in the visage of the mistress of the Nara inn where he and Ashie stayed the previous night. The passage also reveals that the title of the story indicates an optical phenomenon caused by the light at dusk.

The focus on description and the complex and confusing use of flashbacks creates a tale that is quite complicated, mixing humor with a travelogue-style description of food and place in a narrative that is nowhere as atmospheric in its evocation of horror and the supernatural as *The Holy Man of Kōya*. But this comment really applies to the first half of the text only. From chap. 15 the narrative becomes much more tightly focused, and Mimizuku's nausea, which is now severe chest pain, becomes the chief element of the plot. However, the humor remains in such instances as the depiction of an increasingly frantic Mimizuku desperately trying to find an unoccupied toilet late at night in the Kyoto inn in order to rid himself of the contents of his throat and stomach. Perhaps Kyōka's use of humor represents an attempt to write a more up-to-date, entertaining narrative. Charles Inouye, Kyōka's biographer, quotes the Nobel Prize-winning novelist Kawabata Yasunari (1899–1972) as saying that at this time "Kyōka's obscurity was near-total."[37]

The Violet Sliding Door traces the physical origin of Mimizuku's nausea to his consumption of eggrolls in Nara that had apparently been contaminated by a dirty carving knife. The event occurs in chap. 14 as part of an extended flashback recounting Mimizuku and Ashie's trip to Nara. But the psychic origin of his nausea is more complicated. In chap. 4, having come from Nara, Mimizuku checks into the Tamashiba inn in Kyoto. There, retracing in his imagination "the night journey he took to the inn, he felt that he had struck a go-piece, which lodged unpleasantly at the top of his chest."[38] Mimizuku is taken aback by this horrible sensation, and concludes that nothing he has eaten could have contained a go-piece (or go-stone), a checker-like piece used in the Sino-Japanese board game called Go. The notion of a go-piece stuck in Mimizuku's throat recurs from then on throughout the narrative. References to go-pieces and games of Go multiply to a startling degree, and much of the dialogue between Ashie and Mimizuku occurs while they are engaged in games of Go. The go-piece is described in chap. 7: "[T]he go-piece was colored . . . it was like looking at a fine checked pattern criss-crossed on a black texture: blue, powder blue, yellow, white all mixed together, sparkling. I hear that it can be used to essay the quality of gold by rubbing the gold against the black stone."[39] Somehow the various go-pieces that are continually dropping out of the sleeves of the maids, Ashie, and others resemble this type of go-stone: they are elegantly colored, often with a gold filigree inscribed on the shiny black surface.

In chap. 17, while attempting to find a toilet, Mimizuku sees a beautiful and mysterious woman who resembles the mysterious woman in Nara (who was also playing a game of Go) and who is naked in the bath adjoining the lavatory. She is obscured by the steam and is holding a towel when suddenly, "the towel moved upwards, slithered round her upper torso, twisting itself around her, wriggling: the pointed head of a snake appeared, raised upright. It was indeed a serpent."[40] This woman has two snakes—one black and one white—entwined around her arms. Mimizuku cannot believe what he sees and, thinking this is a hallucination, promptly escapes into the toilet and vomits. Yet even after emptying his stomach, he hears a noise that he believes must be the go-stones moving in his body. The noise turns out to be two Kyoto *maiko*, or apprentice geisha, "with printed silk kimono sleeves with matching patterns, in the dark [it is two in the morning], their lanterns flickering in the mist. Holding the earthenware lanterns near their necks, their scarlet kimono collars embroidered in a flower pattern, the women were hitting go-stones, black, white, against their front teeth, bamboo-green amid rouged lips."[41] Startled by Mimizuku, the women disappear, but the go-stones fly upwards and hit Mimizuku, who thinks they are snakes. Discovering exactly the same go-piece described earlier, Mimizuku throws it into the garden of the inn, only to have the stone actually turn into a snake.

In the last three chapters of the novella the pace rapidly picks up. Mimizuku discovers from the maid the next day that the old cottage, an out-building of the inn, contains a Go board and a shrine, where two snakes reside and are worshipped as the "masters of the house" *(uchi no nushi han ya)*.[42] The snakes are but a part of the supernatural presences who inhabit this inn. Mimizuku dreams again of Ashie and, associating her with the snakes, wishes to be devoured by them. When they are finally leaving the inn in a cab to go to the station, Ashie tells Mimizuku of a dream she had: she went to the old cottage and found two Gion *maiko*, who dipped go-stones in oil and then licked them. She also saw the woman from Nara naked in the cottage, and she turned into two snakes and squeezed Ashie into a go-stone case filled with oil. At this point in Ashie's account the taxi hits a blue woman, but the body cannot be found. The narrative proper ends with the information that afterwards both Mimizuku and Ashie are plagued with a mysterious illness. For Mimizuku it lasts a considerable time, but Ashie dies not long after returning to Osaka. Now, says the narrator, Mimizuku is obsessed with snakes.

If the novella were to end at this point, then the reader would conclude that this is a typical Kyōka tale filled with snake women and supernatural presences and very much a study of Mimizuku's barely suppressed lust (for Ashie whom he cannot have on account of his poverty) and envy (of those who, unlike himself, can afford to live the life of luxury, sightseeing in expensive inns). But this is, as Higashi Masao has stated, a modern horror story. After concluding Mimizuku's story with the words, "I told you this in secret," the narrator/author adds a coda stating that there actually exists a secret cult of female snake-worshippers in Kyoto who believe that by consuming oil secreted by women who have been crushed to death by snakes they can become beautiful.[43] They also believe that by polishing their teeth with a white go-stone kept in the go-case where the oil is preserved, they can marry or find a new man. The black stone also has supernatural qualities, enabling the women to become rich. The risk is that by consuming such substances the women may die. An unusually beautiful woman who has invested the go-pieces with snake symbolism leads the cult. The inn, notes the narrator, is a cultic site.

Recent research has revealed that this coda is apparently based on historical fact and thus the typical Kyōka story becomes a somewhat different kind of fiction: in some respects, a tale of ratiocination, with parallels to Edgar Allan Poe's famous 1841 story "The Murders in the Rue Morgue." The supernatural in this tale is partially explained as the mysterious goings-on of an actual female cult that worships snakes and is involved in occult rituals of blood-letting. Hence Mimizuku's hallucinations can be seen to be based on real events that are so far outside his experience or understanding that the only way he can rationalize them is to believe them to be illusions or nightmares; in this sense the story is not, strictly speaking, a melodrama. Yet Kyōka's novella is equally a tale of gothic horror where the horror is actually the inner phantasm of psychological dread—in this case the dread of unfulfilled and, in some sense, illicit desire. Mimizuku's encounters with the blue snake woman, who is not a mere snake worshipper but an actual snake herself— or rather a snake demoness—reflect his voyeuristic longing for Ashie. He often gazes lustily at Ashie asleep, usually when her body is partially revealed, but she is the geisha he cannot possess. Kyōka's tale is also about class, about the large gap that had developed by the 1920s in Japan between the haves and the have-nots. This was a theme also taken up by late-nineteenth-century European gothic romances, and like those romances, *The Violet Sliding Door* may also reinforce social class distinctions with Mimizuku's lingering illness as punishment for his obsession with Ashie.[44]

The alien within the novella is revealed to be Mimizuku's not-so-hidden desires, represented by the blue snake-woman he conjures up out of his fevered imagination, and this aspect of the story maintains the continuity with Kyōka's other gothic tales. Thus the work is at the same time a psychological mystery story and a tale of gothic horror. Kyōka's writing was changing with the times, perhaps more than he himself was willing to acknowledge, but he was still a man of his time, which was more fin-de-siècle Japan than twentieth century. In Kyōka's version of gothic, specifically in *The Violet Sliding Door,* the influences of both eras can be seen.

Sadomasochistic Irony

Tanizaki Jun'ichirō is a much more self-conscious practitioner of psychological fiction than Kyōka. Even in his early fiction Tanizaki appears to be in control of the tropes and metaphors that explode from his pen. Tanizaki is often discussed in the same breath as Oscar Wilde, and like Wilde, Tanizaki was always in control of his material; like Wilde, he was also always ready to try new and different modes of expression to elaborate his ideas.[45] The central motif of Wilde's famous novel *The Picture of Dorian Gray* (1891) is the relationship between the artist and art. The artist is overpowered by his art, and Wilde's prose is replete with sadomasochistic metaphors that express the power that art exerts over the artist. In "Shisei" (The tattooer, 1910), Tanizaki's first mature work of fiction (although he was only twenty-four when he wrote it), the same metaphors of control and slavery are expressed in an explicitly sadomasochistic form.[46] In order to evaluate this work, it is first necessary to investigate the sources of its power, the antecedents of Tanizaki's gothic style.

Tanizaki is often linked to such Japanese authors as Nagai Kafū and Kyōka, who are associated with the Japanese version of gothic. Tanizaki first met Kafū in November 1910; at their second meeting the following month he gave Kafū a copy of "The Tattooer," which had just been published in *Shinshichō.* Kafū responded by writing an article on Tanizaki for the November 1911 issue of *Mita Bungaku* entitled "Tanizaki Jun'ichirō no sakuhin" (Tanizaki's writing), in which he gave much praise to Tanizaki's writing. Kafū argued that there were three characteristics of Tanizaki's fiction: a quiet mystical beauty born out of carnal fear, an obsession with urban landscapes, and a perfect style.[47] Itō Sei claims that when Tanizaki read Kafū's *Amerika monogatari* (American tales, 1908), he was so impressed with the collection that it changed his thinking altogether, which was why he was so anxious to gain Kafū's approval of "The Tattooer," his real debut in the literary world.[48] Nishihara Daisuke argues that *American Tales* is the source for many of Tanizaki's early fictional motifs, including "The Tattooer."[49] Chiba Shunji has argued that Tanizaki inherits Kafū's "reverse Orientalism" and that Kafū's story "Suibijin" (Drunken beauty, 1908), first published in *American Tales,* clearly influenced "The Tattooer."[50]

Kyōka was Tanizaki's senior by thirteen years, but according to Muramatsu Sadataka it was Tanizaki's art that inspired the older writer to climb new heights when his career was in something of a slump.[51] Charles Inouye contends that there was an affinity between the two writers, noting that "we can identify a shared appreciation for Edo culture and also a passionate regard for artistic style."[52] He even claims that "The Tattooer" is inspired by a story by Kyōka entitled "Higedaimoku" (The grave writer, 1897).[53] Kyōka's works are traditionally associated with an Orientalist vision of the gothic rather than the Western version, but as a number of commentators have remarked, the "Orientalism" found in Tanizaki's writing is an exoticized, European product, not something arising out of the Japanese past. As Ken Ito has noted, "[W]hen Tanizaki portrays late Edo as the 'other world,' he not only reflects Kafū's reformulation of European Orientalism, but also displays a distinct skill in naturalizing foreign concepts."[54] This comment refers to "The Tattooer," which as Nishihara notes, "is a classic example of the Orientalist aesthetic."[55] He asserts: "For Tanizaki the Edo era was the same as the Orient for Westerners, mentally separated from the world in which the author and his readers lived. . . . The juxtaposition of the West against the Orient was replaced by Japan against China, modern Japan against Edo."[56] This comment testifies to Tanizaki's deep absorption of Western culture, where the Western exoticized Other becomes Japan's exoticized Other, despite the fact that it was a caricature of Japan's own Asian heritage. Nishihara maintains that "The Tattooer" is a perfect example of a work that is completely suffused with Tanizaki's Orientalism.[57]

The plot of this short story set in the Edo period is simplicity itself. A young tattooist named Seikichi has a secret desire to torment men with his needles, and he also has a secret desire to create a masterpiece on the skin of a beautiful woman. One day in the Fukagawa district, Seikichi sees a woman's foot peeping out from the curtains of a palanquin. He determines to find her, and by accident he does. He drugs the young girl, who is soon to begin a career as a geisha, so that he can begin tattooing her back. But when the girl awakes with a tattoo of a spider on her back, the tables are turned, and she, not Seikichi, is the master.

At no stage during "The Tattooer" is there a double-text such as that in *The Holy Man of Kōya* where the natural phenomena present a text that parallels the text of the plot. The lush, exotic, and therefore artificial atmosphere produced by Tanizaki's style is transparently artificial. Why is this so? It is because the narrative voice is clearly ironic; Tanizaki's narrator—a character in his own right—cannot be read as a subtext or a double narrative hidden within the main text, as can some of the narrators in Kyōka's fiction. The very first sentence, "It was an age when people still held on to the noble virtue of foolishness, unlike the present era where society is in a state of violent discord," exhibits a degree of self-conscious irony lacking in Kyōka's narrators in *The Holy Man of Kōya*.[58] The gothic elements in Tanizaki's tale arise from the performative interaction of the characters, which compete with the ironic narrator for the readers' attention. The melodrama in the story, while clearly part of the psychology of sadomasochism, operates within a stable frame of narrative, a stable other-world, a world of desire rather than the world of dreams. Take, for instance, the sadomasochistic monomania of Seikichi as revealed in the following quotation:

> The heart of the young tattooer concealed a hidden pleasure and a hidden longing. When he pierced the skin with his needle, most men were unable to bear the pain in their blood-engorged flesh and groaned in agony, but, curiously, their moaning gave him an indescribable joy. To use vermilion dye in the tattoo, reputed to be exceptionally painful, injecting layer on layer, delighted him most of all. Pierced by the needle an average of five or six hundred times, after emerging from the bath to heighten the colors, his customers—more dead than alive—collapsed near Seikichi's feet, unable to move a muscle. Coldly gazing upon this cruel sight, Seikichi always remarked, smiling with enjoyment, "My, that must have hurt."
>
> When men without pride, their teeth clenched, their mouths contorted as if in agony at the moment of their death, groaned, struggling for breath, Seikichi said, "You're a son of Edo aren't you. Take it like a man!—My needle is excruciatingly painful. . . ."
>
> . . . For many years he had cherished the desire to tattoo his own soul onto the skin of a dazzling beauty. He had several requirements regarding the attitudes and features of the beauty. He could not be satisfied with a beautiful face and lovely skin alone.[59]

This is a quite transparent revelation of psychology, and in that sense the gothic is on the surface; it is placed in the foreground rather than in the background. The subtext, the dark subtext, or the uncanny, is found in the revelation of a sadistic aspect to the woman, which is revealed clearly and relatively early in the narrative:

> "This picture [of a battle scene filled with corpses] shows your future. All those fallen men will abandon their lives for you." Seikichi pointed to the face of the woman in the painting exactly like her own.

"Please, I beg you, take this picture away now," she pleaded. As if to avert the temptation, and defy the picture, the girl fell flat on the mat, but before long her lips began to quiver once more.

"Master, I confess. Just as you sensed, I possess the same nature as that woman."[60]

Tanizaki's description of Seikichi beginning to work on the drugged woman—the tattooer in near ecstasy—matches the lurid, exotic tones of late European gothic literature, which also often focused on the figure of a woman confined in an enclosed space by male lust or unnatural desire.[61]

Sunlight streamed in glorious reflection from the surface of the river into the eight-mat room, seemingly on fire. Reflecting off the river, the rays of light played over the face of the girl, who was sleeping innocently, and painted gold ripples on the paper of the sliding doors. Seikichi had closed up the partition and, with his tattooing equipment in hand, just stood there for some time in a state of rapture. For the first time he was able to savor to his heart's content the woman's lovely face. Gazing at her immobile features, he thought that if he were to sit quietly in this room for hundreds of years he would still not tire of the sight. Just as the citizens of ancient Memphis decorated the majestic land of Egypt with the pyramids and the Sphinx, so Seikichi was going to embroider undefiled human skin with his adoration.

Presently, with the tip of his brush between his little finger, ring finger, and thumb, he drew a line with the tip of his brush flat against the girl's back, and from above with his right hand he plunged the needle into her. The heart of the young tattooer melted into the black ink and ran onto her skin. The red droplets of vermilion Ryūkyū ink that had been mixed with liquor pierced her skin—his very life-blood. He saw the color of his soul there.[62]

The woman's sadistic nature is revealed fully when the tattoo is completed on her back. However, as Seikichi has foreseen this aspect of the woman's nature, it comes as no great surprise to the reader when her narcissistic cruelty is revealed.

"Master, quickly, show me the tattoo on my back, I must be even more beautiful now that I've taken possession of your life."

The girl's words were like a dream, but her voice had a cutting edge to it.

"Go and have a bath, the colours will be enhanced. It will hurt, but you only have to bear it for a little while," Seikichi whispered into her ear in a sympathetic tone.

"As long as I become more beautiful, I can take it no matter what," she said, with a forced smile, suppressing the pain in her body.

"Ah, the hot water hurts, it hurts . . . master, I beg you, leave me, wait on the first floor. I don't want to be seen by a man in this wretched state."

Unable even to dry her body after her bath, the girl thrust aside Seikichi's proffered hand and, in the throes of agony, threw herself down onto the wooden floor of the bathroom, moaning as if in a nightmare. Her disheveled hair, tangled like that of a madwoman, fell melancholy onto her cheeks. Behind her there stood a small dressing table with a mirror on top. The snow-white soles of her feet were reflected in the mirror.

Seikichi was astonished by the change in her manner since the previous day, but waited by himself on the first floor as he had been instructed, and after about an hour, the woman came up, her newly washed hair hanging loose about her shoulders, her dress newly arranged. No shadow of distress remained in her bright eyes as she leaned against the railing, gazing upwards at the hazy sky.

"I'm giving you this painting as well as the tattoo, you can take it and leave." With these words, Seikichi placed the scroll in front of the woman.

"Master, I've abandoned my timid nature completely—now you're nothing but dung for me to use, the first of many men." She remarked, her eyes glittering like a blade. In her ears, she could only hear a victory anthem.

"Before you go, show me the tattoo once more," Seikichi asked.

The woman nodded silently and took off her clothes. Just then the morning sun shone on her tattoo, the woman's back was on fire.[63]

It may be argued that the changed nature of the woman, her sudden shift from victim to master, and the cruelty that is an essential element of her transformation is fundamentally a construction of Seikichi, in the same way that the character of Naomi is the construction of her mentor Jōji in Tanizaki's brilliant comic masterpiece *Chijin no ai* (Naomi, 1925), but in "The Tattooer" Tanizaki's self-conscious narrator has by a variety of means already hinted at this possibility from the beginning.[64]

The sources of the sadomasochistic motifs in "The Tattooer," motifs that reoccur with increasing frequency in Tanizaki's works, arise from Tanizaki's adventures in literature as well as from more personal roots. The following quotation from his novel *Jōtarō*, first published in 1914 and described by the Tanizaki authority Matsumura Masaie as "an autobiographical work," has long been cited by Tanizaki specialists as referring to Tanizaki's own discovery of sadomasochism: [65]

> Nevertheless, when he was in the first year of his Humanities course at university, by chance he perused a volume by Krafft-Ebing. How great was Jōtarō's amazement, joy, and excitement at that time? This was the first time he had received such a frightening and powerful shock from a book by a human being the same as himself. As he turned the pages and read, a violent shivering spread through his entire body that he was powerless to prevent . . .
>
> . . . What this book taught him was that there were hundreds of thousands of human beings like himself in the world who felt the secret pleasures that he had hidden deep within his innermost heart. . . .
>
> . . . He discovered that from Rousseau and Baudelaire onwards there had been many geniuses who were trapped by their masochistic desires. . . .
>
> . . . Something else that had moved him in his reading of Krafft-Ebing was that Western women, especially prostitutes, in their attitude towards their clients, had a powerful, animated, and stimulating allure, unimaginable by lukewarm matrons, and also possessed a frank temperament easily able to accommodate all the varied demands for pleasure in the sophisticated and complex environment in which they worked. Not only Jōtarō, but many masochists like him longed to meet women who were endowed with cruel, bestial natures. . . .[66]

Tanizaki's discovery of Baron Richard Freiherr von Krafft-Ebing's *Psychopathia Sexualis* (1886), perhaps the nineteenth century's most famous study of sexual aberration, clearly had a deep impact upon him. Inoue Ken has documented the various English translations and summaries of this work that were available for Tanizaki to read at the time he wrote "The Tattooer," and, judging from the quotation above, he put some of the ideas expressed in the book to good use in his characterizations.[67] Other literary sources exist for the use and exploitation of these ideas in literature. Tanizaki translated a Thomas Hardy tale called "Barbara, of the House of Grebe" into Japanese in 1927, and Tanizaki's knowledge of Hardy and Western literature in general provided fertile ground for the adaptation of such motifs taken from late gothic and fin-de-siècle writing. Matsumura Masaie has pointed to the significance of the strange tale of sexual obsession arising out of "Barbara, of the House of Grebe" for various

Tanizaki works, and Anthony Chambers has analyzed the use Tanizaki made of the story in the novel *Shunkinshō* (A portrait of Shunkin, 1933).[68] Tanizaki found gothic and fin-de-siècle writing a useful starting point for many of his own explorations in fiction of the irrational and perverse nature of human sexuality. In this sense he was a Japanese exotic non pareil, and it comes as no surprise that a recent study of his literature has the title *Tanizaki Jun'ichirō to ikoku no gengo* (Tanizaki and exotic languages), for exoticism is close to the heart of his aesthetic.[69] Tanizaki's exoticism derives as much from the Japanese tradition as the Western, but his treatment of it represents an attempt to reintroduce the alien into literary discourse.

Gothic Horror as Doubled Narrative

The alien within as a theme or marker of the gothic is no more perfectly illustrated than in the famous Tanizaki story, "Jinmenso" (The carbuncle with a human face), first published in *New Fiction* in March 1918.[70] This is another example of a story within a story, which takes place in the first two decades of the twentieth century. The embedded story tells of an *oiran,* or high-ranking courtesan, in Nagasaki named Ayame Dayū. Ayame longs to be with her lover, a white American sailor who is referred to only by the appellation *hakujin* (white man). A Japanese beggar who has fallen in love with Ayame agrees to help her join her lover on board a ship bound for America. Ayame hides inside a trunk, which the sailor locks, and the beggar takes from her brothel to the old temple where he dosses down so that the sailor can come and bring her back to his ship. The beggar has asked for the privilege of sleeping with her as payment. For two days he savors the prospect of sex with Ayame, barely able to keep his eyes off the locked trunk. However, Ayame has conspired with her lover to trick the beggar, so when the sailor arrives at the temple, he claims to have forgotten to bring the key for the trunk. Crushed by this deception, the beggar, before throwing himself into the sea to die, pronounces the following curse: "[M]y ugly face will eat into the flesh of the courtesan and haunt her forever."[71]

Crammed into the trunk in the hold of the ship, Ayame notices something growing on her right knee. It turns out to be a carbuncle. Then further changes in the carbuncle occur:

On the inexpressibly soft swollen surface of the carbuncle four tiny heads began to grow. Strangely, the carbuncle did not appear to cause her any pain at all. She pushed at it and patted it. . . . As the days passed, it gradually grew harder, and the four heads slowly assumed a more and more definite shape. The two heads on the top became round like balls, the one in the middle grew into a long thin vertical line, and the one at the bottom twisted eerily like the wriggling of a caterpillar. . . . Once, gazing at the diseased part, she could not help but notice that the two protuberances on top had become like the eyeballs of a living creature. And the long thin pimple in the middle had grown into a nose; the caterpillar shape had turned into something like a mouth. The whole of the swollen surface, she discovered, had suddenly and indisputably turned into a human face.[72]

The face eventually turns into a perfect semblance of the unspeakably ugly beggar. She conceals her carbuncle from her lover, and they depart the ship in San Francisco. One day he discovers the carbuncle and declares that he will abandon her, and, with the fury of a woman possessed by an evil spirit, she strangles him to death. The carbuncle with the human face smiles, a further demonstration of its powers.

Ayame falls into a life of moral dissipation and decay while in the United States, yet she becomes more and more beautiful and voluptuous. The carbuncle also grows in power. She seduces many "white men" for money and then kills them. Eventually she becomes a music hall performer in New York, while also now and then plying her trade as a prostitute. Ayame achieves fame in vaudeville and becomes the darling of the wealthy, moneyed elite of New York. Finally, full of regrets at the evils of her former life, she marries a young European count. However, at a party to celebrate their wedding, Ayame loses herself in joyful dancing and allows the carbuncle with the human face to tear its way through the gauze covering her knee, and all is revealed before the crowd of well-wishers.

That evening in the ballroom, while dancing madly as if in a dream, all of a sudden, bright red blood trickles in a single line down the pure white silk stockings that Ayame is wearing and drips onto the floor. Totally unaware, Ayame continues to dance. The count, who has always wondered at the dressing that his wife wears over her knee, casually comes to her side to examine the bandage—the carbuncle with the human face, using its teeth, tears at the stocking, protruding its long tongue, and, blood pouring from its eyes and nose, begins to cackle.

At that moment Ayame loses her sanity, and while fleeing to her bedroom, plunges a knife into her breast, and with the knife still imbedded in her chest collapses backwards onto the bed. Though she has committed suicide, the carbuncle with a human face appears to survive, still cackling.[73]

Thus the embedded story ends. This wildly improbable tale takes gothic horror to a level far surpassing anything achieved in "The Tattooer," and, despite the many parallels between the two female protagonists, it is a far more overtly melodramatic tale. On the surface it is much closer to Kyōka's gothic fiction than to "The Tattooer." But in "Jinmenso" this inner tale is actually the plot of a five-reel movie called *Obsession* (*Shūnen* in Japanese).[74] About a third of the story is taken up with a description of the movie, but the short story frame gives the movie narrative an entirely different complexion: it acts as an ironic commentary on the movie—so ironic, if read in a certain light, that it can even approach parody.[75]

The protagonist of the full story of "The Carbuncle with a Human Face" is a famous actress called Utagawa Yurie, who returns to Japan after a successful career making movies in the United States. She has heard of the movie *Obsession*, which apparently has her starring as the courtesan Ayame, but she cannot remember ever having made the movie. Actually Yurie's name is the sole credit on the film, which is currently making the rounds of cinemas on the outskirts of Tokyo. Since the movie is being shown out of town, she has not had an opportunity to see it. So she consults Mr. H, a translator and a U.S. agent for Nittō, the company that is showing the movie.

Half of "The Carbuncle with a Human Face" consists of a conversation that Yurie has with H, although H does most of the talking. He tells her that a print of the film, which was made under the aegis of a Los Angeles film company named Globe, was bought illegally from a Frenchman, who procured a copy of the film in Shanghai. H informs Yurie that the film is said to be haunted and that Nittō's best film technician quit the company in fear after trying to clean the scratches from the print. H cannot find any trace of the actor who plays the beggar. He suspects that the film is a composite of several films spliced together that star Yurie and others, but evidence of this is hard to find. In response to H's queries, Globe has stated that they did not make the film, but various scenes from their movies may have been patched together to make the composite.

Yurie begs to know why the film is so frightening. H confesses that the close-up of the carbuncle in the last scene not only scares the wits out of viewers with its horrible leer, but that the faint cackle emanating from its mouth rendered one viewer, sitting alone in a darkened room, unconscious. Tanizaki's Japanese readers understand perfectly well that the film is a black-and-white silent movie, and therefore what H is saying about a cackle does not make sense. H feels that the film is possessed, and walking over to the windows in his office, he unrolls the film to show Yurie the face on the carbuncle (the beggar), which he now sees clearly has been spliced onto the film as a double exposure. Yurie responds that she has no idea who the face is. The story ends with H wondering what will happen when they sell the film back to Globe, as Globe will copy the print and sell it all over the world.

The frame story is different from the movie described in the tale in several respects. Nothing supernatural or even horrible occurs in the calm conversation between H and Yurie, and nothing they say approaches the lurid plot of the film. Virtually all of H's comments about the effects that the film has on audiences can be explained rationally, even the cackle of the carbuncle can be attributed to the audience's heightened imagination, especially that of a single viewer alone in a darkened room. Other contradictions that seem to indicate the film is no ordinary movie can be explained as products of the new film techniques of double exposure and composite splicing. Tanizaki leaves the reader to contemplate a double narrative: the conversation between H and Yurie, which can be interpreted as intensifying the mystery behind the horror film or which can be read as an ironic commentary on the nature of gothic horror as a highly charged product of the human imagination. The story literally incorporates the two worlds of the gothic: the lurid otherworld of the movie and the normal everyday world of Yurie and H's conversation; the two worlds are placed in ironic juxtaposition and capable of various interpretations. "The Carbuncle with a Human Face," written eight years after "The Tattoer," reveals how much Tanizaki had matured as an ironist, and how the gothic had become for Tanizaki a much more complex exploration of the human psyche and the narrative form than was possible in the earlier work.

In a detailed study of the narrative published in 2003, Nozaki Kan contextualizes the story against the background of the emerging film industry. Tanizaki was fascinated by the new art form of the cinema and had already in 1917 written an article on the subject in which he expressed his admiration for the new medium and his preference for the cinema over live theater. He also wrote scripts for two films that were later produced.[76] If the reading of the story as an ironic counterpoint to the movie is adopted, then H's comment about the film being given a wide theatrical release by Globe could indicate Tanizaki's real fears about the fledgling Japanese film industry being swamped by the emerging power of Hollywood. Nozaki argues that one can read the text as an extended metaphor for the pervasive epidemic-like power of the film industry; the haunting referred to in the narrative and its mesmerizing effect on the audience is a horrific consequence of this new technology. Thus Nozaki sees yet another subtext or meta-text hidden within Tanizaki's narrative.[77] Nozaki also points out that the key question is whether Yurie's participation in the film could be completely faked—if it is faked, then the very issue of the movie being haunted is brought into doubt. It hinges on new technology of the cinema that was not yet available in Japan: innovative special effects like double exposure and the close-up.[78] Tanizaki's intimate knowledge of these techniques is also a noteworthy feature of the text, which imitates the film narrative by using them as literary tropes.

Another intriguing reading Nozaki proposes is that the text plays with the notion of the real. By this he means that Ayame is a purer version of the female (seen as an ideal) than Yurie. Reading Tanizaki's narrative in the light of Plato's concept of Form—as Socrates remarks in the *Phaedo,* there must be "an absolute essence of all things"—Ayame becomes the very embodiment of desire, evil, and sexuality, and possessed sexuality at that.[79] Nozaki contends that Tanizaki provides one hint as to the possibility of this interpretation in the following section of H's monologue: "No, not only you, but us as well, it's really weird that we know nothing about that guy [the actor who played the beggar]—where on earth did he come from? The role of the flute-playing beggar, you have to say that it's a performance that goes beyond powerful, his expression after becoming the carbuncle, unbelievably nuanced; the only actor I can think of who could play that role is someone like [Paul] Wegener, who starred in *Der Student von Prag* [The Student of Prague, 1913] and *Der Golem* [The Golem]." [80]

Both of these films are acclaimed horror movies, classics of the German silent film. In the plot of the former, a drama student proffers his image, that is, his doppelganger, to a magician in order to gain the affection of a rich countess. The notion of the doppelganger, of one's shadow (or soul) being stolen by another, obviously has parallels to the relationship between Ayame and the beggar and also between Ayame and Yurie. In this reading, Ayame represents the Platonic Form of Yurie: her real essence. Both German films are based on the Faust legend of selling one's soul to the devil. Echoes of other Faustian dramas, such as Robert Louis Stevenson's famous novel *The Strange Case of Dr Jekyll and Mr Hyde* (1886), are also obvious in the story.[81] The idea of Ayame being the shadow of Yurie (or the reverse) prompted Nozaki to see the double narrative of Tanizaki's tale as a variation on this theme.[82] In a very real sense Ayame is the alien within the real self of the famous actress Utagawa Yurie (who is, of course, a fictional character created by Tanizaki).

The allusions to German expressionist cinema are no accident and stress how self-referential Tanizaki's literary art was becoming. This is why Tanizaki's version of gothic is modern, indeed modernist, in its realization. Nozaki also notes that the carbuncle is something of which Ayame is deeply ashamed and seeks to keep hidden, wrapped in silk stockings and gauze. Inevitably perhaps, Nozaki is led to make a case that the carbuncle actually stands for Ayame's genitals; such a reading is also supported by the kind of analysis that appears in Krafft-Ebing's *Psychopathia Sexualis* and that Freud and Havelock Ellis were carrying out in various publications at the time.[83] Nozaki sees the carbuncle as a site of aberrant desire, a conjunction of the hidden and the shameful combining to create an eroticism that embraces that which is most repugnant and ugly. Tanizaki's reader, Nozaki claims—perhaps the reader crafted by Tanazaki—gains an erotic charge out of a kind of masochistic desire, a perverse gaze.[84] The blood that pours out of the nostrils and eyes of the carbuncle in the last scene of the movie may strengthen Nozaki's argument for Ayame, but the character of Yurie, who is described as an action heroine playing female pirates among other physical roles, does not fit this analysis at all.

This difficulty in logic can be avoided if we invoke a Jekyll-and-Hyde juxtaposition, with Yurie posed as the healthy neurosis-free modern woman of 1920s Japan and Ayame the courtesan as a dark reminder of Japan's past, with its long history of prostitution. Such an analysis also fits neatly with the European gothic genre of fiction, for numerous commentators have read gothic writing as an exploration of what Susanne Becker calls the "monstrous-feminine."[85] Becker analyzes the European gothic using Julia Kristeva's notion of "abjection," where "abjection . . . means (phobic) fear and (physical) repulsion. The fear of the evil involved turns out to be fear of the other, fear of evil-the-feminine."[86] Becker argues that in gothic texts the female body "becomes a target for . . . suppression," specifically in three aspects: "female sexuality, the power of procreation, and the 'two-faced mother.'"[87] Aspects of Becker's argument work well with Tanizaki's text and help explain why the two female characters are so different: Ayame is a celluloid construction of the "monstrous-feminine" or "evil-the-feminine," while Yurie is her polar opposite, the healthy "Westernized" Japanese woman of contemporary cinema and typical of Tanizaki's ideal woman at this time. This figure is most notably realized in Naomi, the protagonist of his 1925 novel *Naomi*, although his ideal was to change later.[88]

Tanizaki utilized Western notions of the gothic drawn from his extensive reading of Western literature, as well as from the numerous horror films (which he mentions in his text) that were increasingly making their way to Japan, to craft his complex and ironic vision of modern horror and the gothic. When subjected to a close reading, Tanizaki's double narrative discloses even more meta-narratives than at first may appear, as revealed in Nozaki's acute analysis. The reader is never sure just what is going on with "The Carbuncle with a Human Face." The alien within has two dimensions: the carbuncle as the embodiment of evil, especially a sexualized evil, and the notion of Ayame as Yurie's doppelganger, the bad girl hiding within the good. Another interpretation sees the alien within as a symbol of the dark past of Japanese womanhood contrasted with the shining future of a Westernized Japanese female. Tanizaki's superb narrative is at the same time a classic example of gothic horror and a modern commentary on the nature of the gothic itself.

Concluding Note

While the same dark elements found in the works of Kafū and Kyōka that underlie their conception of the human soul, and indeed the world itself, can be seen in Tanizaki's fiction, thus creating a unifying thread of gothic excess, these authors differ in many respects. Tanizaki's use of the gothic mode of narrative is a more self-conscious working of the tradition, and this is probably because he was much more familiar with it than Kyōka was, as has been pointed out by many Japanese commentators. Although Tanizaki was, like Kyōka, influenced by *kusazōshi* and by earlier Japanese gothic authors like Arishima Takeo, he read much more widely and borrowed much more overtly from late-nineteenth-century Western practitioners of gothic.[89] Imitating Kafū's modernist "self-referential" tendencies, Tanizaki deliberately played with the form, much more so in his later stories, and his influence on Japanese writers in the modern era was so great that many of them came to see gothic as merely one mode of romance or one mode of expression that was at their disposal as authors. He is the final link in that sequence of writers who established the gothic as one of the foundations of modernism in Japan.

CHAPTER 5

GOTHIC STYLISTICS
Arishima Takeo and Melodramatic Excess

I never knew such happiness. I never knew such happiness could
    exist.
Not that the dark world was removed or brightened, but
Each thing in it was slightly enlarged, and in so seeming became its
True cameo self, a liquid thing, to be held in the hollow
Of the hand like a bird. . . .
      —John Ashbery, from *Flow Chart*

I am not so afraid of the dark night
As the friends I do not know,
I do not fear the night above,
As I fear the friends below.
      —Stevie Smith, from "Dirge"

The connection between the gothic and the melodramatic mode of writing is how a foreign style of writing, indeed a foreign mode of expression, came to dominate Arishima Takeo's (1878–1923) fiction. It was in this sense that Arishima incorporated elements of the gothic in his fiction although the sources of this style lie not only in Western literature but in Edo literature as well. Arishima discovered the exotic, the alien within—within the highly wrought language from which he constructed his fiction—and without, in the choice of subject matter of much of that fiction. In subject and expression the notion of the alien held a great attraction for him.

Gerald Figel in his 1999 study, *Civilization and Monsters: Spirits of Modernity in Meiji Japan* has argued that "the fantastic allows the modern to be thought." [1] The fantastic has affinities with the notion of the alien as used in this study but, more pertinently, Figel links the notion of "otherness" to the foreign:

What we see occurring simultaneously with the colonization of the "outer territories" *(gaishi)* is an endocolonization of the demons and spirits of the "other world," a world conceived as other both spatially (rural periphery) and temporally (past beliefs). In the case of modern Japan, external *and* internal sources of blackness were thus at the disposal of the builders of a nation-state, the cultural, political, and social integrity of which would rely on an overdetermined spiritual ethnos to mask domestic differences *and* foreign similarities. The foreign took over the role of present Other while the *fushigi* of the folk was consigned to an anachronistic but respected past of national essence and origins.[2]

The taking over of the Other by the foreign is a response to modernization, as Figal notes, and this idea constitutes one of the central arguments of this book. This chapter will examine various aspects of Arishima Takeo's "foreignizing" style, using the notion of the "melodramatic imagination" as developed by Peter Brooks in his 1976 book of the same name. Such a study will not only provide a general insight into the gothic as it was manifested in Japan but will also illustrate how Arishima incorporated the alien into his fiction and thus illuminate his overall oeuvre. We begin by briefly considering the overall stylistic landscape in Japan when Arishima began writing and explore how Arishima's style fits or does not fit the conventional schematization.

Towards an "Un-Japanese" Style

Yamamoto Masahide in his magisterial *Kindai buntai hassei no shiteki kenkyū* (A historical study of the birth of the modern style, 1965) links the victory of the colloquial style *(genbun itchi)* with the domination of Japanese letters by such Naturalist writers as Shimazaki Tōson (1872–1943) and Tayama Katai (1871–1930).[3] By 1910 this process was complete, and writers belonging to the anti-Naturalist school, most notably Natsume Sōseki (1867–1916) and Mori Ōgai, (1862–1922), had brought a new richness and freshness to literary style. However even the anti-Naturalist writers, because of their classical education, were still fond of using recondite Chinese characters and occasionally preserved Sino-Japanese *(kanbun)* features in their work. Yamamoto argues that the final break with the past was made by writers associated with the Shirakaba (White Birch) literary coterie.[4]

The break occurred after 1910 because the young Shirakaba writers did not share the same educational background in the Japanese and Chinese classics as their predecessors. Yamamoto observes that a knowledge of Western rhetoric was needed to bring about this final severing of past traditions, and the *White Birch* magazine was one of the leading advocates of things Western in art and literature in the Japan of the time.[5] Thus the writers associated with the magazine were uniquely placed to bring the Japanese colloquial style to maturation. The writer whom Yamamoto finds most identified with an exotic, European tone is Arishima Takeo.[6] Yamamoto's analysis is echoed by many commentators. From the time Arishima began writing to the present, critics have accused him of adopting an un-Japanese, "foreign" style. They have sensed the influence of English constructions and idioms in his writing, and comments on foreignness are usually intended to be pejorative.[7]

In this connection the remarks by novelist Akutagawa Ryūnosuke (1892–1927), which were recorded by his fellow author Eguchi Kiyoshi (1887–1975), are most apposite:

> "Tanizaki Jun'ichirō is said to have admired Arishima Takeo's *Descendant of Cain,* but to have been impressed by a work like that Tanizaki shows how old-fashioned he is."
>
> Then Akutagawa stopped talking, and smiled as if in satisfaction, and added, "Arishima's novels are just like listening to a record of Western music."
>
> "How do you mean?"
>
> "Because I can't help feeling how wonderful it would be *if they were the real thing.*"[8]

Nakamura Akira's detailed stylistic analysis of Arishima's masterpiece *Aru onna* (A certain woman, 1919) confirms these perceptions.[9] Nakamura shows that Arishima is far more inclined to a mode of writing that differs in several respects from his contemporaries and that certain features of this mode of writing have been traditionally associated with translations from Western languages. To cite a few specific findings: a detailed statistical analysis of the occurrence of simile and metaphor in *A Certain Woman* demonstrates that Arishima uses both rhetorical devices to a much greater degree than his contemporaries did.[10] Arishima's use of metaphor is highly wrought and intellectual; in other words, it arises more from the author's conceptual categories than from nature.[11]

In addition to using figurative expressions that seem almost as if they are direct translations from Western languages, Arishima's rhetoric employs a contradictory, conceptual logic that marks his style as "un-Japanese" in intention and effect.[12] Curiously, Nakamura's analysis of Arishima's style matches almost exactly Tanizaki Jun'ichirō's celebrated characterization in his *Bunshō tokuhon* (Prose primer, 1934) of the imported "translation-style" as un-Japanese in his comparison of Theodore Dreiser's *An American Tragedy* (1925) with traditional Japanese prose style. Tanizaki finds the English prose style unutterably wordy. Tanizaki emphasizes the point later when he demonstrates how Arthur Waley's translation of *The Tale of Genji* destroys the compression and fluidity of the original by the addition of several passages (necessitated by the nature of the English language) not in the original.[13]

Nakamura argues that Arishima was attempting to develop the metaphor into something not hitherto seen in Japanese fiction; in other words, he was attempting to write a new kind of fiction. As we saw in Chapter 4, Noguchi Takehiko makes similar claims about Izumi Kyōka's technique in his much acclaimed study *The Language of the Novel*.[14] In Noguchi's analysis, the critic Iwano Hōmei's achievements as a theoretician and practitioner of the modern novel allowed the Naturalist movement to make significant advances in the art of writing fiction. The inheritors of this triumph of Naturalism included writers like Arishima, although the writer who took Japanese fiction into a new kind of conceptual poetics was Izumi Kyōka, as argued earlier. I believe that Arishima traveled the same journey as Kyōka, and thus my analysis diverges from Noguchi, but to understand what that journey represents it is necessary to consider Noguchi's argument in more detail.

Hōmei's polemical essay "Gendai shōrai no shōsetsu teki hassō o isshin subeki boku no byōsharon" (My thesis concerning portrayal which will reform conceptions of the novel now and in the future, 1918) is the starting point for Noguchi's discussion. This essay criticizes Naturalist writers like Shimazaki Tōson for claiming that objectivity is a normative possibility.[15] All fiction, Hōmei asserts, is necessarily subjective, for it is seen through the eyes of a subjective protagonist. Noguchi claims that Hōmei carried out these precepts in his own fiction, where the third person merges with the self. As a consequence, we find no instances of the protagonist speaking of events that only the author, and not the protagonist, could know. This approach to writing created a subtler, more complex relationship between author and narrator than the Naturalist credo permitted. Noguchi uses the phrase "destructive subjectivity" *(hakaiteki shukan)* to describe Hōmei's distinctive novelistic technique.[16] In Hōmei's fiction the tension between the author and author as character lies in a kind of antithetical humor. Realist fiction, the category in which Noguchi places Arishima, could only arise after this more sophisticated approach to narrative had emerged.[17]

As noted in Chapter 4, Kyōka takes fiction, or to be more specific, narrative technique, one step further. Noguchi argues that Kyōka's use of metaphor evokes an other world, an anti-real world.[18] This argument I will return to shortly, but it is worth noting that another eminent critic keenly interested in the poetics of the novel, Yoshimoto Takaaki, finds Arishima to have taken a step similar to Kyōka in the area of literary style in that he "added something new to the territory defined by Sōseki . . . and Satō Haruo."[19] Yet another critic, Niwa Kazuhiko, argues that by this step Yoshimoto means the construction of a fantasy space *(gensōkūkan)* opposed to society.[20] At this point it is necessary to consider the notion of the gothic or, more specifically, the notion of the melodramatic imagination.

The Melodramatic Imagination

Arishima's stylistic excess as manifested in his rhetorical intensity bears some similarity to certain literary forms that have taken on a new significance in light of the scholarship over the past four decades or so. Recent approaches in literary theory have reinterpreted many of the fundamental critical tropes of the nineteenth century, perhaps the most prominent being Romanticism. The concept of Romanticism has expanded enormously beyond earlier definitions. In any examination of Arishima's mode of excess, two substrata of Romanticism immediately come to mind: the gothic and the melodramatic.

The connection between the two is elucidated clearly by Peter Brooks in his penetrating study *The Melodramatic Imagination.* Brooks argues that the two forms nourish one another. To restate the case, the gothic novel represents a "quest for the numinous"; it reasserts the presence of forces that lodge within the unconscious rather than the conscious mind.[21] Thus the gothic is yet another reaction to the loss of the sacred; mythmaking in a romantic or post-romantic world could only be individual. In 1987 Brooks elaborated upon this by remarking that gothic fiction involves "a willingness, a desire, to enter into the delusional systems of texts, to espouse their hallucinated vision, in an attempt to master and be mastered by their power of conviction."[22]

Melodrama, asserts Brooks, is more optimistic, unlike the gothic novel, in that it is a drama of morality, rather than a drama of the "moral occult."[23] These insights arise from a study of nineteenth-century fiction and if directed solely to the pursuit of literary history would still be useful for an understanding of Arishima, for he, no less than his Western counterparts, was equally a product of the intellectual ferment created by the last decades of the nineteenth century. For Brooks melodrama is not merely a literary-historical phenomenon relating exclusively to developments in European theater at the end of the nineteenth century. Rather, Brooks chooses to use the adjective rather than the substantive, and the adjective "melodramatic" signifies

> the mode of [certain fictional] dramatizations, especially the extravagance of certain representations, and the intensity of moral claim impinging on their characters' consciousness. Within an apparent context of "realism" and the ordinary, they seemed in fact to be staging a heightened and hyperbolic drama. . . . They seemed to place their characters at the point of intersection of primal ethical forces and to confer on the characters' enactments a charge of meaning referred to the clash of these forces. Reading these [late-nineteenth-century] novelists with a full awareness of their ambitions more and more appeared to me to pose problems and to demand understanding of the melodramatic mode: a certain theatrical substratum used and reworked in the novelistic representations.[24]

Hence for Brooks the notion of the melodramatic is a hermeneusis, a mode of expression, or to use Brooks's words "a mode of conception and expression."[25] The "melodramatic imagination" is not merely a central fact of the modern sensibility, itself a product of the Romantic impulse, but is fundamentally opposed to Naturalistic expression. The chief instrument of the melodramatic imagination is the metaphor. Significance is transferred from the surface to deeper, more complex contexts. Commenting on the prose of Balzac and Henry James, Brooks notes that both authors weave a rich texture of metaphor in their writing, and the metaphors create an expanded moral content for the narrative.[26] These remarks are equally true of Arishima.

Indeed, in regard to Arishima the importance of Brooks's insights cannot be overstated. Any reading of Arishima's dark fictions—the epistolary nightmare of *Ishi ni hishigareta zassō* (The weed crushed by the stone, 1918), the ever darker exploration of the human psyche in *Jikkenshitsu* (The laboratory, 1917), the tortuous descent into madness described in the second half of *A Certain Woman,* all immediately bring to mind the gothic novel. And the characteristic exaggeration, the tense and ornate language, compose a style almost identical to what Brooks defines as the melodramatic mode of excess.[27] Thus it is possible to apply Brooks's comments on these stylistic techniques to Arishima's writing: "We must attend to melodramatic rhetoric. This will have the advantage of permitting us to confront what much criticism has simply dismissed from embarrassment: the overstatement and over-emphasis of melodrama, its rhetorical excess. These are not accidental to but intrinsic to the form." [28]

Using Brooks's insights, we will now examine two early works of fiction by Arishima. The focus of the investigation will be metaphoric troping, but we will also take into account the complex role of the narrator. These developments in fictional technique have been identified by Noguchi Takehiko as marking a fundamental step forward, a step beyond the bounds established by the Naturalist literary tradition. It is the same step forward taken by Henry James for English literature, a step into the modern only made possible, as Brooks confirms, by the melodramatic imagination.

Exoticism as Rhetoric: *Kankan mushi* (Rust-chippers)

Rust-chippers was published in *Shirakaba* in October 1910, but, as is well known, an earlier draft of the work, which differs in several respects (though with no major plot differences) from the published version, was completed in 1907. Arishima had written it the previous year while he was in Washington.[29] The fact that Arishima chose to shift the locale and characters from Yokohama, where the story was originally set, to Russia not only indicates an intention to "place" the narrative in an exotic context but also suggests a strong interest in politics, with ideology emerging as a major theme.

The narrator of *Rust-chippers* is a former Volga boatman and assistant cook, now working as a wharf laborer chipping rust off the ship *Odessa*, which is anchored in Kherson harbor, a port on the Black Sea. The story takes the form of a conversation between the narrator and Yakov Ilyich, his boss. Yakov is proud of his illiteracy, his working-class origins, and his work. His conversation constantly refers to the deplorable working conditions of the laborers, whom he calls "grubs" *(mushi)*, highlighting the contrast between them and their employers, the "humans" *(ningen)*. Yakov talks of his fear of the secret police, the inequality between the police and the laborers, and of his own act of defiance in striking a policeman. He points out the hypocrisy of conventional morality by telling of the attempts of two nuns to convert the laborers to Christianity.

Yakov relates how Ephrahim, a Turkish laborer, has fallen in love with his daughter Katya. However, Yakov and Katya feel that a certain Gregori Petonikov working on the site as an accountant is a better marriage prospect. Katya even attempts to seduce Petonikov in her pursuit of material wealth. Her father, while scornful of Katya's mercenary nature, urges her on in her efforts to entrap Petonikov, as life with a "human" is infinitely preferable to living with a "grub." If Ephrahim wishes to prevent Katya from becoming Petonikov's mistress and instead take her as his own wife then, declares Yakov, he must win her for himself either by money or by force. During an inspection of the ship, Petonikov is attacked and severely wounded in a general riot by the laborers. The police come to investigate but cannot discover the ringleaders. Yakov's dialogue is interspersed with a continuous stream of abuse directed against the "humans" and the unequal class society that they control.

This work has been labeled as exotic virtually from the time it appeared in print. Nakamura Kogetsu in his November 1910 review in *Waseda bungaku* appears to have been the first to use language like "exotic" and "Gorky-like" to describe it.[30] Arishima's friend Asuke Soichi even suggested that Arishima wrote *Rust-chippers* as a prank to tempt critics into arguing that the work was a translation from Gorky, and not an original work.[31] This would have appeared as quite plausible to Arishima's contemporaries, since Arishima was an avid reader of Gorky in English translation.[32] Modern critics like Nishigaki Tsutomu and Uesugi Yoshikazu have continued the tradition by praising both the exoticism and the elements of Western realism in the story.[33] Perhaps the most extreme advocate of this viewpoint is Matsumoto Chūji, who claims that Arishima's technique in *Rust-chippers* represents "in the main the genuine realism of Western literature."[34] However, many critics have expressed reservations about such opinions. One of the most prominent doubters was Senuma Shigeki, the most distinguished of Arishima's biographers. Senuma wrote in 1968, in an article entitled "Takeo no buntai nado"(On Arishima's style): "I have some doubt that Arishima's style can be classified as Western," further remarking that it could just as easily be described as belonging to the Asian tradition.[35] By this Senuma meant the tradition to which Arishima's brother, the novelist Satomi Ton (1888–1983), belonged, a stylistic tradition of richness and density, a tradition identified with Izumi Kyōka, and one which was made manifest in the early fiction of Natsume Sōseki. Finally, Senuma used the term *amasa* to characterize Arishima's rhetoric, a critical word signifying an overly florid style.[36]

While noting here the similarity in argument to the points made by Noguchi and Niwa, this notion is worth examining in a little more detail. Nishigaki and Okuda Kōji both assert that *Rust-chippers* can be claimed as much for the Romantic tradition as for the Realist.[37] But a more recent critic, Matsuura Takeshi, goes further and declares without the slightest hesitation that the work portrays a romanticized world, a world bearing no resemblance whatever to anything like reality. Indeed it is the absence of realistic description that Matsuura finds impressive.[38] Matsuura insists that Arishima's style not only strongly resembles that of Izumi Kyōka, but also that the overall thrust of the writing is symbolic, subjective, not in any sense objective.[39]

Here is a clear clash of opinions. How can two points of view that seem to be in clear contradiction of one another be reconciled?

Perhaps, rather than reconciliation, an acceptance of the strains may lead back to Brooks's paradigmatic expression of excess, the "melodramatic imagination." As Brooks remarks of the romantic mode of expression, "the emotion and signification found in the gestures of reality, extrapolated from them and postulated on them, is in excess of the representation itself."[40] Thus if we apply Brooks's insight to Arishima, it can be argued that the romantic elements in *Rust-chippers* are consciously exaggerated in an overly dramatic or overly aesthetic fashion to create a significant tension—a tension no doubt inspired by a similar sense of excess in Gorky, and a tension used to sharpen the dissonance or contrast between the narrator's descriptive tableaux and Yakov Ilyich's monologue. In the narrator's set pieces can be found such sentences as: "The various muddied hues of water were concealed in shadows, and as seen in paintings by Monet, the sea, sky, ships, and people were dyed a single fierce monochrome brilliant to the point of vertigo." Such lush rhetoric clearly clashes with, jars against, the harsh crudity of the wharf laborers' argot, and consequently Yakov Ilyich's monologue acts as a reminder of another reality altogether: "Oy, hammering away in the belly of the ship, we bash and clang, bash and clang so we're the clangers, I get that, I get that, but clang-clang grubs, why the fuck grubs . . . we might be factory seconds but a human being's a human being, right? It gets right up me nose that people gotta throw dirt at us like that."[41]

Contrasts or dissonances like these recur throughout the narrative. One moment the narrator is likening the laborer Ephrahim's eyes to Chopin's, and in the next the laborers' tactics are compared to Napoleon's marshaling his troops.[42] Arishima's style is truly hyperbolic, but hyperbole here serves a purpose.

Whether, as Matsuura argues, Yakov Ilyich's monologue, and indeed the portrait of the wharf laborers generally, is more fantastic than realistic, the fact remains that they match the narrator's metaphorical flights of fancy, for they are painted in equally lurid colors. One has the gutter language of the Yokohama slum (in keeping with the first draft), the other uses the rich palette of an educated aesthete, more Arishima than a self-educated youth.[43]

The intensity and richness of the two narratorial streams gradually converge as the story reaches its climax. At the end, using one of Arishima's favorite stylistic effects, the physical atmosphere echoes and reinforces the psychic atmosphere:

> In the roiling tide, waves formed large ridges; the afternoon sun, which had begun to set over the docks, blazed across almost horizontally. A squall swirled about in a vortex on the horizon; in the silence before the storm the surface of the sea calmed, as if reduced to a syrup by boiling. Even in Kherson, with a large admixture of fresh water from the Danube, the sea was the sea. Although there was no wind, since it was evening the scent of brine wafted in from nowhere and enveloped all in moisture. The twilight murmurings from Kherson sounding like a swarm of mosquitoes and the staccato thump of the steam tug pulling the massive barge matched exactly my unsettled, restless mood.[44]

The mood of urgent expectation, of the calm before the storm, presages revolution, or at least rebellion, in the heart of the narrator and in the anger of the laborers; it signifies not merely an emotional reflex, but also a political gesture, an act of defiance. The very air itself is charged with tension. This overarching trope or metaphor of the sea and waves, which mirror and sometimes counterpoint the moods of the narrator and Yakov Ilyich, recalls Brooks's comment on Balzac's technique in *La Comédie Humaine*: "[T]he narrative tends to move towards moments that clarify the signs it uses, moments of confrontation and explication where signification coincides, momentarily, with representation."[45] Or, and here the emphasis is on revolution, "one particular object or person or identity can constantly be seen in a claim of metaphoric mutations."[46]

Arishima's characteristic lushness, his fondness for the elaborate metaphor, is thus recognized in this fiction as a strategy to heighten the contrast between an intense, bright surface (the sun is always "blazing") and a hidden, dark, vengeful menace, the menace of revolution. The author makes full use of the "melodramatic imagination" to create a complex interweaving of symbolic and psychic excess.

The same excess can be glimpsed in a typical sample of writing from Kyōka, say in *The Holy Man of Kōya*.[47] In this respect Niwa Kazuhiko's notion of a "fantasy space" links the stylistic technique of both writers, and then Brooks's paradigm may add yet another to the chain. But the interior, psychic forces in *Rust-chippers* relate to the "daylight self" (Marxism, the quintessentially materialist philosophy) not to the numinous, and thus it is not until Arishima's later fiction that troping can be found that approaches the gothic in its journey into a self that comes out of darkness rather than light.

Gothic as Moral Occult: "Gasu" (Fog, 1918)

Arishima's most gothic creation is *The Weed Crushed by the Stone*, closely followed by *The Laboratory*, but as both these works deserve separate studies, we will not examine them here.[48] Instead, another small work of fiction, written a year or so before them, approaches the gothic both in the extravagance of its troping and in what Brooks calls the "epistemology of the depths," that is, the traps laid for the conscious by the unconscious.[49] For it is the "moral occult," the realm of inner imperatives and demons, that denotes the gothic, although, of course, much of this is shared with the melodramatic imagination. "Gasu" (Fog) was written in July 1916 and published in its final form in 1918. This short piece is, according to Yamada Akio, based upon an actual event that Arishima experienced in 1901.[50] The story is simplicity itself. The anonymous narrator is traveling by ship from Muroran to Hakodate in Hokkaidō, when during the night the ship steams into a thick northern fog called, in the local dialect, *gasu*. It is so thick that nobody can see. The ship is forced to stop; an alarm bell rings. All is in a state of confusion; the narrator ponders his mortality. When the fog clears, the passengers see that they have just avoided running aground on the rocks of Mt. E peninsula.

The rhetoric Arishima employs in this short piece matches Brooks's description of melodramatic rhetoric perfectly: "hyperbole, antithesis, and oxymoron."[51] But the personification of the sea, of the fog itself, assumes a quality of menace, a sinister quality that points to a darkness, a deeper fear that is the source of the narrator's apprehensions. The origin of this deeper fear is Death, the stock villain of the gothic novel. Eleanor Sickels gives this figure the name "King Death" in her study of eighteenth- and nineteenth-century gothic fiction.[52] And it is not unusual that death lies behind many of the most frightening apprehensions of the narrator.

Is there any reason that Arishima should turn to such a theme at this particular time? There is a diary entry for June 26, 1916, a mere three weeks or so before the first diary indication that Arishima is working on the piece, that reveals the following English meditation on death, prompted by Arishima's gloom about his wife's, Yasuko's, tuberculosis: "I came face to face to the surmountable dark wall on which no letter is written, but a pointed finger that directs the path to Death. The meaning of Death has ever so much meaning to me than anything else."[53]

In "Fog" death comes in a variety of disguises: first as cloud, a "she-devil" to be precise. "The peak of the Rebunge ridge was so hazy that it appeared to be the tip of the early summer cloud disheveled like the locks of a she-devil."[54] Then death becomes night, swallowing the sun, whipping the clouds in the most hyperbolic of rhetorical flights: "The sun sank while slashing asunder with its whips of light the cloud mass that was threatening to devour it. . . . The cloud . . . was bathed in its own vertiginous blood. . . . As a dying person hurries towards death, so the sun hurried towards night. The sun lay in eternal death, surely nothing was left alive. Such were his frightened thoughts."[55]

After the narrator plays out this elaborate drama of the death of the sun—he is, after all, only watching a sunset—the fog appears. The fog is a "taut black curtain," death garbed in traditional attire, "advancing with the terror of a nightmare."[56] The fog has a preternatural presence, and the narrator's worst imaginings seem to be coming true. He asks himself, "But has not the dense bank of fog trampled into dust the efforts of humanity for thousands of years?"[57] When the narrator senses the other passengers milling around confused in the darkness, he is filled with a "wordless grief."[58] The ship itself is no more than a "diseased leaf sunk to the bottom of the great river of fog." After this metaphor the passengers are overcome by "extremes of anxiety." In his mind the narrator feels he has been "seized by Death."[59] And, finally, the fog in its final imagined form appears as a "towering demonic barrier."

Arishima's metaphors are exaggeration itself. The ship's whistle is likened to the "howling of cattle dragged to the slaughterhouse"; the ship's bell is "funereal." Vehicle is not merely overcome by tenor, it is practically drowned by it. Psyche overpowers the material world; rhetoric—the sign—triumphs over the signified. Here the language is so symbolic that the terms melodramatic or gothic hardly suffice. But like all romances, indeed like a dream, it ends. And in

this dream-reality of language we apprehend a fantasy-space of dramatic pro-
portions. "Fog" is by no stretch of imagination naturalistic fiction, it is almost
grotesque in its use of language, a grotesquerie that could only be created by an
author who had absorbed both the dark intimations of the mature Romantics
and the psychological explorations of the Naturalist school. In other words, only
a modern writer, modern in all the senses of the word, could have written this.

Sources of Japanese Gothic

The question of the sources of the gothic in Arishima's fiction remains to be
further explored. Senuma Shigeki pointed to the Japanese tradition rather than
the Western as being the prime inspiration, singling out in particular Sōseki and
Kyōka. This is only natural since the use of the term "gothic" clearly takes on
quite different implications in a non-Western context, although as argued here
the literary affinities in terms of stylistic excess and theme allow the comparison
to be meaningful. And, as noted in Chapter 4, gothic literature was widely read
in translation by twentieth-century Japanese writers. The model of Kyōka seems
inescapable, although as suggested earlier, it may be that Arishima developed in
parallel to Kyōka, rather than simply following in his footsteps. Moreover, there
is no reason to deny the influence of both the Western and Japanese tradition
on the evolution of Arishima's style. A careful reading of Arishima's masters'
thesis (awarded by Haverford College in Pennsylvania) soon reveals his mastery
of many of the late Victorian tropes that characterized English prose at the turn
of the century, and gothic fiction was far from dead at this time. Kōda Rohan
has been mentioned by Mizutani Akio as a stylistic progenitor to Arishima.[60]
These problems remain open to more detailed investigation.

　Nakamura Miharu has described the style that Arishima adopted for his late
fiction as "expressionist."[61] The same term is used by Brooks, who argues that
expressionism "justifies the theatrical and heightened vehicles of representation:
the summary gestures, excessive statements, extreme antitheses, hyperbole and
oxymoron."[62] It may be that this notion, which Nakamura has linked to a number of essays that Arishima wrote on art towards the end of his life, can be given
a wider application. In his stimulating study of Arishima's *Kain no matsuei* (The
descendant of Cain), Nakamura draws attention to the relationship between the
narrator and the protagonist, Nin'emon. This relationship, Nakamura argues,
involves a symbiosis where the narrator and the object *(taishō)* merge, thus
an objective narrative *(kyakkan shōsetsu)* becomes possible.[63] This argument

recalls Noguchi Takehiko's like-minded analysis of Iwano Hōmei's polemic on fiction.

Komori Yōichi, in his 1988 study *Kōzō to shite no katari* (Narrative as structure), argues along semiological grounds for a much more complex picture—one that pays a great deal more attention to the problem of who is speaking to whom—regarding the evolution of modern style than that offered by earlier scholars like Yamamoto Masahide.[64] Komori's move was paralleled in the West, as can be seen in Paul de Man's work towards a reevaluation of poetic language and therefore literary history.[65] There is also the growing body of translation theory referred to in Chapter 1, which will help to reframe questions regarding the nature of intercultural or interlingual exchange. However, there is no doubt that Brooks's revolutionary reevaluation and restatement of the melodramatic imagination and the nature of the gothic adds immeasurably to an understanding of Arishima. For, as Nakamura Miharu has demonstrated, Arishima is a most conscious fabricator of fictions, not merely in regard to the message that his writings conveys but also in the linguistic structure of the message itself.[66] As Arishima wrote in 1921: "[Words] seem dead but are alive. Words have will." [67]

CHAPTER 6

FEMALE SHAMANS

Ōshiro Tatsuhiro and *Yuta*

Mark what radiant state she spreds,
In circle round her shining throne,
Shooting her beams like silver threds,
This this is she alone,
Sitting like a Goddes bright
In the center of her light,
　　—John Milton, from "Arcades"

Cruelty has a Human heart
And Jealousy a Human face,
Terror, the Human Form Divine
And Secrecy, the Human Dress.
　　—William Blake, from "A Divine Image"

Itherto this book has examined examples of the "other" or the "alien" taken from the prewar corpus of mainstream Japanese literature, or more properly, literature from mainland Japan. This chapter studies an example of postwar literature written in Okinawa, by a writer born, raised, and resident in Okinawa.[1] Okinawa here means the prefecture of Okinawa, not simply the island of this name; it is an archipelago located some four hours from Tokyo by plane. Here I propose to treat the literature of Okinawa as an "Other," as alien to mainland Japan and its culture. Until 1879 Okinawa—or the Ryūkyū kingdom as it was then known—was an independent state, which had close relations with both China and Japan; however, in that year the kingdom was incorporated into the Japanese empire by force. Even acknowledging that "the Ryūkyū kingdom had for centuries served two masters, China and Satsuma, paying tribute to both," as Donald Keene recently wrote, does not vitiate the significant differences in culture and language that separated Okinawa from Japan proper.[2] These differences have been compounded by Okinawa's period of servitude to another master, the United States of America, from 1951 to 1972, when the United States took control of the island chain and administered it as an American territory.

Okinawan attitudes toward Japan have always been complex, as is evidenced by the large number of Okinawans who died in defense of the Japanese empire during the climactic battle of Okinawa in 1945.[3] Okinawan attitudes towards the mainland also changed during the period of the American interregnum, as more and more residents of Okinawa came to adopt a version of the standard Tokyo dialect in everyday speech rather than using the myriad dialects of the Okinawa islands.[4] Nevertheless, Okinawa has retained its distinctive cultural identity to the present day, not simply because of the existence of the many dialects of Okinawa but also because of the numerous physical differences in topography and climate between Okinawa and the mainland.[5] These very real differences have not simply resulted in the sense of alienation that Okinawans writers often experience when they leave their home islands to journey to the mainland but also the strong sensation of the exotic that mainlanders experience when encountering Okinawa and its culture and language.

This collision of the exotic and the familiar, the alien and native, has characterized much of the literature written on Okinawa and by writers based in Okinawa. This chapter is concerned with one of the most distinctive features of Okinawan culture, *yuta*, or female Okinawan shamans, as explored by one of the most famous authors to emerge from Okinawa in the postwar era, Ōshiro Tatsuhiro (b.1925), who was awarded the prestigious Akutagawa Prize in 1967 for his novella *Kakuteru pātii* (Cocktail party).[6] How to communicate the "alien" to readers is a complex and intriguing problem, and as will be demonstrated, Ōshiro's treatment of this issue has something profound to say about the nature of Okinawan society and its relationship to mainland Japan itself.

Ōshiro and *Yuta*

In 1991 Ōshiro Tatsuhiro wrote an article in the *Nishi Nippon* newspaper about *yuta*, or female Okinawan shamans. He begins by discussing how even intellectuals such as himself may automatically think, when hearing of someone taken ill, of the phrase *ugan busuku*, or "not enough prayers." This attitude derives from the belief that illness and other troubles can be helped by prayer.

Such a belief is not confined to Okinawa, of course. It may well be that a majority of the peoples of the world would agree with such a sentiment. However, Ōshiro goes on to link this belief with the phenomenon of shamans. *Yuta* differ from other kinds of female mediums, such as *itako,* found in northern Japan, because they are quite ordinary people, who for the most part live quite ordinary lives. Ōshiro notes how this explains the fact that the numinous is perceived as being a matter of everyday life in Okinawa.

Ōshiro tells the story that when he worked at the prefectural museum, he would see women prostrate, intoning prayers in front of stone or porcelain funerary urns. These funerary urns are traditionally quite large and contain bones, not ashes as is usual on mainland Japan; they are often made in the form of dwellings. The prayers are improvised, not learnt, and Ōshiro discovered that after a period of extended mental or spiritual anguish such women could become divinely possessed. This signaled the beginning of the process whereby they would become *yuta.*

When he was a boy, Ōshiro thought that *yuta,* like the village priestesses found in rural areas called *noro,* would gradually disappear. But if anything, he writes, they seem to be on the increase. Over a decade earlier, in 1981, Ōshiro wrote his first story about *yuta,* called *Mumyō no matsuri* (The dark festival). Since writing that tale, he had written many more stories on *yuta* and had gradually come to feel that *yuta* performed the role of scapegoats for contemporary Okinawans. The need for this role had increased under the American occupation.[7]

The story that is the subject of this chapter, *Zushigame* (Funerary urn), was first published in the literary journal *Gunzō* in 1986. It was later reprinted in a collection of four novellas, all on the subject of *yuta* (it included *The Dark Festival*), published in 1992 under the title of *Gushō kara no koe* (Voices from the next world). The essay summarized earlier serves as the postscript to this collection. The fact that Ōshiro decided in 1981 to take up the theme of shamanism, to be precise the particular variety of female shamanism practiced in Okinawa, does not by any means represent a departure from the main thrust of his writing. On the contrary, the subject of *yuta* may well seem to be a theme that was fated to become a part of Ōshiro's fictional output, since from the very beginning of his career as a writer, Ōshiro was concerned with the depiction of the ordinary, day-to-day experience of the Okinawan people.

In the early 1950s Ōshiro took part in a heated debate with several younger Okinawan postwar writers in the pages of the *Ryūdai bungaku* literary journal. Ōshiro argued forcefully against the prevailing trend of realism that was rooted in the socialist conception of literature adopted by these younger novelists. Literature is not propaganda, stated Ōshiro, it is something "from which the human spirit and life itself overflows."[8] Ōshiro continued, saying that he saw his task as a writer to describe life, in whatever form it might take.[9] The critic Okamoto Keitoku believes that this credo can be applied to Ōshiro's work throughout his career.[10] That being the case, it was inevitable that he would take up the theme of *yuta*, for they occupy an important, if not fundamental, place in contemporary Okinawan society.

In a famous essay entitled "Okinawa de Nihonjin ni naru koto" (Becoming a Japanese in Okinawa), written in 1970, Ōshiro pondered his own life as he debated the question of the relationship between Okinawa and Japan. He pointed out that the Okinawan people are deeply religious, indeed, that religion was a part of virtually every Okinawan household. Okinawans worshipped their ancestors, unlike mainland Japanese, whose folk beliefs had become tied to Buddhism and who had been forced to become nominally Buddhist during the era of Christian persecution in the seventeenth century. Ancestor worship, whether accorded the status of religion proper or not, is for the people of Okinawa the center of their religious worldview.[11] As seen in *The Dark Festival*, *yuta*, because they intercede with the ancestors, have a pivotal role to play in negotiating between this world and the next.

This chapter will treat the phenomenon of *yuta* in the literary context created by Ōshiro's tale, but precisely how this phenomenon relates to the world outside, or how religion manifests itself in the psyche of the characters described in the story, is a question that cannot be answered in full in this analysis. This point needs to be stressed, for it is important to note the limitations of literary criticism in respect of religion. Northrop Frye's words on the relationship between religion and criticism should be kept in mind when reading and reflecting on Ōshiro's story:

> In criticism, as in history, the divine is always treated as a human artifact. God for the critic, whether he finds him in *Paradise Lost* or the Bible, is a character in a human story; and for the critic all epiphanies are explained, not in terms of the riddle of a possessing god or devil, but as mental phenomena closely associated in their origin with dreams. This once established, it is then necessary to say that nothing in criticism or art compels the critic to take the attitude of ordinary waking consciousness towards the dream or the god. Art deals not with the real

but with the conceivable; and criticism, though it will eventually have to have some theory of conceivability, can never be justified in trying to develop, much less assume, any theory of actuality.[12]

Some of these ideas will help tease out the meanings of Ōshiro's tale, but as Frye suggests, they can never exhaust its possibilities.

Funerary Urn

Funerary Urn begins with the intrusion of a *yuta* called Higa Tsuruko in the lives of a small Okinawan household. The *yuta* turns up out of nowhere one day insisting that the resting place of the family's ancestors be located. Maja Etsuko, the wife of a fireman called Kōichi, lives with her mother-in-law, Toshi, and is most disturbed by the *yuta*'s demands. Etsuko, the main protagonist of Ōshiro's tale, has been suffering from a hallucinatory daydream, in which she sees a funerary urn in her garden. Etsuko is even more disturbed when she learns that the *yuta* needs to know this in order to help heal the sickness of her husband's illegitimate baby son. Toshi denies that she knows where her son's ancestors' remains are interred, and this is confirmed by a series of mental flashbacks. Kōichi is the result of a liaison between Toshi and an Okinawan laborer during the war. The father quickly disappeared, and Toshi has always assumed that he deserted her and was caught in the fierce fighting of the Okinawan campaign. Etsuko has been told all this, but she has been totally unaware of Kōichi's affair with a bar-hostess named Ashitomi Chie.

Toshi wins her verbal battle with the *yuta* and later that day, when Kōichi returns home from work, forces Kōichi to confess his adultery and beg for Etsuko's forgiveness. Etsuko is terrified by the prospect of losing her husband to Chie, especially since Chie has been able to bear a son, while Etsuko's own son died at the age of three. She fears that Toshi, who dominates Kōichi, will see Chie's child as the only means of continuing the family name. After some discussion, they decide to have the child legally registered as Kōichi's son, and Etsuko and Toshi resolve to visit Chie to discuss the matter. Various of the *yuta*'s pronouncements seem to be coming true, for Etsuko recalls that the *yuta* demanded that they pray to their ancestors since Kōichi's child is a substitute for Etsuko's dead son.

Etsuko is even more horrified to discover that Chie, at Kōichi's urging, has given her child the same name as her dead child. Chie refuses to allow the boy to be adopted into the Maja family and says she will not permit registration of the boy as Kōichi's son. But Kōichi insists the baby boy be so registered. After hearing Chie's words, Etsuko sinks even further into despair. Visions of the funerary urn continually haunt her, and she eventually takes to her bed, plagued by terrible headaches. Chie demands that the Maja family find their ancestors' resting place, so that her child will be cured in accordance with the advice of the *yuta*.

By the time the New Year has passed, Etsuko's visions have multiplied to an alarming degree: one day she warns her husband not to go the next day on an area inspection to explode unexploded bombs. Kōichi goes and finds the *yuta* Higa praying in front of an urn where, she claims, his father's ashes are interred. Kōichi recalls his wife's warnings but insists that the *yuta* leave before the explosion occurs. Meanwhile, Etsuko undergoes a strange dream: she is confronted by the spirit of her husband's father, who explains that he did not desert the family but died honorably. He also explains that he has returned to assist Etsuko, to ease her anguish. On the basis of an earlier dream, Etsuko rushes to Chie's home to look in a mirror where she believes she can converse with spirits. From Chie's house she continues on to the location of her father-in-law's ashes, which she has discovered by herself. They lie in one of the urns placed at the prefectural museum. There are various minor threads relating to the urns at the museum, Etsuko's fears that Chie will usurp her relationship with Kōichi, and Etsuko's struggles with Toshi, but these are all joined in a kind of resolution when Kōichi and Toshi go to the museum to find her.

Etsuko is now a *yuta,* as Chie had earlier prophesied; she is praying in an ecstatic trance. Kōichi rushes to embrace her after she collapses, still engrossed in her prayers to save the boy's life and to worship her family's ancestors properly. This is the climax she has half-wished for. Kōichi prays fervently that he has saved his wife from madness, and perhaps, saved his marriage.[13]

The Birth of the Divine

Ōshiro's novella unites several threads present in present-day Okinawan society. Tensions between mothers-in-law and daughters, struggles relating to the inheritance and continuation of a family's name, the legacy of the war both in terms of Toshi's sudden liaison and its consequences, and the physical reality of unexploded bombs still menacing the people of Okinawa: all these elements, and others besides, combine to constitute the complex material reality created in the text. Twisting through the shifting pattern of contending psyches in this story two threads link and re-link the various character and plot-elements together: the discovery and shock of adultery and the equally unsettling presence of the *yuta*.

When Toshi first catches sight of Higa Tsuruko, she remarks: "*Yuta* really are frightening creatures." [14] And very soon after the appearance of the *yuta*, the other thread in the psycho-drama is revealed when the *yuta* bluntly states: "Kōichi has fathered a child." Two lines later, readers are informed of Etsuko's reaction: "Hearing this, Etsuko's breathing stopped, she steeled herself against the feeling that the blood-vessels in her brain were about to burst." [15] In a sense, the linking of the world of everyday reality and the numinous world of the spirit—the two worlds joined in the presence of the *yuta*, which occurs here—acts not merely as the touchstone for all that follows, but also signals the larger conflict that overshadows the particular struggles both within and outside the Maja family. This larger conflict is that of the material world against the spiritual world, and this conflict takes place within Etsuko's psyche.

It is no coincidence, therefore, that after the revelation of adultery Etsuko's brain is described as about to burst, for at the end of the story, her husband, Kōichi, wonders, more or less, whether her body itself can survive the birth within Etsuko of the divine. The relationship between the damage done to Etsuko's sense of self by her husband's betrayal—not merely the psychological damage but the material damage in the sense of her standing in society and in the family—and the disintegration of her mental stability and its reconstitution in the form of possession by the divine is ambiguous and changing. Nowhere is this relationship clearly defined in the novella. If the literary critic follows Frye's example, and treats the divine as a human artifact, then nothing in the story will necessarily contradict such an interpretation, but, equally, nothing in the story will necessarily support it either.

This very ambiguity is even more emphasized by Ōshiro's revealing postscript where, in the article summarized earlier, he reveals his own experience, remarkably similar to the final scene of the novella, of witnessing *yuta* praying in front of the funerary urns in the prefectural museum where the author once worked. No particular meaning can be attached to this revelation, for none is implied. It is simply given as an autobiographical fact. Yet Ōshiro's choosing to place this particular incident, written five years after the story was composed, in the postscript to the collection may also be not wholly accidental. In the same postscript, Ōshiro ends his reflections on how Okinawan intellectuals flee from the implications contained in the phrase "not enough prayers" by stating that *yoso de* (a phrase that may be interpreted as meaning outside Okinawa), he avoids ridiculing such notions; indeed, he "refrains from putting [such notions] into words."[16]

An examination of the fleeting remarks made by the other characters in the story, which relate to this larger conflict within Etsuko, reveals this ambiguity clearly. The story is divided into five chapters, and events clearly accelerate after the beginning of the New Year, a month or two from the time the *yuta* appears at the Maja household. This occurs at the beginning of chap. 4, the next to last chapter, and the last two chapters chart the course of Etsuko's divine visions and the resolution, if that is what it is, which follows. Early in chap. 4, Etsuko is lying in bed assailed by dreams, or are they hallucinations? Etsuko is not sure. The palpitations of her heart are so violent that she fears she may die. She "thought she might tell Kōichi of her visions but held her peace, feeling that he would laugh at her and accuse her of becoming like a *yuta*."[17] Shortly after she has this thought, she apologizes to Kōichi, who is beside her bed, for not being able to go to work. "He, on the other hand, made a disagreeable face. For Kōichi, who thought that his wife's illness might be his fault, could not help but feel that her remarks sounded like sarcasm."[18]

After Etsuko has a long communication with the spirit of her father-in-law, the action speeds up. Etsuko hastens to Chie's house; her motivation is complex, but underneath there is always the fear that she may be supplanted by Chie. Toshi and Kōichi are shocked to discover Etsuko's absence and also rush to Chie's house. When they arrive, Etsuko has already left for the museum. But Chie, who remains a somewhat enigmatic figure throughout, startles them by stating something they are afraid to contemplate. Toshi and Kōichi are wondering where the funerary urn containing the ashes of Kōichi's father could be:

> Neither Toshi nor Kōichi had the slightest idea where the ashes might be but guessed that Etsuko might know the secret.
>
> Both feared to put this thought into words.
>
> "Etsuko's turning into a *yuta*, isn't she?" Chie said these words without any expression.
>
> "Don't say that!" yelled Kōichi.[19]

In Kōichi's reaction, the unstated reality, just barely hinted at earlier, takes concrete form. However, it takes quite some time for Kōichi and Toshi to be able to face this fact. The relationship between possession and madness, between the psychic shock of adultery and hallucinatory dreams, is not stated in either of the scenes. Indeed, it is not made explicit anywhere in the novella. This is quite deliberate. Ōshiro is attempting to go beyond Frye's strictures: his art is hinting not only at the conceivable but also at something beyond. Such connections, however, as Frye points out, cannot be expressed in art, for art, by its very nature, is a fabrication. However, fabrication can press against the actual, and there is no doubt that in the evocation of *yuta* in this novella, that is exactly what Ōshiro is attempting to do.

The Truth of Art

In early 1997, at the International Symposium on Okinawa Studies on the Occasion of the 25th Anniversary of Okinawa's Reversion to Japan, held in Naha, Ōshiro Tatsuhiro spoke of the difficulties of conveying the reality of Okinawan dialects while writing in standard Japanese.[20] *Funerary Urn* is written in the standard form of Japanese, that is, in the Tokyo dialect, but in various places Ōshiro uses snippets of Okinawan dialect to establish the mood. This usually happens in the speech of the *yuta*. Here can be found the impossibility of conveying the quite different reality of Okinawa using standard Japanese only, which, despite its genetic affiliation with Okinawan, is nevertheless sufficiently different to be considered by some linguists a separate language. Ōshiro has often written about the problems arising from the differences between mainland Japan and Okinawa. These problems are greater than that of language and touch upon the issue of *yuta*.

In a book of autobiographical essays entitled *Kōgen wo motomete* (Seeking out the light source, 1997), Ōshiro notes that Okinawa's history began a thousand years after that of mainland Japan.[21] This time gap left Okinawan civilization with a number of difficulties. Modernization in Okinawa occurred in a society that had not experienced a medieval period; this was quite different from the case of mainland Japan. The phenomenon of *yuta*, Ōshiro argues, arises from this very difference.[22] Ōshiro notes that modern civilization has left the Okinawan people with a schizophrenic personality. This is especially the case for people who have lost their identity; they need to create a separate world in which to live, and this is how they become *yuta*.[23] In order to discover why it is that they suffer so, such individuals have an overwhelming urge to seek their identity in their past, in their ancestral heritage. This is the reason why they fantasize about their ancestors in funerary urns, observes Ōshiro.[24] As a consequence, the function of *yuta* is a direct result of the anguish caused by the loss of identity suffered by modern Okinawans in the course of their recent history. The Okinawan people have been trapped in the triangle of Okinawan, Japanese and American culture.[25]

This explanation is perhaps the most detailed rationalization yet that Ōshiro has advanced concerning *yuta* and their place in contemporary Okinawan society. The real world of Okinawa today and the fictional world created in *Funerary Urn* do not coincide exactly, though they overlap. Frye uses the notion of an "ordinary waking consciousness" as opposed to a dream-state to characterize the relationship between art and reality, and this is a most apposite metaphor when considering the place of dreams in Etsuko's transformation into a *yuta*.[26] The metaphor may also be emblematic of the relationship between Ōshiro's essays and his fiction.

In the dream or trance state, where Etsuko can communicate with her dead father-in-law, only the realities of the heart matter. Their dream dialogues are not concerned with the more mundane realities of the material world but with the emotional issues that trouble Etsuko. In her first dream dialogue with her father-in-law, Etsuko can speak frankly of the desires of her heart. In the following dialogue, Etsuko remarks, in connection with the possibility that the spirit of her father-in-law will be destroyed by detonation of the unexploded shells in the cave where his funerary urn is located: "But wouldn't it be good to be with Kōichi?"[27] In this moment Etsuko contemplates her husband dying in the cave:

"Are you Kōichi's father?"

"Yes."

"Did you die in the war?"

"I managed to get away to the end of the island, but it did me no good."

"You were about to die a second time from an exploded shell, then."

"I don't want to die twice in war."

"But wouldn't it be good to be with Kōichi?"

"You wouldn't like it. You don't want to lose him."

"That's right. Kōichi is mine."

"Grab hold of him and don't let him go. He's a good man."[28]

This direct declaration of her love is something that Etsuko cannot articulate in the usual conversational exchanges she has with her husband. Only in this trance-state, when she becomes a *yuta*, can she speak the truth of her heart.

Similarly, in the final scene, when Etsuko is deep in prayer in front of the funerary urns at the prefectural museum, she confesses to her father-in-law in the following dialogue.

"Now I can truly rely only upon my ancestors, so I've never been as happy as this."

"Kōichi loves you most of all. Toshi always worries about you. If you're bitter towards people, it will be only you who suffers."

"I don't feel any bitterness. . . ."[29]

At the end of their dialogue, still in a trance, Etsuko is told by the spirit of her father-in-law that he may never know any rest, for the prefectural museum itself could be blown up in the future. Etsuko responds with a most significant remark: "In this world, it may well be that even the power of our ancestors is not enough."[30]

At this point, more than any other in the novella, art intrudes upon, presses against, reality. The truth of the fascinating fiction that Ōshiro Tatsuhiro has created in *Funerary Urn*—that the truth of the heart is as much compounded with the pain of betrayal as with love—is what lingers in the mind, more than the mundane actuality of life itself. Indeed, if it were not for the truth of art, as many critics and artists alike have insisted, it would not be possible to know anything about life at all. For it is only in art that we can contemplate the totality of life: art gives shape to life in our imagined conceptualization of it. Or, as Frye wrote in a different context:

It is a fact of experience that the world we live in is a world largely created by the human imagination. . . .

. . . It is the resemblance between vision and hallucination, ecstasy and neurosis, the imaginative and the imaginary, that impresses itself on sense.[31]

This truth of art is what Ōshiro captures in Etsuko's experience. For despite Etsuko's forebodings, she is rewarded for her forbearance and her faithful prayers by the safe arrival of her husband by her side, just as the spirit of her father-in-law has promised, and as the *yuta* Higa has foretold. This is a truth that the reader anticipates, a vision of suffering being prompted by virtue, the virtue of love, and this suffering being rewarded with good: in this case Kōichi is saved from death by his wife's prayers. On the other hand, Kōichi's evil, the evil of his betrayal of Etsuko by his adultery, is not rewarded; as the very last sentence of story makes clear, Kōichi is praying for Etsuko's deliverance from her possession, but this is by no means certain, as Kōichi clings to the hope of his faith alone.

Yuta as Symbol

Wayne Booth, in his influential 1988 study, *The Company We Keep,* discusses the metaphoric worlds that authors create and reminds his readers that most authors have "explicitly offered their works as criticisms of false views of the world, false cosmic myths." [32] There is no doubt that Ōshiro is doing this. The truth of fulfilled expectations is a moral truth, and this truth is one of many that Ōshiro is illustrating, advocating, creating as metaphoric reality in *Funerary Urn.* In his *Seeking Out the Light Source,* Ōshiro castigates those Okinawans who see all *yuta* as frauds because, among other things, they use invocations in their prayers like "Amaterasu Ōmikami" (the Sun goddess, putative ancestor of the Japanese imperial family), which obviously do not derive from native Okinawan religious sources. Ōshiro argues that Okinawan religiosity has been stolen from Okinawa by mainland Japanese culture, which has achieved dominance over the native culture through the imposition of the Japanese education system.[33]

In *Funerary Urn* the figure of the *yuta* serves (albeit only indirectly) as symbol of a lost or not-quite-lost culture—a culture in a state of resistance, so to speak—and also as a symbol of female culture. It is worth remarking that the psychological battles Etsuko fights are primarily against women. Her first antagonist is the *yuta* Higa Tsuruko, who, from the very beginning of the story, adopts a hostile, accusing tone. Higa appears at the garden of the Maja household asking an innocuous question or two about the flowers, but she soon moves in for the kill with her pointed query: "Do you make offerings with these flowers when you worship your ancestors?" [34]

A more literal translation would direct the question at "in your household" (*otaku*), thus Higa's query is, in reality, a sharp attack on the Maja family's neglect of their ancestors' resting place.

The next antagonist with whom Etsuko is forced to contend is her mother-in-law, Toshi. This a stock conflict in Japanese fiction, and in the fiction of many other societies besides, but in the Okinawan context the conflict is directly linked to Etsuko's ability to provide an heir for the continuation of the Maja line. Given the importance of ancestor worship, the subsequent emphasis on the family lineage comes as no surprise. Once she learns of her, Etsuko constantly fears that Toshi may encourage Kōichi to supplant her with his erstwhile paramour, Ashitomi Chie, since Chie has been able to bear Kōichi a son, who, unlike Etsuko's child, still survives.

The last female enemy against whom Etsuko must battle is the paramour herself. Etsuko is obsessed with the thought that Kōichi may turn to her rival. At times, Chie seems like a *yuta* herself, for she is able to discern things about Etsuko that no one else can. These struggles, which make up the bulk of the narrative dynamic, are conflicts about the relationships between women: they focus on the role of women in modern Okinawa. The transformation of Etsuko into a *yuta* is symbolic of a particularly female crisis of identity. This crisis is predicated upon the dual roles that women play in Okinawan families as preservers of the family line through their religious observance and as reproductive agents who make continuation of the family lineage possible through their roles as mothers.

Why do women feature so prominently in Okinawan culture? In an article published in 2000, the historian Kawahashi Noriko summarizes neatly the nature and significance of the woman's role in Okinawa. I will quote the relevant passage in full as an understanding of this issue is crucial to any reading of Ōshiro's fiction that treats women in general and *yuta* in particular.

One of the most striking characteristics of Okinawan religious culture is its gendered nature and its allocation of authority to females. The complete domination by women in the rituals of the various Okinawan social institutions, such as household group, kin group, village community, and, formerly, the state, illustrates that women monopolize control of the religious sphere even when that sphere's relevance extends to the whole society. As has been observed by many researchers, nonsubordinate roles of women in the religio-cultural life of Okinawa significantly differ from those found in other cultures, where women are traditionally excluded from religious leadership.

Ordinary Okinawan women serve conspicuous religious functions as sisters and daughters on the one hand, and as wives and mothers on the other. Okinawan women, regardless of the official priesthood, are assigned a culturally recognized role as spiritual guardians. In general, while sisters are traditionally believed to fulfill the role of spiritual protector toward their brothers throughout their lives, married women are assumed to protect their household members as housewife-priestesses of the hearth deity. That is, Okinawan religious culture appears to have chosen a particular modality of sacred beings in which women in general are imbued with extraordinary strength.[35]

It is striking that Kawahashi offers this statement to argue against a 1990 book on Okinawan women by Horiba Kiyoko, in which Horiba puts the case that women are oppressed by men in Okinawa. In support of her thesis, Kawahashi cites the anthropologist Henrietta Moore, who notes: "When researchers perceive the asymmetrical relations between women and men in other cultures, they assume such asymmetries to be analogous to their own cultural experience of the unequal and hierarchical nature of gender relations in the West."[36] This remark is a timely reminder of the danger of simplistically and uncritically assuming an easy identification of the gendered Other in Ōshiro's fiction with any putative equivalent in Western literature. But such power granted to the women of Okinawa also imposes heavy burdens upon them, as is clear from the dilemma that Etsuko faces. Since Etsuko has failed to ensure the continuation of the Maja name as a mother, she is forced to assume a much more dominant role in religious observance by becoming a *yuta*.

Yuta are representative of an older Okinawan religious tradition, a tradition at odds with mainland religions, such as Buddhism, which are dominated by male clergy. In this sense it can be argued that *yuta* act as a culture of resistance against the dominant religious culture of the mainland. In *Seeking Out the Light Source*, Ōshiro points to the dominant position of women in Okinawan folkways as one of the five key differences between Okinawan and Japanese mainland society.[37] Dominance in this context denotes the traditional religious dominance of women over men.

In *Funerary Urn*, Etsuko's transformation into a *yuta* is seen more as a response to victimization and trauma than as anything else. To put it another way, Etsuko becomes a *yuta* to resolve an identity crisis peculiar to Okinawan women. This can be read in both a positive and a negative sense. It can be read positively as a reaffirmation of *yuta*, not as frauds, but as women exploring an important role that serves both a therapeutic and religious function. Or, conversely, the therapeutic function of *yuta* can be read as a criticism of male infidelity or of male dominance generally, which necessitates such a social and psychological safety-valve for women.

In any case, the metaphoric world constructed by Ōshiro in *Funerary Urn* can, in the readings proposed above, be seen to take on very real political and social implications. That Ōshiro's novella contains so many possible readings should not be in the least startling. It is the mark of significant literature that it is open to various readings that serve to interrogate not merely the truths of art but also those of the world art seeks to represent. In doing so, Ōshiro Tatsuhiro creates more than a vision of the female, or the family, but a vision of Okinawa. Ōshiro's vision is not simply another version of the Japanese nation but reveals a culture that differs significantly from what is normally thought of as Japanese. In Ōshiro's writing, Okinawa is not an exoticized tropical paradise but an alternative way of envisioning Japan; it offers a different set of possibilities for the Japanese people.

CHAPTER 7

HISTORY/FICTION/IDENTITY
Ōshiro Tatsuhiro and the Uncanny

To communicate with Mars, converse with spirits,
To report the behavior of the sea monster,
Describe the horoscope, haruspicate or scry,
Observe disease in signatures, evoke
Biography from the wrinkles of the palm
And tragedy from fingers; release omens
. . . .
Men's curiosity searches past and future
And clings to that dimension.
       —T.S. Eliot, from "The Dry Salvages"

It is like what we imagine knowledge to be:
dark, salt, clear, moving, utterly free,
drawn from the cold hard mouth
of the world, derived from the rocky breasts
forever, flowing and drawn, and since
our knowledge is historical, flowing, and flown.
       —Elizabeth Bishop, from "At the Fishhouses"

Chapter 6 explored Ōshiro Tatsuhiro's vision of *yuta,* the female shamans of Okinawa, but this chapter is concerned with *noro,* women who in some respects have played similar roles to *yuta,* but whose significance for Okinawan history was much more momentous. There is no mainland equivalent in medieval or modern Japanese history to *noro,* although some similarities may be found to a female seer named Himiko, a possibly mythical figure dating from Japan's distant past, the third century CE. Ōshiro's writing on *noro* attempts to stake out the very real differences between mainland and Okinawan culture and to dramatize the clash between them. But his literature also raises many other important questions: what is the connection between literature and history, between religion and myth expressed as literary art? Does the specific history of Okinawa influence its literature in theme or style in a way that is different from other literatures, including Japanese literature itself?[1] This chapter attempts to answer these questions and several related issues by examining Ōshiro's novel *Noro*. The exact meaning of the word *noro* will be investigated later, but we will translate it here as "mantic woman" or "seer." *Noro* was first published as a single volume in 1985 and republished in a corrected form in 2002.

Okinawa and Its Literature

The interpretation of modern Okinawan literature has often focused on political readings that seek ultimate justification for the work in its links to society, in the way in which the work creates or contributes to a dialogue on the many political issues that confront contemporary Okinawa. I take it for granted that we can speak of "Okinawan literature" in a way that we cannot, perhaps, speak of the literature of Shiga prefecture or Kanagawa prefecture, that is, we can consider it to possess a certain inherent coherence in theme or language, a kind of literary "self-consciousness." To put it more bluntly, it is a literature that presumes an identity distinct from (but not necessarily utterly separated from) Japanese literature.

Today such a statement is not necessarily controversial even on the Japanese mainland, let alone in Okinawa. The fact that the Ryūkyū islands once existed as an independent kingdom until their forcible incorporation in 1609 into the Satsuma domain is not questioned by any historian. The invasion had been sanctioned by the ruler of Japan, Tokugawa Ieyasu, and thus the Satsuma conquest of the Ryūkyūs foreshadows the absorption into Japan proper as the prefecture of Okinawa in March 1879. Modern Okinawan literature has had to deal with the consequences of the deliberate destruction of the once independent kingdom of the Ryūkyūs. Donald Keene has summarized the complex history of Okinawa thus: "The status of [Okinawa] had long been ambiguous. In 1186 the shogunate had given the founder of the house of Satsuma the title of *'jitō'* (manor lord) of Okinawa. . . . [W]arfare among the three kingdoms of Okinawa . . . led one of the kings to send a mission to the Ming Court in 1372, asking Chinese help in unifying the country; he also asked to become a feudatory. The Chinese agreed and gave the country the new name of Ryūkyū. This change in relations with China did not end the long-standing tributary relationship with Japan."[2] And as Keene concludes: "The Ryūkyū kingdom had for centuries served two masters, China and Satsuma, paying tribute to both. This was the only way a small country with few resources and no military strength could maintain its existence."[3]

Keene's interpretation of Okinawan history reflects the traditional view in mainland Japan, but in recent years historians such as Kuroshima Satoru have argued that the Ryūkyū kingdom had more freedom and autonomy than was previously assumed. Thomas Nelson, using Kuroshima as his source, argues that as late as 1570, "[f]ar from being in awe of their northern neighbors, the Okinawans had enough strength and self-confidence in their dealings with powerful figures in Japan to place islands within sight of the mainland of Kyushu under their own tutelage, albeit briefly."[4] This view of a strongly independent Ryūkyū kingdom tends to be the one held by Okinawan historians, again emphasizing the difference in perspective between the mainland proper and Okinawa.

The fact of the "foreignness," or to use the terms emphasized in this book, the alien, exotic nature of Okinawan folkways, customs, and languages is well known, as can be seen in the Tokugawa government still regarding Okinawa as a foreign country insofar as diplomatic usage was concerned. And this "foreignness" has been the source of many instances of discrimination that Okinawans have experienced over the course of the last two centuries.[5] Not only are the distinctive culture and the various languages of Okinawa a source of the separate identity of the Okinawan people, but this same distinctness has in recent years stimulated many Japanese to rethink the notion of Japan itself, as I have argued at the end of Chapter 6. Such revaluations include the novelist Shimao Toshio (1917–1986), who argues for a new vision of Japan as a Pacific rather than an Asian culture, which has led him to coin the word "Yaponesia." They also include the recent study by the sociologist Oguma Eiji, *"Nihonjin" no kyōkai* (The boundaries of the Japanese), which argues that Japan's history as a colonial power created an identity for the Japanese that is fundamentally multicultural.[6]

The debate over Yaponesia was most likely sparked by the famous anthropologist Yanagita Kunio's (1875–1962) seminal 1961 study *Kaijō no michi* (The ocean road), which argued for an alternative view that Japanese ethnicity arose in Okinawa.[7] Following this trend, a mere nine years later, the Nobel Prize-winning author Ōe Kenzaburō published his *Okinawa nōto* (Notes on Okinawa), in which he wrote that his journey to Okinawa was an attempt to "transform myself into an un-Japanese Japanese."[8] It is worth noting, however, that this quotation comes from a chapter titled "Nihon ga Okinawa ni zokusuru" (Japan belongs to Okinawa).[9] In Ōe's understanding, Okinawa and its culture became an "Other" inside Japan, a mirror in which Japanese can re-envision and reinterpret their own cultural and literary tradition.

The American interregnum from 1951 to 1972—when Okinawa was administered by the United States—gave the citizens of Okinawa the dubious privilege of a second colonization of their culture. Thus modern Okinawan literature can be categorized along the lines summarized by Okamoto Keitoku in his 1996 book *Gendai bungaku ni miru Okinawa no jigazō* (Okinawa in contemporary novels and dramas). In this work Okinawan indigenous cultural influences, the shadow cast by America in the postwar era, and the post-reversion rediscovery of an even more nuanced sense of Okinawan identity all combine to make its literature a complex fusion of traditional and contemporary themes.[10]

To restate the proposition, Okinawan literature has an identity separate from the literature of mainland Japan because of the historical, cultural and linguistic differences of the inhabitants of Okinawa. Does this mean, therefore, that the literature of Okinawa can be evaluated primarily through the lens of the sense of identity that it possesses?

Seers and Shamans

Ōshiro Tatsuhiro came to prominence on the Japanese mainland in 1967 when he was awarded the Akutagawa Prize for his novella *Cocktail Party*, but he had been well known in Okinawa for a much longer period.[11] During the 1950s Ōshiro was one of the major figures in the development and formation of postwar Okinawan literature, quite apart from the several posts he held in the government, which were often positions relating to the preservation of Okinawan culture. Okamoto Keitoku argues that Ōshiro's early fiction frequently took up autobiographical themes—a dominant strand of prewar and immediate postwar Okinawan fiction—but after the publication of *Cocktail Party*, which dealt with Okinawan identity, the U.S. occupation, and the war—as Michael Molasky notes, the central theme in postwar Okinawan writing until the 1970s—his range as a writer expanded considerably.[12]

Ōshiro maintained a keen interest in traditional Okinawan culture, especially the role women play in modern Okinawa in maintaining and passing on traditional cultural practices, and this emerged as an important topic in his writing from the 1960s onwards. His 1968 story "Kamishima" (Divine island), for instance, features a female *noro,* or shaman, called Futenma Yae as the main character, and the story deals in part with her religious responsibilities during World War II.[13] Similarly, Ōshiro's 1979 novel *Hanabanashiki utage no ato ni* (After the splendid banquet) has another *noro,* named Akamine Matsu, as its chief protagonist.[14]

The issue of *noro* raises again the more general question of how to approach seers, shamans and shamanism. Literary critic Harold Bloom, writing in 1996 in his book *Omens of Millennium,* questions the thesis that shamanism arises "from social conditions of change and uncertainty." Bloom argues: "[R]ather, the evidence is that shamanism was and is universal and primal: always it has been the resource of groups and of individuals who refuse to resign all power to God or to the gods."[15] Bloom goes on to say: "Innate divinity is the center of shamanism as it is of the various offspring of shamanism . . . shamanistic trance is utterly fused with possession by spirits, and I can hardly know what it would mean to call such possession an illness."[16]

Bloom's words provide a useful background against which to situate Ōshiro Tatsuhiro's view of *noro.* The subject of seers, shamans, and mantic women who are able to predict the future and influence events yet to come also brings to mind Freud's discussion of the uncanny. In his essay on the subject, Freud remarks: "It is true that the writer creates a kind of uncertainty in us in the beginning by not letting us know, no doubt purposely, whether he is taking us into the real world or into a purely fantastic one of his own creation. He has, of course, a right to do either; and if he chooses to stage his action in a world peopled with spirits, demons and ghosts . . . we must bow to his decision and treat his setting as though it were real for as long as we put ourselves into his hands."[17] Freud's argument resembles the literary maxim of the suspension of disbelief as a precondition for reading fiction and speaks directly to Ōshiro's unsettling mixture of history and fiction in this novel that all but demands assent to the notion of the uncanny or to the uncertainty created by it, for it is an integral part of Ōshiro's conceptualization of *noro.*

There is another dimension to the novel that also demands attention. The work is an historical novel dealing with real events in Okinawan history. So, before examining the novel's fictional treatment, I will give a brief account of the events described, relying largely on the historian George Kerr's classic study *Okinawa: The History of an Island People,* first published in 1958.

The Kingdom of the Ryūkyūs

The novel *Noro* is set in the middle of the fifteenth century and opens during the reign of the sixth king of the first Shō dynasty to rule the kingdom of the Ryūkyūs. This was Shō Taikyū, who reigned from 1454 to 1460. Taikyū was the fifth son of King Shō Hashi, who reigned from 1422 to 1439 and was, according to Kerr, "one of the great men of Okinawan history." [18] Kerr notes that at his death Shō Hashi "left Okinawa under a unified administration and in a position of importance and prosperity among the islands along the western Pacific rim." [19]

However, King Shō Taikyū was altogether different from his father. As Kerr observes, "Shō Taikyū appears to have come increasingly under the influence of Japanese missionary priests and been led into a course of lavish patronage for Buddhist temples and Shinto shrines. At least four new temple foundations were created and endowed. . . . [T]hese temples were not built in response to popular demand nor based on popular support; the king's resources were squandered in building on a scale unwarranted by the position of Buddhism in Okinawa." [20]

The main character in Ōshiro's novel is Shō Taikyū's son, the next king of Okinawa, Shō Toku, who reigned from 1461 to 1469. Unfortunately, Toku inherited a difficult situation from his father, as Kerr explicates:

> The pious king [Shō Taikyū] died in 1460, leaving to his heirs and court officers the problems of an impoverished treasury. Temple building, metal casting, religious ceremonial, and luxurious entertainment at the palace had consumed the surpluses accumulated by Sho Hashi and his successors. The late king's extravagance now had severe political consequences.
>
> His son Toku was a headstrong youth of twenty-one years when he became king. This was at a time when nearby seas were full of swash-buckling Japanese pirates and privateers, who preyed on shipping along the China coast. . . . Sho Toku decided on an overseas military adventure. In 1465 Okinawan forces embarked for an invasion of Kikai Island, which lay to the north, on the trading route to Japan. The young king himself took command, adopting the banner of Hachiman, Japanese God of War. . . .
>
> The invasion of Kikai Island was not difficult, for it lay nearby, virtually unpopulated and undeveloped. The young king nevertheless treated the expedition as a great success; an officer was appointed to hold the island in the king's interest; the Asato Hachiman Shrine was erected at Naha in token of gratitude;

and Hachiman's crest (the three-comma *Mitsu-domoe*) was adopted as the crest of the royal house.

This much, and no more, the conventional histories tell us. Future studies may bring evidence that Sho Toku had indeed attempted to link the fortunes of his principality with those of the powerful *wako,* the freebooters and buccaneers who were terrorizing the seaboard provinces of China. Whatever his motivation, it became evident at once that he did not enjoy support among his chief officers at Shuri.

Kikai Island had no economic value. No new resources and no important harbors were acquired by Sho Toku's expedition. The whole adventure proved a drain on the Chuzan treasury without adequate return. Kanemaro, the royal treasurer, and a number of other important figures withdrew from the court and retired to their estates in the countryside. Tradition says that the headstrong young king about this time became enamored of the chief priestess of Kudaka Island, to which he had gone on pilgrimage, and that while he dallied with her, far from the court at Shuri, a conspiracy ripened into open rebellion. This led to the king's death in his twenty-ninth year.[21]

Kerr also tells us about another important character in Ōshiro's novel, the treasurer (in Kerr's words) who served King Shō Toku. In Kerr's account he is called "Kanemaro," but in Ōshiro's novel and in Japanese reference sources he is known as "Kanamaru," so from here on, this name will used. Here is Kerr's account of Kanamaru's early life and career:

[Kanamaru] went down to Shuri and found employment in the household of Sho Taikyu, who was then the Prince of Goeku.

As the years passed his talents attracted attention: from one position of trust to another he rose steadily in favor. Here in Shuri and Naha he could give play to his skills as a manager. When Taikyu became king, Kanamaru was taken into the royal household organization. Ultimately he became the king's treasurer.

This meant that the excessive expenditures made by Taikyu on behalf of temples, shrines, and ceremonies passed through Kanamaru's hands. None knew better than he the state of the Okinawan economy, the total revenues of foreign trade, and the probable effects of unlimited and injudicious spending. When his patron Taikyu died, Kanamaru was expected to carry on management of the royal finance. We can only guess that he disapproved of Sho Toku's military adventure to Kikai, and that the headstrong young king paid little attention to his treasurer's conservative advice.

Kanamaru by this time had an estate of his own in the countryside, and to this he withdrew after resigning his offices at court. Influential officers nevertheless continued to seek him out for advice and guidance, and it may well be that here in the seclusion of his farmhouse the plot was hatched which led to Sho Toku's downfall.[22]

Kerr's account provides the bare bones of historical fact which Ōshiro's novel fleshes out.

Should Ōshiro's novel be read basically as a historical fiction that seeks to enlarge and embellish a period of history, which, as Kerr observes, "gave rise to the tales of romance and loyalty which form the classic body of Okinawan song and tradition"?[23] An alternative reading of the work might see it as an exploration of myth and Okinawan religiosity that is not fundamentally concerned with history at all. The work could be read as an allegorical tale that seeks to reclaim a sense of Okinawan identity torn from the Okinawan people by history itself. As we analyze the novel, we will consider these questions, but first we need to consider how Ōshiro himself conceived of his role as a writer and what view he held concerning the history of Okinawa.

History and Literature

One of Ōshiro's most significant statements concerning Okinawan history appeared in the *Asahi Jānaru* magazine in 1972, the year Okinawa was returned to Japanese sovereignty from American overlordship:

An antimony was born from the colonial government established by Satsuma. [In the seventeenth century] Satsuma, while ruling and exploiting the Ryūkyūs as a colony, ordered Okinawans to think of themselves as part of Satsuma. This can be said to be the model of the policy centuries later of forcing Okinawans to think of themselves as Imperial subjects when Okinawa became a colony in the Japanese empire. . . . I am convinced now that, as far as Japan is concerned, Okinawa is a military colony.[24]

Later in the same essay Ōshiro spelled out the implications of Okinawa's past for literature:

In the prewar period, the modern literature of Okinawa mostly dealt with the theme of liberating ourselves from Yamato [Japan]. After the war, the pattern was exactly the same except that the USA replaced Yamato. . . . [Since the 1980s] in our Okinawan literature we have tried to appeal to the world. This is our response to the global information age, to the age of multiculturalism. Can the indigenous culture of Okinawa be made universal? [25]

A quarter of a century later, in his 1997 autobiographical *Seeking Out the Light Source*, Ōshiro took up the change in direction in his writing that occurred in the 1980s:

At this time a new development occurred in the themes of my fiction. It was my attempt to describe the depths of Okinawan history and the Okinawan people. There is a theory that Okinawan culture, originally, was a female culture. This may well have influenced me at the subconscious level since I was born and raised in the women's quarters . . . the most important element of [Okinawan] female culture is that preserved by *yuta*. I began to write a series of novellas on this theme. . . .[26]

A few pages on, Ōshiro elaborates upon his experience of *noro* and the traditional culture that they represent.

Coincidence or not, what survived in good health right up until the postwar era was festivals: at least one on the main island of Okinawa, and on Miyako Island and on Yaeyama. These festivals were the Izaihō festival of Kudaka Island, the Uyagan ritual on Miyako Island in the Karimata region, and, on Yaeyama, the Akamata and Kuromata ceremonies of Miyara, Kohama, Aragusuku, and Komi. These esoteric rituals transcend by far the wisdom of modern civilization.

I was privileged to witness these three festivals. What all these festivals share is a world—time and space—known only to the participants (that is, the *noro*). They are completely immersed [in this world]. As far as I can see, the female participants—all the participants are female—are completely oblivious to this world. As soon as all the festival activities have finished, they attain a state in which they can return to this world. The Karimata festival is truly a horrifying event. The *noro* (in Sakijima they are called *tsukasa*), their hair all dishevelled, are stupefied for a time, then they slowly return to this world. . . . There is no doubt that that world is where the world of the past is alive. The first destruction of this world occurred with the Izaihō festival of Kudaka Island. As the festival only occurred every twelve years it was relatively easy to get rid of; at any rate, life grew difficult on the island also perhaps because [the island girls] married men from outside, [and] they were no longer bound to the island festival. . . .

. . . In these cases, modern civilization wrecked the traditional, communal nature of the village. Originally, festivals were built upon the unity of traditional communal bonds, and they were linked to the hopes in life of their members. But this no longer became necessary.[27]

Ōshiro's view of *noro* and the traditional culture of Okinawa is stated clearly. He sees as a writer of historical fiction that he should attempt to recreate an important aspect of Okinawan history and religious practice that is now lost. The sense of mission outlined in *Seeking Out the Light Source* reveals that through his writing Ōshiro is attempting not merely to critique the history of colonialism experienced by Okinawa but, by reconstructing the history of the Ryūkyū kingdom, to reinvent an Okinawa free of its historical burden as a colonized state for contemporary readers, both in Okinawa and on the mainland.

Noro as Ideal History

To define the word *noro*, I will quote from Carmen Blacker's *The Catalpa Bow*, first published in 1975, a classic study of shamanism and related phenomena in Japan. It is important to note that Blacker's book was based almost entirely on the author's many years of fieldwork in Japan.

We have the *nuru* or *noro*, a majestic sacral woman, a priestess who exercises spiritual power over a village or group of villages. Until some sixty years ago [that is, until 1915] her life was one strictly regulated by the demands of ritual purity. She was forbidden to marry; she avoided funerals and houses where a death had occurred. Even today she does not sleep with her husband during ceremonial periods, nor does she perform rituals during her period of menstruation. She possesses a personal *kami,* who is in fact the apotheosis of her own ancestry, and who provides her with a direct link with the spirit world. Her residence is a shrine where these ancestors have their tablets, and where her special panoply of clothes, which includes a necklace of *magatama* beads and sometimes a bronze drum, are kept. In former times she used to travel to the villages under her jurisdiction on a white horse, accompanied by a male acolyte.[28]

It is interesting to note that Blacker compares *noro* to the Korean *son-mudang* and argues that parallels exist with sacral women in various other parts of Japan. Writing over a quarter of a century ago, Blacker also notes that "in former times [*noro*] used to travel to the villages under her jurisdiction on a white horse," which would seem to indicate that she sees *noro* as a phenomenon belonging to the past rather than the present. But that view is contradicted by a recent book, entitled *Minami no seishinshi* (A spiritual record of the South), by the novelist Okaya Kōji (b. 1929), who has often written about Okinawa.

This work is an account of the various spiritual practices of Okinawa, and *noro* feature prominently in a chapter entitled "Unjami matsuri no kisetsu" (The season of festivals celebrating the gods of the sea). This chapter concerns Iheya Island, where the author traveled to seek out Okinawan religious ceremonies. He arrives at the oldest village on the island, called Dana, and goes to a house called the "Danaya," which is famous as a female *noro* residence. He interviews a male festival official who complains that no one wants to celebrate the ancient ceremonies any more. As Okaya observes: "The *noro* who once were supplied with farms by the Ryūkyū kings and benefited economically now had lost these privileges; they had even lost the support of the village. The fact that there was a shortage of women willing to become *noro* was only natural." [29] Nevertheless, *noro* do survive: the author is careful to note that one of the *noro* was a pretty young woman.

Okaya describes a ceremony conducted that morning at the Danaya where to welcome the gods from Nirai Kanai (the land across the sea) the female *noro* pretend to shoot wild boar with bows and arrows and also performed a ceremony to enhance the fishing catch.[30] Finally the *noro* travel to the eastern shore of the island where they mount horses prepared for them to travel in a procession, exactly as Blacker describes. Okaya's description of the prayers and other ceremonies performed by these women match almost exactly the ceremonies described in the novel that Ōshiro sets 500 years in the past.[31] Perhaps Ōshiro's portrayal of *noro* is not as historical as it seems, especially for Okinawan readers.

From *Seeking Out the Light Source,* however, we have what Ōshiro himself has written about *noro* and how he relates his understanding of these women to his fiction:

> The world of the *noro* has, in one regard, connections to the world of the *yuta* but also contains significant departures from their world. From my point of view, both worlds in ancient times contained the same shamans (people possessed

by the divine). Plotting to use his spiritual powers to unify the country [of the Ryūkyūs], King Shō Shin appointed a shaman to the post of overseeing religious ceremonies in the villages. This was the *noro*. . . . Accompanying the establishment of this state religion, those who were appointed to these duties used their spiritual powers to save individuals from their spiritual malaise, and these were the *yuta*. This was the point when the shamans in ancient times were differentiated [into two types]. . . . Within me was born the desire to investigate literature that seeks out *yuta*—the root of Okinawan ethnicity—and *noro*, and also their roots in history. . . . I wanted to trace the course of modern culture deep back into the past. When and how was female culture taken over by male culture? [32]

The chief product of Ōshiro's investigations into *noro* was the novel *Noro*, first published in 1984 in the March and April issues of the *Subaru* magazine. In September 1985 it was republished as a single volume and is now available in volume 4 of Ōshiro's collected works. This same volume also includes two other long novels about Okinawan history that feature *noro* prominently. The first, *Ten'nyo shisu tomo* (The heavenly maiden dies), first published in 1987, deals with the *noro* Yosoidon and her political role as the "queen mother." Yosoidon was Kanamaru's second wife, so the events in this novel follow chronologically the events described in *Noro*. The last of the *noro* trilogy is *Hana no hi* (The flower maid), first published in 1985. This novel is set in the eighteenth century and deals with Okinawa after the Satsuma invasion. Like these two works, *Noro* is one of Ōshiro's longer novels, with the single-volume edition totaling some 227 pages. Ōshiro summarized the work and its origins in *Seeking Out the Light Source:*

> [After the *Subaru* editor suggested that Ōshiro write a long novel]
> I started on it immediately. I narrated the circumstances behind the love affair between King Shō Toku and the *noro* Kunikasa, which led to the king's downfall. The story is of the revolution led by [the general] Kanamaru and [the male shaman] Asato Ufuya, the principal rebels. I wrote of how female culture represented by Kunikasa's supernatural powers was replaced by male culture represented by the crime jointly committed by Kanamaru and Asato.[33]

Ōshiro also revealed in an earlier book, entitled *Hāfutaimu Okinawa* (Halftime Okinawa, 1994), another reason why the theme of *noro* struck such a strong resonance in him:

For the Okinawan people, modernization has come to be nothing other than Japanization. Our enemy is Japan. . . . At the beginning of the modern era, the Japanese government preserved *noro* as part of its systemization, by viewing them as the illegitimate children of Japanese Shinto, and broke our spirits by forcing on us a unified system. While we Okinawans suffered from an inferiority complex, we lived a false identity by the linking of our collective sense of the numinous with the Japanese collectivity. . . . [After 1972] In every respect, the tide has turned, with our differences from the mainland becoming prominent. This is a movement to revive our free gods from the Japanese system.[34]

Through *Noro*, a historical novel set in the fifteenth-century independent kingdom of the Ryūkyūs, Ōshiro has sought to carry out what British critic Stuart Hall, writing of minority peoples who have been subject to the rule of a majority culture, describes as a search for a "collective 'one true self' . . . . which people with a shared history and ancestry hold in common."[35] This is a search common among peoples who have seen their sense of identity subsumed, forcibly or otherwise, into a larger cultural formation. Such a search reaches back to a past with symbolic effects, as Hall put it, on the present.[36]

Ōshiro's attempt to revive the "true self" of the Okinawan people is not without its dangers. Commenting on Frantz Fanon's quest to "endlessly [create] himself," Homi Bhabha writes, "Fanon recognizes the crucial importance, for subordinated peoples, of asserting their indigenous cultural traditions and retrieving their repressed histories. But he is far too aware of the dangers of the fixity and fetishism of identities within the calcification of colonial cultures to recommend that 'roots' be struck in the celebratory romance of the past or by homogenizing the history of the present."[37] Within Okinawa the range of responses to Okinawa's history of colonial predation is far too complex to summarize here and, properly speaking, outside the scope of this study. It is safe to say, however, that many of the debates swirling about the relationship between colonial (or postcolonial) history and literature conducted over the past three decades in the English-speaking world have already been rehearsed and rehashed among Okinawan intellectuals many times since the late nineteenth century. Ōshiro played a prominent role in the immediate post-World War II environment in Okinawa debating just these issues. His resuscitation of tradition in his historical fiction is neither accidental nor injudicious. His choice of sacral women such as *noro* and *yuta* as the focus of this attempt to recreate Okinawan tradition in literature is equally deliberate. The spiritual dimension of identity has been a central concern for Ōshiro and has continued into his more recent stories on *yuta*. Bloom's comment on shamanism, cited earlier, squarely faces this issue and should be taken into account in any reading of *Noro*.

Toku and Kunikasa

The brief prologue to *Noro* presents a paradisal scene: a female narrator named Kunikasa is making love to a king. The description is filled with imagery suggesting a congress of the gods: the symbol of a white horse stands for Kunikasa, the narrator, and the sun for Tedaosoi, the king. Then chap. 1 sets the scene. We are in the Ryūkyū kingdom in the fifteenth century. The protagonists are introduced: Kanamaru the noble serves Prince Taikyū, the heir of King Shō Hashi, as advisor for thirteen years, and then begins plotting to ensure that Taikyū rather than one of his brothers succeeds to the throne after his father's death. He also acts as advisor to Taikyū's son Shō Toku. By the age of forty-five, Kanamaru has been appointed as a minister of state in Naha by Taikyū, who has assumed the kingship, but after Taikyū's death three years later, Shō Toku inherits the throne at the age of 21. Kanamaru serves Shō Toku for nine years but he is unable to influence the youthful, willful king or to moderate his thoughtless campaign of bloody conquest to subjugate the neighboring islands.

An old male shaman named Asato Ufuya tries to persuade Kanamaru that destiny awaits him, that Kanamaru should lead a rebellion against the cruel king. However, Kanamaru has to wait until the right moment, specifically, when King Toku determines to build an invasion fleet and subjugate Kikai Island. Kanamaru strongly opposes this course of action and retires from the king's service to Uchima Island. The king's invasion fleet is badly damaged during a storm, and Toku and some 800 soldiers are driven to take refuge on Kudaka Island. There Toku meets Kunikasa, the chief *noro* of the island. The two feel a strong mutual attraction, but Kunikasa is dismayed by Toku's advocacy of Buddhism rather than the native Okinawan deities.

Chap. 2 details the relationship between Kunikasa and the king as it develops during his stay on Kudaka Island. Kanamaru and Asato journey to Kudaka, but Kanamaru is reluctant to foment rebellion while the king remains on Kudaka, fearing the power of the local *noro*.

Chap. 3 chronicles the further development of Kanamaru's and Asato's plot to commit regicide. Toku resolves to mount another expedition against Kikai

Island, this time with fifty ships and 2,000 soldiers. However, the island is warned of the impending invasion by Kunikasa's father, and when the battle is joined, there are heavy casualties on both sides. Kunikasa joins Toku on a warship in order to get to Kikai, where she hopes to find her brother Matsugane, who has been shipwrecked on the island. However, in a surrealistic, almost cinematic sequence, Matsugane—who has lost his sight during the shipwreck—is enveloped in flame and dies during a vicious assault by Toku on the Kikai troops.

Chap. 4 sees the final subjugation of Kikai Island. But Toku's victory is not without complications. So many die on either side that after returning to Shuri, the capital, even the king himself wonders whether he has truly won, or has he actually lost? The king gains a wife, a *noro* called Suetsuru, the elder sister of a farmer that Toku has killed in a fit of rage, and this act is the catalyst for the cycle of violence that follows. Toku goes back to Kudaka to tend to a weakened, distraught Kunikasa, who has miscarried the king's child and is convinced that she has lost her power.

Finally, Toku returns to Shuri and is reciting the Hannya Shingyō (The essence of Prajñāpāramitā) sutra—all is the void—when Kanamaru seizes his moment and commences the insurrection. Soldiers attack the palace and kill the princes and princesses, but they allow Toku to flee. Fearing the consequences of regicide, Kanamaru permits Toku to escape to a boat, to return to Kudaka, perhaps to be with Kunikasa? The last paragraphs of the chapter record the king's last moments on the boat:

> Kunikasa, who gave me such joy, will she bring me to destruction? Does the hell that I long for lie beyond the slope of the sea? Does this mean that Nirai Kanai is the land of death?
>
> When this awareness melted away, the stars vanished in the heavens, the darkness surrounding the split between the heavens and the sea melted away. In the faint light before dawn, which had melted away, a buzzard soared above. It came closer. It cut through the vast sky. It was directly on top of his head. He wished it could alight on the mast. He wanted to rest his oar for a while and stare at it. I wonder why it doesn't appear to be landing on the mast. Doesn't it see the mast that pierces to the heavens? Didn't you once lead me to Kudaka, your brave eyes glittering? Look, this mast! Shō Toku stood up and stretched out his hand, trying to touch the mast. His hand fell through the air, his upper body swaying, finally the boat was unable to support his legs. The buzzard, he imagines,

is perching not on the mast but on his shoulder, and thus does Shō Toku melt away, body and soul, into the sea.[38]

The final chapter, an epilogue, records the accession of Kanamaru to the kingship—he assumes the name Shō En. He wishes the *noro* to recite the *teruru*, or chanted prayers, as before, an implied rebuke to the previous king's policy of replacing the Okinawan gods with deities imported from Japan or elsewhere. However, Kunikasa cannot reconcile herself to her lost love, the new regime, or her own violation of the sacred grove. The final sentences of the novel chronicle her end:

> How long has it been since the white horse disappeared? Since the time when Tedaosoi [the sun-king, that is, Toku] drowned in the slope of the sea? But today I will surely see him. On the tip of the sandbar on the slope of the sea, I will surely meet him. I will surely meet him. . . . Kunikasa's body grew hot, she began to shudder, she had already immersed herself up to her waist in the tide.[39]

This summary does not do justice to the complexity of the narrative, which is at once poetic and mystical, filled with mysterious symbols, like the white horse and the seabirds, and also suffused with religious imagery. Much of the story is taken up with discussions about Nirai Kanai, the nature of the gods, and the connection between the numinous and *noro*. One can make the argument that, in this novel at least, history takes second place to the mysterious interweaving of myth and belief.

Myth as Symbolic Representation

The intermingling of myth and history to the point that they fuse into one highly poetic narrative can be seen most transparently in two sequences. The first occurs in the prologue, where the narrative foreshadows a scene in chap. 2 when King Toku and the *noro* Kunikasa make love in a sacred grove overlooking the beach. This act of lovemaking is a violation of the grove; it results in Kunikasa's becoming pregnant and then in a tragic miscarriage when Kunikasa is tested by her fellow *noro* to see if the gods favor her. The tragedy is compounded by the fact that Kunikasa is distracted at a critical moment during the test by her enemy Asato Ufuya, who cries out that he is responsible for her brother's death. All these complications lie in the future for the unwitting reader, who is from the very first page thrust into the mysticism of ancient Okinawan religion and the ecstasy of carnal love. The narrator of this passage is the *noro* Kunikasa, but the reader is not informed of the significance of who Kunikasa is or what this means for the story until the end of chap. 1:

He is whinnying. Can you hear me? He sent his whinny far away. He is chasing after his whinny.

"Ah faster!"

The wind swirls. The grasses wave. Like a storm, he embraces me. Raising high his hind legs, piercing the earth with his hooves, bending backwards, his front legs embracing my breast, the sun invades me. My moon greets him in attack. Locked in mutual assault, the night turns to day, both night and day cease, and the sun and moon alike climb coruscating to the Heavens. . . .

"Kunikasa!" he cried, and I responded,

"Sun warrior!"

. . . .

The sea roared in my body. The tide flowed from him into me, I was filled with it, shuddering, my shuddering voice called the whole world into my body, my body gave way beneath the burden. The tide encircled my body, passed outside my body, it flowed out into the open sea, along the road of light, reached the split between the heaven and earth and kept flowing, and climbed into the unending universe caught between light and darkness, seeming to appeal to the gods but at that moment it returned to my body. My body is seething. The tide flowed evermore into infinity, the world grew infinitely massive, the light from the sun and the moon contended.

"The world . . ."

"Will end . . ."

The wind suddenly ceases. Have I died?

. . . .

Where am I? Lying down in a space like darkness, like night, I passed the time dazed. The sun warrior returned his shining body back to the ocean road and headed out to the open sea. The sun warrior is both the sun, and he who attacks (rules)—the king. Where will the soul of the king of our land go now?

"There lies the road to death!"

I cried out, but no voice emerged; the sun killed my voice, the world had turned to day. Stifling my voice, the sun grew languid and simply floated on the universe.[40]

In this opening passage the course of the ensuing narrative is foreshadowed, and the major themes of *Noro* are given expression, but this revelation of character, the tale of King Toku, the sun warrior, and his tragic love affair with Kunikasa, the powerful *noro* from Kudaka Island, are put into poetic, symbolic prose. The initial erotic encounter is transfigured into the mystical symbol of the white horse that reappears throughout the narrative, seemingly dancing on the white breakers far out on the distant horizon. Blacker has already documented the traditional link between *noro,* their male acolytes, and white horses. The symbolism of the sun and moon is pregnant with meaning, as can be seen in the opening verse of the *Omoro sōshi.* The first verse of this great Okinawan song-cycle—the Ryūkyū equivalent to the great Japanese mythohistorical text of origin, *Kojiki,* and Japan's foundation poetry collection, *Man'yōshū*—reads:

Kikoe ōgimi giya	Kikoe Ōgimi
Orete asubiyowareba	Come down and celebrate the rites
Teni ga shita	The world under heaven
Tairagete chiyoware	Rule in peace [41]

As Hokama Shuzen explains in the notes to the modern Japanese version, the *noro* Kikoe Ōgimi becomes a sun god and grants her spiritual power to the king to rule the Ryūkyū kingdom in peace. This is precisely the kind of ceremony that Kunikasa is conducting in the prologue. However, the sexual congress between the king and Kunikasa violates the ceremony, and this results in Kunikasa's foretelling of the end of the king. In Yamato [Japanese] religious myth, the sun god is a female, Amaterasu Ōmikami, who is the source of the Japanese imperial line, but in the prologue here the sun warrior is the king, who is granted his spiritual power by Kikoe Ōgimi. As Hokama observes, absolute power rests with Kikoe Ōgimi, a *noro* who has the ability to transform into a sun-goddess—this is clearly a different arrangement from mainstream religious belief where absolute power is vested in the person of the emperor.[42] In Ōshiro's novel the female principle embodied in the *noro* is represented by the moon. Quite apart from the different but similar religious traditions of Okinawa and Yamato, Ōshiro is evoking an intricate vision where motifs from several strands of Japanese religious feeling entwine and entangle, enriching as well as complicating the plot line.

The other passage where a similar mix of religious elements combine to create a contrast in traditions is at the end of chap. 1. King Shō Toku's first attempt to conquer Kikai Island with a fleet of warships has failed, and the king is ship-wrecked on Kudaka Island. There the king meets Kunikasa, the charismatic *noro* of Kudaka for the first time. The king, who appears to have forsaken the older gods of Okinawa for the newer gods of Buddhism brought from Yamato, has a conversation with Kunikasa in which the polarities of male and female power, the clash of religions, indeed of civilizations, and the hybrid possibilities that the king holds out for his Okinawan subjects are revealed:

[King Shō Toku:] "I was fourteen at the time. I clearly saw the wretchedness of the world for what it was. My father the king told me this once. The reason why you feel uneasy even on the most peaceful of days is that secretly you sense that this day will come. Eventually this will befall you too so keep this in your heart . . . . Perhaps this is why my father the king accepted the way of the Buddha from Yamato, or because he was deeply troubled."

[Kunikasa] "What is the way of the Buddha?"

Shō Toku smiled gently, "I see. The people of Kudaka are ignorant of the Buddha. The Buddha is far away in this world, in a place beyond the sea, that's right, beyond the divide between the heavens and the sea over there. He protects us from there. And he grants us salvation after death."

"In Kudaka, the gods dwell beyond the cliffs. The gods of Nirai Kanai. The gods of Kikai Island are there also. I saw a white horse. . . ."

Kunikasa dimly felt the clamor of blood in her body but held her breath and kept it to herself.

"A white horse? Is there a white horse in Kudaka also?"

Shō Toku wondered if the white horse was the same as the one in his dream. But that was on Kikai.

"I don't know why it's there. From ancient times we were told it existed. And I've seen it. Beyond the divide between the heavens and the sea. . . ."

Shō Toku gazed toward the far horizon. The color of the heavens had dissolved away, the color of darkness was growing ever darker. It seemed to be on the verge of extinguishing the divide between the heavens and the sea.

Was the white horse the Buddha's salvation? But it ate the sun; what did this mean? [43]

The king is caught between the foreign religion of Buddhism taught to him by his father and the old religion of Okinawa practiced by the *noro*. He is also tempted by the prospect of the power to defy the gods whoever they may be—a classic struggle between, in Ōshiro's words, the secular authority of male power and the traditional spiritual power of women. The struggle is more complicated than religion alone, for it also involves a clash between traditional Okinawan culture and imported Japanese culture. This passage already hints that a hybrid mix of religions is emerging. Whether this is a compromise or a capitulation is left to the imagination of readers.

A King Revealed

The novel is not merely constructed from symbolic interactions between *noro* and from the political struggle over leadership of the Ryūkyū kingdom. If it were simply a collection of such episodes and did not create a certain verisimilitude for the historical figures portrayed, then those figures would remain two-dimensional and not come to life as people. But Ōshiro strives hard to create complex, realistic characters, as can be seen in the many-faceted portrait of King Shō Toku. The king's savage, impulsive nature is revealed in a scene in chap. 1 where he beheads the leader of a group of farmers who are seeking relief from payments to the king. The scene begins with Shō Toku berating the farmers:

> "You must apologize. Your annual tax is a tribute to the gods. You must never think that it is a gift to the Lord of the realm. This Shuri Forest palace is a garden of the gods who protect the sun-king [*tedaosoi*], the lord of the realm. To neglect your contribution to the lord of the realm is fail in your gift to the gods."
>
> "My deepest apologies."
>
> Their shoulders shivered at [Shō Toku's] voice, which reverberated with such force as to split their chests asunder; one, two, three men shuddered, their backs quivering. The sunlight gently filtering through the trees shifted. Suddenly, Shō Toku's sword created an especially violent disturbance. Without warning, he forced one of the men down by pulling him by the neck.
>
> "Tribute must be given to gods! Why were you negligent!"
>
> "My deepest apology."
>
> "Silence!"
>
> A sudden flash of light ran across Shō Toku's blade, fresh blood drank the screams of the severed head and scattered all about. In an instant, shocked cries melted into the shadows of the sacred trees, the light in the holy grove was unmoved. Fresh blood spattered branches, fallen leaves, and the top of the severed head, its eyes still wide open.

"One life saves many!"

All of a sudden this cry burst out of Shō Toku's throat, shaking the holy grove.[44]

The scene created by the self-righteous tone of Shō Toku's voice and his bloodthirsty anger is reinforced later when the king has a violent dream that prefigures his end. In his dream he recalls a baby who died, crushed beneath the hooves of the horse that he was riding:

> My father the king lived for war. He sacrificed his daughter and his wife to establish the kingdom. I hate my father. So I trampled the child to death. Because I love, I hated everyone. . . . That child reported that I intend to kill you, Kanamaru. When that child was trampled beneath my horse's hooves, it was you who really killed him, Kanamaru. Here I come, Kanamaru! He tried to stride forward with his blade drawn, at the ready, but could not move. The ground was covered with unclean things, human waste, and he could find no footing.[45]

Later in his dream, he encounters the farmer whom he beheaded, who warns him of the danger of attacking Kikai Island. The farmer tells Shō Toku: " 'Nirai Kanai is that kind of place.' From long ago it had been said that a pure land called Nirai Kanai lay beyond the sea but is this Kikai Island? 'Yes,' replied the farmer." [46]

Despite these warnings, Shō Toku's hubris does not permit him to heed the warning of his dream, and the king embarks upon his two disastrous campaigns against Kikai Island.

If the vengeful king portrayed so far by Ōshiro remained without any significant development to his character, the novel would fail to present a realistic characterization, but the king falls in love, and his character changes, although only to a limited degree. He is still driven by pride and ambition, but his love for Kunikasa reveals a softer, more humane side. This aspect of his character is revealed most vividly when he contemplates the ruin he has created on Kikai Island after his second, successful campaign to subjugate its people to his rule. The king asks Kanamaru whether his deeds will be recorded:

> "The [diary record] will remain as a symbol of the sun-king's virtue and glory."
>
> What is virtue and glory?—in his heart Shō Toku was repelled by the words, he did not speak again. This servility was out of place for Kanamaru, feelings of hatred rose again and again in his breast.

Virtue and glory, it was the exact opposite. Shō Toku was tormented by this thought. Was his subjugation of Kikai Island a victory, or a defeat? . . . Through this battle for victory both Matsugane and the white horse had been lost.[47]

In this passage the terrible cost of war is revealed. The slaughter of thousands, combatants and noncombatants alike, have sickened the king. At the same time readers are made aware that the conquest of Kikai Island is actually part of the plot by Kanamaru's spiritual advisor, Asato Ufuya, to bring down the king. Thus Kanamaru does not escape his share of the blame for the slaughter.

The author reveals the king to be a complex, troubled character who may, indeed, be the victim of his upbringing in the home of yet another bloodthirsty, ambitious king. The end of the novel poses the reader a question: will the new king Kanamaru be any different from his predecessors?

Conclusion

In the foregoing analysis of *Noro*, two sides to the novel have been highlighted: the mystical, religious element symbolized by the *noro* themselves— the women who are possessed, often violently, by the gods. Their supernatural powers are feared and respected by all, and they clearly represent an aspect of what Freud called the uncanny. But the lives of the *noro* themselves are rigidly circumscribed by custom. In this respect they, too, are victims of the society in which they live, and they also, in an even more piteous sense, are mere playthings of the gods. Kunikasa is a rebel, and because she loves Shō Toku and becomes pregnant by him, she ultimately pays the penalty of forfeiting her powers, the chief determinant of her identity.

The love affair between Kunikasa and Shō Toku is part of the novel's other aspect: the all-too-human struggle for love coming up against the political machinations of the principal actors, which cause the deaths of thousands for the sake of secular power. The twin motifs of the secular power possessed by males and the sacred power of women are carefully interwoven in Ōshiro's narrative. The novel is not two disconnected narratives but an attempt to describe what Ōshiro sees as the reality of human experience and Okinawan history where the spiritual and the political dimensions are fused together into one unbroken thread.

Okinawan readers are already familiar with many aspects of the story because it is a part of their history. The contemporary Okinawan novelist Matayoshi

Eiki (b. 1947) has commented that the story the novel tells is central to Okinawan myth and legend. He also notes that for him at least, the most compelling part of the narrative concerns the portraits Ōshiro painted of the *noro,* which he describes as being all too human.[48] This comment recalls what Okaya Kōji wrote: that *noro* still practice their beliefs, their ceremonies, and their divinations even now in Okinawa. The discovery of the human in the divine that Matayoshi highlights thus takes on a certain real-life significance for Okinawan readers that might not be apparent to readers elsewhere.

The novel is clearly part of Okinawa's unique cultural heritage, and it takes on a special meaning since the status of Okinawa has again been reduced to that of merely another Japanese prefecture. This is not to say that sacral women have not and do not exist in other regions of Japan. Nor does this mean that that there is no other body of literature celebrating or, at least, recording the lives of these women. For Ōshiro the existence of sacral women both in the present and past is more than just an ethnographic or historical fact, as his writing demonstrates, the existence of *yuta* and *noro* is a necessary and ineradicable condition underlying the existence of contemporary Okinawa. Such an understanding represents something quite different from that of the rest of Japan and its literature.

The novel also has obvious political overtones—it speaks to contemporary Okinawans and Japanese alike about the sources of culture and identity. Hybridity—the fusion of an Okinawan cultural ethos and that of Yamato— and its linguistic, religious, political, and ethnic consequences has been one of the major themes of Ōshiro's fiction. In *Noro,* Ōshiro redefines the culture of Okinawa, which remains, in a very real sense, an alien within the body politic and within the culture of Japan; it approaches, or more specifically, begins to assume a hybrid identity. The notion of hybridity can also cast a different light on the mainstream Yamato culture of Japan, and such a process of reexamining the sources of Japanese identity itself may be glimpsed in the novel as well.[49]

CHAPTER 8

THE ALIEN WITHOUT

Murakami Haruki and the Sydney Olympics

you faint & the city's
there like a pillow

you wake in the morning
each street is a beach—

others have armchairs
& opinions about things
. . . .
the city's still hearing
when they're dead & gone
   —John Forbes, from "Sydney"

But here I am in Sydney
At the age of sixty-one
With the clock at a quarter to bedtime
And my homework still not done.
   —Kenneth Slessor, from "I Wish I Were . . ."

This chapter will focus on a single volume by the acclaimed Japanese author Murakami Haruki (b. 1949)—*Shidonii!* (Sydney!)—published in January 2001 by the Bungei Shunjū company in Tokyo. Three-quarters of this 409-page book, published originally as a single volume and then in two volumes in paperback, consists of Murakami's *Shidonii nisshi* (Sydney diary), which records in twenty-three daily entries the minutiae of his life in Sydney and his observations on the Sydney Olympics. The diary also contains many reflections on Australia and its life and culture. This chapter will examine the *Sydney Diary*, rather than the remaining quarter of the book, which consists of diary entries before the Olympics written in Atlanta and Hiroshima, and four brief pieces written after the Olympics set in Tokushima and New York, which discuss Takahashi Naoko, the winner of the Sydney Olympic Women's Marathon.

Travel diaries are a fascinating form of expression, several examples of which (in both the English and Japanese tradition) have been critically acclaimed as important works of literature. In general, travel diaries focus on exotic locales and especially on the odd practices and customs of the inhabitants of these (usually) faraway places. Murakami's *Sydney!* is no exception to this rule. The travel diary is well represented in the history of Japanese literature, one of the most famous examples being undoubtedly Matsuo Bashō's (1644–1694) *Oku no hosomichi* (The narrow road from the deep north, 1702). We will begin with a consideration of the travel diary form and then examine other travel works by Murakami, before examining his *Sydney Diary*.

The Travel Diary Genre

Travel diaries are an old genre in Japanese literature. Travel accounts by monks, aristocrats, and others have been preserved from Japan's distant past. Donald Keene, in the first volume of his acclaimed history of Japanese literature, cites the travel diary by the monk Ennin (793–864), which describes a journey to China, as one of the most important of the numerous such accounts that are extant.[1] Many of these works approach the status of literature and have long been recognized as such in Japan. A standard dictionary of Japanese literature begins the entry on travel literature *(kikō bungaku)* with discussion of three travel diaries dating from classical times: *Tosa nikki* (The Tosa diary, ca. tenth century), *Kaidōki* (Journey along the seacoast road, 1233), and the *Izayoi nikki* (The diary of the waning moon, ca. thirteenth century).[2] Earl Miner has analyzed one of the most important of the literary travel diaries, Bashō's *The Narrow Road from the Deep North*. In his 1996 book entitled *Naming Properties*, Miner compares Bashō's work to a number of other travel accounts, principally Samuel Johnson's *A Journey to the Western Islands of Scotland* (1775). He has a number of useful observations on the problems involved in reading and evaluating travel diaries, so we will take his observations into account when reading Murakami's Sydney diary.

The first issue is that of the relationship between the writer of the account and the persons and places named in it. To quote Miner: "The problem turns on the traveler's capacity to give meaning to the names of those people and places. . . . No doubt all narrative involves not merely sequence but continuum to some telos, an end often realized in the sequential process itself."[3] Miner is considering here the larger problem of reference in his discussion of the nature of fiction and factuality. This is important to the investigation of travel accounts because it helps to determine how to read these accounts: if literature is essentially a fictional construction, then what of travel narratives that are essentially factual? Another issue Miner addresses is the aim of such a narrative, which in the case of a travel diary may well be realized by the progression, or sequence, of entries. Yet another of Miner's useful insights is that a travel diary is a portrait of a personality, the projected personality of the author. He notes:

> [D]esign argues personality, what we can understand as . . . psychological and moral character. And what is character in our understanding of [him] as [an] individual is ideological in cultural terms. . . . In writing about largely unfamiliar people in mostly unfamiliar places, [he is a] historian traveling into territories largely unknown. . . . In seeking to understand [him], we naturally bring our own selves into play. We too have ideologies, and with them our limits. Many things lie beyond our capacities, and it is common experience to find ourselves missing something important or to discover that we are convinced that we understand what we cannot explain.[4]

This argument is very similar to that argued by Wayne Booth, discussed in Chapter 3, where the notion of personality is diverse. As Booth writes: "I am not an individual self at all, but a character, a social self, a being-in-process, many of whose established dispositions or habits belong to others—some of them even to all humankind."[5] The relationship between reading about a character or characters on a page and the choice of self or selves that individual readers make is not at all simple, nor is it yet a matter of clear scientific consensus, but Booth's formulation contains truths that are exceedingly useful in assessing fictional narratives. The notion of beings-in-process also has obvious implications for the reading of travel narratives and in that respect bears some affinity to Miner's stress on the connection between the design of the narrative (Miner is thinking specifically of the travel narrative) and the projected personality of the author read in terms of the ideology, the cultural context, that is created by the narrative.

Miner's argument attempts to claim literary status for travel narratives, expressly for the narratives he is investigating, and to redefine the notion of fiction itself. As Miner notes:

> The complex "dialectic" of fact and fiction and other elements in historical writing has been described in great detail . . . and in brief as "the actual refiguration of time, now become human time through the interweaving of history and fiction.". . . [G]iven these considerations, the decision whether a given literary expression is factual or nonfactual is literally not simple: it incorporates *both* fact and nonfact. . . . It further follows that for the literary version of the aesthetic a fact-fiction distinction is inadequate.[6]

The notion of history in this passage incorporates travel writing, for Miner argues that contemporary accounts of social phenomena are historical narratives. Writing of Johnson's account of his tour of Scotland, Miner remarks: "Observing poverty, deforestation, and underpopulation in Scotland, why should Johnson not synthesize these facts into a factual whole that yet derives much of its force from the fictional energies of his desire for causal connections and motives that are not demonstrably factual?"[7] That travel narratives can be and have been great literature is the starting and end point of Miner's argument.

It may be objected that the travel accounts Miner treats are indisputably great works of literature, and no one reads them as anything else. Therefore it may be difficult to conflate his logic into an argument that could apply to any travel diary. The point is not that all travel accounts are great literature, but that some certainly are and that by and large the genre itself needs to be seen and read as belonging to the category of literature, or at the very least the category of history, which itself often intrudes into the literary domain, and thus arguments and analysis of such accounts should be taken as much from a literary-critical perspective as any other. This is the approach we will take to Murakami's work. Another objection might be that Miner's argument is based upon a travel diary written some three hundred years ago. In response, can a more recent example of the travel diary genre be found that can qualify as literature, if not great literature?

It is easy to answer that question in the affirmative because numerous examples come to mind. In nineteenth-century Japan, the famous author Mori Ōgai's *Doitsu nikki* (German diary, 1937), a rewritten version of a number of early diaries kept by Ōgai during his period of study overseas, but not published until well after his death, is justly famed as literature.[8] In *Modern Japanese Diaries*, Donald Keene has published an analysis of and translations from the *German Diary*, and he has observed that Ōgai may well have intended to publish it. This seems entirely plausible, given Ōgai's rewriting of the early diaries.[9] Keene's study translates and discusses passages from numerous travel accounts written by Japanese in the modern era, and he often remarks on their literary qualities. Keene observes of diaries in general:

> It is hard for a person with literary gifts to keep from improving on the truth even when relating something that happened that day, and the temptation to embellish is all the greater when he describes the events in his diary. He may relate events that never really occurred, simply because life is generally not as artistic as the artist might desire. But even if we can demonstrate that certain diary entries must be untruthful, they may nevertheless reveal much about the diarist: as products of his imagination, they are certainly more important than the weather and other more mundane aspects of everyday life.[10]

Other examples of travel diaries cited by Keene for their literary excellence include journalist and essayist Narushima Ryūhoku's (1837–1884) *Kōsei nichijō* (Journal of a voyage to the West, 1880–1884) and various of the Christian evangelist Niijima Jō's (1843–1890) diaries describing his journeys to the United States and Asia.[11]

In twentieth-century Japan also, one can find numerous examples of important travel diaries. It is rare for such works to be either translated or the subject of academic study in any language other than Japanese, but recently substantial extracts from Yosano Akiko's *Man mō yuki* (Travels in Manchuria and Mongolia, 1928) were rendered into English for the first time by Joshua Fogel, and some English-language studies of Japanese travel diaries have appeared over the last decade or so.[12] In another recent book Atsuko Sakaki has probed several travel accounts of China written by Tanizaki Jun'ichirō, based on journeys he made to China in 1918 and 1926.[13]

Among the numerous twentieth-century travel diaries not yet translated, the famous ethnographer Yanagita Kunio's *Kainan shōki* (South Sea notes, 1925) stands out as an acclaimed example of the genre.[14] It may be argued that the travel diary is the very foundation of Yanagita's work, as various examples of this genre occur in his oeuvre. Several other examples of travel diaries long recognized as possessing literary merit spring to mind: poet and dramatist Yoshii Isamu's (1886–1960) *Michinoku kikō* (Trip to Michinoku, 1936), included in Yoshii's volume of travel essays, *Wabizumi no ki* (A record of a solitary life, 1936); novelist Hayashi Fumiko's (1903–1951) *Minami no hate no shima* (Island in the far South, 1950), which was later retitled *Yakushima kikō* (Trip to Yakushima, 1952); and novelist Ibuse Masuji's (1898–1993) *Bizen kaidō* (Road to Bizen, 1956). It is well known that Ibuse also wrote a large number of stories and travel accounts about Hiroshima, where he was born, not to mention his masterpiece, *Kuroi ame* (Black rain, 1965–1966), about the atomic bombing of Hiroshima, which was based on the diary of a survivor. These are by no means isolated phenomena; many other examples could be cited, such as works by novelist Nogami Yaeko (1885–1995), who wrote over five hundred short travel accounts, many about Oita prefecture, her birthplace.[15]

Travel diaries written in English and other European languages have an equally long history, but it would be a pointless exercise to list all of the most important—a few will suffice to indicate the importance of the genre. Johnson's *A Journey to the Western Islands of Scotland* was mentioned earlier, but the European travel diary long predates Johnson. It is not necessary to trace the influence of the travel diary from classical literature as it wended its way into medieval Europe, nevertheless a number of famous examples of the genre suggest themselves immediately: Marco Polo's (1254–1324) account of his travels in Asia was already available in English by 1579, and it became the model for numerous imitations, whether based on fiction or fact. The novelist Peter Ackroyd, in a chapter on travel writing in his book *Albion*, moves rapidly from accounts of monks written in the eighth century to the fourteenth century, where he examines the "joy in the arcane places of the earth" with the mythical Sir John Mandeville's *Travels*. In his summation of various medieval travel accounts, Ackroyd observes that: "We may say that English travel-writers define their nationhood by describing other nations; it is an instinctive form of reassurance," a comment that may well apply to travel accounts written in the twentieth century and in languages other than English.[16] Another influential book cited by Ackroyd is Richard Hakluyt's compilation, *The Principall Navigations,*

Voiages and Discoveries of the English Nation, first published in 1589. Ackroyd notes that these works created a taste for exotic lands across the sea; it is possible to argue that Japanese travel accounts have had a similar impact.

Modern English examples of travel diaries are as ubiquitous as those written earlier and include several hundred written about Japan alone, many by well-known authors. A few travel accounts of Japan published by notable Australian authors would include the novelist Hal Porter's (1911–1984) *The Actors* (1968) and the novelist Peter Carey's (b. 1943) *Wrong about Japan* (2004).[17] A number of authors writing in English have even adopted the travel diary as their major genre, including Bruce Chatwin (1940–1989), who came to fame with his *In Patagonia* (1977) and *The Songlines* (1987), written about Aboriginal Australia; Paul Theroux (b. 1941), whose most famous travel diary is *The Great Railway Bazaar* (1987), about a journey across Europe and Russia to Japan; and V. S. Naipaul (b. 1932), perhaps more celebrated for his fiction, but also an accomplished writer of travel diaries, notably, *An Area of Darkness* (1964) on India. Naipaul was awarded the Nobel Prize for Literature in 2001.

The fascination of Western travel writers with exotic lands is evident in any brief survey of the genre, which as Ackroyd noted, is perhaps as much a comment on their own societies as those they visit. The American travel writer Peter Matthiessen (b. 1927), whose most famous travel account is *The Snow Leopard* (1978), based on a trip to the Himalayas, uses Zen Buddhism (he has been ordained as a Zen priest) as a means to comprehend nature. But, as Garvin Perram remarks, "the depiction of landscape [in Peter Matthiessen's writing] goes beyond a mere description of natural features . . . into a psychological and mythopoetic response . . . [that] might seem somewhat paradoxical when one takes into consideration . . . that a very characteristic feature of his work is a strongly journalistic documentation of experience."[18] As will soon become evident, these comments may also be applied to Murakami's writings on Australia.

Murakami Haruki's Travel Diaries

Before the publication of his *Sydney Diary,* Murakami Haruki also penned other travel accounts.[19] But first I will briefly outline Murakami's career up to 2008. Murakami was born in Kyoto in 1949 and grew up in the salubrious surroundings of seaside Kobe. He went to Tokyo for his degree and graduated from the literature and theater school of Waseda University in 1975. His graduation thesis was on the journey motif in American cinema. Murakami was, then, an American specialist, and even after becoming a full-time writer in 1981, he continued a career as a translator of some of the greatest modern American writers into Japanese. His translations include works by F. Scott Fitzgerald, Truman Capote, J. D. Salinger, Raymond Carver, John Irving, and Tim O'Brien.[20]

Murakami has won most of the major Japanese literary awards. His best-known novels include the trilogy *1979 Nen no pinbōru* (1979 Pinball, 1980), *Hitsuji o meguru bōken* (A wild sheep chase, 1982), and *Dansu Dansu Dansu* (Dance, dance, dance, 1988). He has also written much nonfiction, including his well-known study of the Sarin gas attack by the Aum terrorist group on the Tokyo subways, *Undāguraundo* (Underground, 1997). All of his major novels—which now number over ten—and some of his nonfiction (including *Underground*)—have been translated into English. Already four books have been written in English on Murakami, and, no doubt, there will be many more. He has lived overseas for long periods, mostly in Europe and the United States, often in an attempt to escape media attention. One important fact to keep in mind is Murakami's excellent reading and speaking skills in English.

Philip Gabriel in his 2002 study of three of Murakami's travel books: *Tōi taiko* (A distant drum, 1990), *Uten enten* (Days of rain, days of fire, 1990), and *Henkyō kinkyō* (Borders near and far, 1998) explains that travel writing is one of the more popular genres of contemporary writing in Japan and notes that "during the decade of the 1990s [Murakami]'s travel books were arguably among the most popular and best-known examples of travel writing in Japan."[21] He contends that Murakami's travel narratives share "a concern for memory, a nostalgic sense of loss, as well as a foregrounding of the limits of knowledge and representation. . . . Murakami's writing . . . spirals inwards, an ostensible attempt to confront the exotic and the unfamiliar . . . [and] ends up obsessed with the familiar."[22]

The first two of these travel books—*A Distant Drum* and *Days of Rain, Days of Fire*—arose from the three years Murakami spent in Italy, Greece, and surrounding areas from 1986 to 1989, and they coincide with the writing of his novel *Noruwei no mori* (Norwegian wood, 1987), which had sold 8.26 million copies by the end of 2004.[23] Gabriel notes about the two volumes: "One is tempted to see these early travel books . . . in the light of V. S. Naipaul's comments on his own early travel books . . . namely as 'autobiography and landscape.'"[24] *A Distant Drum* chronicles Murakami's search for a quiet place to work, while *Days of Rain, Days of Fire* describes two trips, first to the sacred

Athos monastery of Greece and then to Turkey. Gabriel finds familiar patterns in the two works: a certain amount of detail about various localities "yet always depicted in a decidedly hesitant, distanced way," and at the end of the journey a "negative view of the foreign land, a rush away . . . away from the unfamiliar and back to the familiar." [25] This leads Gabriel to the idea "that one returns to the familiar only to find it has become now the defamiliarized, the *un*familiar." [26]

Another interesting point about Murakami's travel books is his method of composition. *A Distant Drum* was not composed in real time but was a collection of sketches woven from fragmentary jottings he did during the three years abroad. [27] *Borders Near and Far* is similarly a composite narrative consisting of seven essays written and published separately over a period of about five years. For example, in the brief preface to the first essay, "Iisuto Hanputon: Sakka tachi no shizukana seichi" (East Hampton: A sacred ground for writers), Murakami explains: "It was in the autumn of '91 when I was asked by a certain editor of a credit card PR magazine to write something about East Hampton. Because I was competing in the New York City marathon, I thought it would be easy to go there afterwards and so I accepted the commission." [28] East Hampton, on Long Island in New York, is described in Murakami's essay as a writers' haven, where such notable authors as Thomas Harris (b. 1940), the author of the Hannibal Lector novels; E. L. Doctorow (b. 1931), the distinguished winner of the National Book Critics Circle Award for his novel *Ragtime* (1975) and a popularizer of "faction," novels that mix fact and fiction and use real people as characters; and Nelson Algren (1909–1981), the author of *The Man With the Golden Arm* (1949) have lived at one time. [29] The importance of modern American literature to Murakami, a prolific and distinguished translator of U.S. fiction, is clearly visible in this essay.

The next essay is about a trip Murakami took in 1990 to Karasu tō (Crow Island), an uninhabited island in the Japanese Inland Sea. The third essay takes place on a grand tour of Mexico undertaken in 1992, and like the previous essay, was serialized in a magazine. This essay is the longest in the book. The fourth concerns a trip to Sanuki on the island of Shikoku, famed for its thick *udon* noodles, and so the purpose of the trip is primarily gustatory. This essay was also written for a magazine. The next trip, commissioned by another magazine, was to Nomonhan in Inner Mongolia and took place in 1994. In 1939 Nomonhan was the site of a fierce battle between the Soviet Union and Japan, and this battle forms the centerpiece of Murakami's long novel *Nejimakidori kuronikuru* (The wind-up bird chronicle, 1994–1995). The sixth essay, written for a magazine in 1995, was based on a trip across the United States. The seventh and last essay, entitled "Kōbe made aruku" (Walking to Kobe), was about a walk that Murakami took from Nishinomiya to Kobe (about eighteen kilometers) in 1997. Murakami grew up in Kobe, and many of his stories are set in the area, and Kobe was also the site of the massive 1995 earthquake, the subject of another nonfiction work by Murakami.[30]

The pattern of a trip overseas and then back to Japan is highlighted by Gabriel, who sees this as representing a "nostalgic sense of alienation," the rediscovery of the familiar through a process of defamilarization.[31] In the postscript to the paperback edition of *Borders Near and Far,* Murakami confides to readers that he loves travel diaries and has delighted in reading them from childhood.[32] But the present is an unhappy era for such works, Murakami asserts, because the sense of adventure, of journeying to a faraway place, has been lost; what is important to Murakami now, however, is the change in consciousness in the traveler that traveling brings about. This is "the real meaning" of travel narratives.[33] It creates a border area *(henkyō)* inside oneself: a journey like that undertaken by Bashō hundreds of years ago is an internal journey, exploring the alien within ourselves. Is this true for Murakami's *Sydney Diary?*

Constructing the Self

Passing, fugitive references to Australia occur in some of Murakami's fiction, rather the way distinguished French novelist George Perec (1936–1982) uses Australian place names in his writing or the Italian philosopher and novelist Umberto Eco (b. 1932) composes his famous essay on the platypus (and Kant). For example, in the short story "Shidonii no guriin sutoriito" (Green Street in Sydney, 1982), Murakami writes: "Frankly speaking, Green Street is the greenest, leafiest street in Sydney."[34] The story is a charming confection based on word play arising from the English character actor Sydney Greenstreet's (1879–1954) name. Another interesting feature of the story is the appearance of sheep, and the sheepman. Apart from its referencing Australia's most famous export product, sheep remind readers of the mysterious sheepman who appears in *A Wild Sheep Chase* and *Dance, Dance, Dance.* In short, Australia is a source of exotica, so the odd kangaroo bounding through Murakami's fiction is a sharp reminder that for most non-Australian intellectuals, Australia represents a mythic land of exotic beasts located at the end of the earth. As far as I am aware, the visit to the Olympics was Murakami's first trip to Australia.

However, Murakami has written on the Olympic Games before. In 1987 he published *The Scrap: Natsukashi no 1980 nendai* (The scrap: The good old 1980s), in which he constructed a portrait of the United States during the decade of the eighties by combing American magazines and newspapers from the era for interesting stories. In this book he comments in the form of a diary on the 1984 Los Angeles Olympics.[35] Obviously Murakami did not come to the Sydney Olympics without significant experience of writing both travel literature and an Olympic diary.

The structure of the *Sydney Diary* is similar to his other travel diaries: the first narrative is entitled "1996 shichigatsu nijūhachinichi Atoranta" (28 July 1996 Atlanta), which is followed by another entitled "2000 rokugatsu jūhachinichi Hiroshima Orinpikku kaikaishiki made ato hachijunichi" (18 June 2000 Hiroshima: 89 days until the Olympic Opening Ceremony), and only then does the actual *Sydney Diary* appear. It is divided into twenty-three entries, all dated, and is followed by a second travel narrative entitled "2000 nen jūgatsu hatsuka Tokushima" (20 October 2000 Tokushima). This is in turn divided into two separate narratives and concludes with a final narrative entitled "2000 nen jūichigatsu itsuka Nyūyōku" (5 November 2000 New York).[36] However, most of the book is the *Sydney Diary*, with the other four narratives making up barely 20 percent of the text as a whole.

As Murakami notes in his postscript to the volume, *Sydney Diary* was the first time he wrote so much in such a short time.[37] At several places in the text he tells his readers that he is actually typing his reportage of a specific event on his laptop at the actual venue while the event is taking place. As he puts it, this is "real-time" writing. Not all of the diary entries are composed in this way, however, as most were written at night in his Sydney hotel after the day's events were concluded.[38] Also, it is important to note that this is a real diary—Murakami records what he had for breakfast every morning on each of the twenty-three days of his diary, how much it cost, what the weather was like while he was jogging or bike-riding around the Sydney Opera House and Botanical Gardens (his regular morning route), how long it took him to complete the circuit, and what clothes he wore each day.[39] Thus the diary is an intensely personal document, and Murakami's diary persona (who bears a strong resemblance to the eponymous hero—simply called *boku* or "I"—who appears in many of his fictional narratives) becomes the reader's friend.

In assessing the text as a whole, the most appropriate approach is to focus on the narrative structure of *Sydney:* reading the diary as a species of "life-writing" or "autobiographical fiction," a genre that has become one of the dominant modes of late-twentieth-century writing. Miner has already suggested something like this approach, and many of the observations made by the other authors on travel narratives confirm the utility of this approach. There is no doubt that the intimate, frank portrait that Murakami has painted in this book presents a compelling subject for readers and presupposes a reader who can get to know this most famous of contemporary Japanese authors on a personal, intimate level. The reader Murakami projects is partly a product of the authorial persona Murakami creates, "a character, a social self, a being-in-process," as Booth has asserted. The portrait of Australia that Murakami paints is as much a product of his construction of self as it is of the events he is describing, and thus the design of the narrative assumes crucial importance. As Miner remarks: "[D]esign argues personality, what we can understand as . . . psychological and moral character," which is in turn intimately intertwined with the environment that constitutes the other of the self's ruminations, an exotic environment to be sure, but one that complements the self of Murakami's narrative. The author "Murakami Haruki" already exists in readers' minds, so what the diary reveals is something elaborated upon, not something invented from scratch.

Japanese readers do not need reminders of Murakami's fame; in all likelihood, it is precisely because of his fame that they are reading the book. In the book itself, Murakami makes only a few passing references to his fame: in an interview with the literary columnist of the *Australian,* Murakami answers a question as to why he has come to cover the Olympics, saying: "I like taking trips and writing about them, so this will probably end up as a piece of travel writing connected to the Olympic Games." In another interview, with a Korean TV journalist, he notes the way in which the journal and the publisher sponsoring and paying for his visit respond to his every need immediately.[40] Tickets that can be only bought from scalpers for exorbitant prices for events like the opening and closing ceremonies, the 400 meter final involving the star Aboriginal runner Cathy Freeman, are all obtained for Murakami instantly.[41] The day after it is stolen from his Sydney hotel room, his expensive Mac laptop is replaced by his benefactor (or should it be "minder") employed by the publisher.[42] When purchasing some books on Australia at a bookshop, Murakami buys two copies of the English translations of his novel *Kokkyō no minami, taiyō no nishi* (South of the border, West of the sun, 1992) to give as presents to people.[43] However, all these references are made openly—Murakami is staggered by the benefi-cence of his sponsors—or so it is made to appear: he cannot believe how much these tickets cost.[44]

Murakami repeatedly tells his readers how much he dislikes the Olympics, how appallingly boring most of the events are. At one point he writes the word *taikutsu* (boring) several times in the same sentence just in case readers have not gotten the idea.[45] This criticism is balanced by mention of the strange paradox that the Olympics are, nevertheless, astonishingly compelling, and Murakami has no regrets whatever about being dispatched all the way from Japan to the end of the world to report on them.

Readers are given to understand that this is one man's, one writer's, view of the Sydney Olympics and Australia in general: Murakami revels in his own idiosyncrasies. Several times, he addresses the "dear reader," who may well have a completely different view of the Olympics from TV viewing, and that view may be the correct one. While such rhetoric may protect Murakami from criti-cism that his reporting is subjective, the real motive for it lies in the creation of a cantankerous, maverick friend called Murakami, who is so intimate with his readers that he will disclose to them exactly what he really thinks, just as a close friend should. In other words it is a rhetorical strategy (probably a perfectly sin-cere one) designed to create a special kind of relationship between author and reader, one that goes far beyond mere journalism.

Constructing the Other

I will now examine specific segments of the text to ascertain exactly how Murakami "creates" Australia for his Japanese audience, and what kind of Aus-tralia he creates. It should be noted first, though, that the diary entries are con-cerned overwhelmingly with meticulous description of various Olympic events in which Murakami is interested—especially the men's and women's marathon. Only three or four entries out of the twenty-three concentrate on Australian life and culture; other observations on Australia emerge simply in passing.

I also mostly exclude the numerous mentions of Australian flora and fauna that Murakami sees in koala parks, zoos, and museums and emphasize instead his analysis of Australian history and society. However, it is worth noting that there are a number of two- or three-page digressions on topics of particular interest to the author—koalas, sharks, shark attacks, poisonous snakes, spiders, bushfires—which usually incorporate much detailed information that he has apparently gleaned from the various reference works by well-known authors like Eric Rolls, Gerry Swan, and Terence Lindsay (these Murakami purchased in bookshops and museums and lists in the bibliography).[46] These digressions follow the time-honored tradition of focusing on the weird and wonderful that has historically characterized travel diaries as well as providing much useful information for future visitors to Australia.

Like the early European explorers of Australia—whose accounts Murakami has read in Tim Flannery's *The Explorers,* which he cites now and again—Murakami comments several times on how strange and weird the Australian landscape is. The view from the airplane flying over the vast deserts of Australia, is, he says, "like a Tim Burton movie"; he is transported to another dimension.[47] He notes that Australia is the hottest, driest continent and recounts the migration in antiquity of marsupials and aboriginals from other land masses to this sunburnt country.[48] However, the western suburbs of Sydney are less romantic: they lead inland to a giant suburban sprawl away from the more up-market beach suburbs. The view during a train trip from his hotel in downtown Sydney to Parramatta, an outer Western Sydney suburb, reveals a crumbling, faded cityscape.[49] His comment comes from the entry for 12 September when Murakami journeyed to Parramatta to see the Olympic flame relay.

The didactic design of the novelist can be seen in his minihistory of Parramatta, from its first Aboriginal settlement through colonial times to the present. Clearly Murakami is intending to educate his audience about Australia. He also lets readers know that Australian English, or "strine" as it is sometimes called (based on an abbreviation of the word "Australian"), puzzled him at first, but his ears quickly make the adjustment, and for the rest of his stay he has no trouble understanding Australians, although he discusses the peculiarities of their dialect from time to time, notably the habit of abbreviating everything: salt-water crocodiles, he writes, are called "salties."[50]

Murakami's analysis of the symbolism of the opening ceremony on 15 September is insightful. He sees the panorama as an attempt to promote a post-reconciliation brand of patriotism—to do away with memories of the convict past and the dispossession of Aboriginal lands by white settlers and reconcile the white and black (Aboriginal) populations of Australia. These observations follow a brief history of Homebush, the western Sydney suburb that is the site of the Olympics, where Murakami outlines the history of white exploitation of Aborigines, seasoned with a touch of Rousseau-like nostalgia for the lifestyle of the noble savage:

Homebush was originally a trading post for the coastal Aborigines who lived in Sydney Cove and the inland Aborigines who lived in the interior. Both groups brought their distinctive products there for the purpose of exchange. This was because it was a site where the sea and the interior came together. As if symbolic of this, the creek water near Homebush was a mixture of seawater and freshwater. That is, from its earliest origins, Homebush was a point of encounter for alien cultures. . . . It is said that the Aborigines gathered here to perform their ceremonies and to compete in various skills. Apparently it was like an Aboriginal Olympics. The objects of trade were mainly shells and hard stones. Hard rocks could not be obtained on the coast, and, naturally, shells could not be found in the mountains. They used stones and shells to fashion tools.

Out of the blue British colonists arrived carrying guns. Then at the hands of the settlers, the relaxed way of life that the Aborigines had followed for many generations was destroyed at its foundations. The Aborigines who were nomadic hunter-gatherers had no concept of private property, but for the British private property was a social condition more important than any other. The British defined Australian land as land abandoned by the indigenous inhabitants, and thus not owned by them; they took possession of the land, used it productively, and interpreted their exploitation of the land as legally just. The two ways of thought were totally at odds with one another. . . .

In the near three hundred years since Captain Cook came in his ships and arrived here, this land [Homebush] was tossed to and fro by the exigencies of fate. It was developed, thrived, defiled, and abandoned, and then was rescued once again. A truly industrious series of transformations! During the entire period of 60,000 years prior to this point, Aborigines were exchanging shells and pebbles. If they had been left to their own devices, the Aborigines would probably still be exchanging shells and pebbles today and would not have felt inconvenienced in the slightest. Civilization is a strange beast. By remedying inconvenience, does it not continue to manufacture privation?[51]

For Murakami, the politically correct version of patriotism exemplified in the opening ceremony is tendentious but also rather countrified.[52] His comment on the theater of the opening ceremony is that it is a load of "bucolic mummery."[53] He earlier allows that the architectural excellence of the main stadium surprises him: there is nothing as sophisticated in Japan.[54] The description of the opening ceremony permits Murakami to pontificate upon nationalism:

When I think about the amount of time, labor and intellect wasted on some-thing like this [the opening ceremony], and the fact that none of this will be repaid—even though it has nothing to do with me—I can't help but feel how sad and meaningless this all is. After witnessing the mass games enacted at the opening ceremony, from somewhere deep inside I felt a strong desire not to see an Olympic opening ceremony held in North Korea for some time to come. That man [Kim Jong Il] would surely put on a mass opening ceremony that would last at least ten hours . . . it is not a "festival of sport." It is an event formed from the fusion of interest between the state and big business. . . . Watching the opening ceremony, waves of unease welled up within me." [55]

On 19–20 September, he drives up the coast from Sydney to Brisbane, the capital of the northern state of Queensland. He goes with a friend in a Ford Falcon, a typical Australian family sedan, to see Japan play Brazil in a prelimi-nary soccer match. He is staggered at the vastness of the territory, and a massive bushfire he encounters on the way. The country cop who pulls him over for speeding is proud of this bushfire, which has been burning for a week. Apart from his shock at how law-abiding Australian motorists are—Japanese drivers always speed on highways, and no one cares, he says—he is intrigued by the Australian attitude towards bushfires. After enjoying the luxury of a five-star hotel in Brisbane, he journeys to the soccer match. The stadium is full of young Japanese waving rising-sun flags. Murakami reflects that although this is uncon-troversial now, he wonders how many of the same Japanese youth are aware of the Japanese bombing of Darwin, Australia's northernmost city, in World War II, and of the large number of casualties that resulted.[56]

Apart from the casual mention of Australian novels he is currently reading, like *Voss* (1957), by the Nobel Prize-winning author Patrick White, which he describes as "old fashioned in its style, and constructed along classical lines," or Peter Carey's *The True History of the Kelly Gang* (2000), it is clear that Murakami gains most of his information from newspapers.[57] As part of his morning rou-tine, he trots to the nearby convenience store to buy copies of the local papers, *The Australian, The Sydney Morning Herald,* and the *Daily Telegraph,* which he reads from cover to cover and cuts out articles of interest to peruse further at night. He frequently quotes from the papers—summarizing their daily content for his readers. One topic that he mentions several times in the lead up to Cathy Freeman's victory in the 400 meters final on 25 September is the hate mail she attracts from newspaper readers who object to her lighting the Olympic torch and, after her win, her waving the (unofficial) Aboriginal flag, an emblem of black pride. In his entry for 26 September, he analyzes the pressure on Freeman and disagrees with criticisms of her assertion of Aboriginality.

However, the most detailed analysis of Australia comes in his 28 September entry, which Murakami styles *seishin byōriteki ni mita Ōsutoraria no reki-shi—Murakami kanryakuhan,* or "a short history of Australia (from the First Fleet to the Olympics) from the perspective of a disturbed individual, that is, Murakami." For this entry he obviously draws upon Flannery's research as well as Geoffrey Blainey's *Short History of Australia,* which is cited in both its original edition and the Japanese translation. He notes that half of the convicts carried to Australia by the First Fleet in 1788 committed serious crimes—they were not all Fenian rebels. And the fact of Australia's being founded as a penal colony determined its destiny, which was in contrast to the United States. The American rebels deliberately broke their ties with Britain to pursue their separate dreams. As he notes:

> In the U.S., they sought out new territory, new possibilities and new freedoms; of their own free will many people came to a new land—the origins of the U.S. were utterly different from those of Australia. Like Australia, the U.S. is a nation established with Britain as the fatherland, so to speak, but if I may use the metaphor of a person, the U.S. possesses a clear ego and purpose. As he grew and gained in strength, he boldly stood up against the control of his father . . . and left home to become independent. At about the same time that the U.S. established its independence, the huge colony called Australia made its appearance, but unlike the sense of ego possessed by big brother America, Australia's will was weak.[58]

Australia—at this point Murakami uses the metaphor of Mother England and her faithful child—and, especially its ruling class, tried to win its mother's affection by volunteering to fight in war after war that had no connection with Australia—the Sudan conflict, the Boer War, Gallipolli (World War I), and so on. He describes the huge Australian losses in the Gallipolli campaign fought in Turkey, Germany's ally, as a sacrifice to erase the convict stain. But when Britain sent its forces to Europe to fight Hitler, and thus abandoned Australia (which was facing the might of imperial Japan), Australia was forced to turn to its big brother, the United States, for help. In the postwar era Australia became the United States's deputy sheriff in the region. For Murakami, this clinging to other nations for security reveals Australia's anxiety over its identity, its failure to articulate its own sense of destiny.[59]

However, after Australia's participation in the Vietnam War, and the strong opposition to the conflict that emerged at the time, a new sense of identity was born. Murakami links this to the birth of the multicultural ideal in Australia. Returning to his Freudian metaphor, he argues that Australia conquered its childish separation trauma and grew up to develop mature relations with its Asian neighbors. The one remaining thorn under the skin of Australian identity is the question of the Aborigines. Murakami notes that they were not counted in the national census as citizens until the 1960s. Australia's attempts to impose its own standards of human rights on its Asian neighbors has failed because of this blatant hypocrisy, he argues. Once Australia moved towards reconciliation and celebrated the national "Sorry Day," when white Australians demonstrated their solidarity with black Australians by saying "sorry" for the destruction of traditional Aboriginal society at a series of national events, then in this respect as well Australia began to mature as a nation. This leads him to Cathy Freeman.

Cathy Freeman's maternal grandmother was a victim of the "stolen generation." This phrase refers to the generation of Aboriginal children removed by the welfare authorities from their parents, ostensibly because of their parents' inability to care for them properly, and handed over to white foster families to be raised. The policy was specifically aimed at children who were of mixed Aboriginal and white genetic heritage. At the root of this policy Murakami discerns an economic motive. The politics of racial separation were designed to create a cheap serf caste of Aboriginal laborers and stockmen. He discusses the failure of High Court cases to recompense Aborigines for their suffering arising out of being forcibly separated from their parents. Murakami describes the verdict of the Supreme Court of New South Wales in the Joy Williams case as a "political judgment." Compensation and an acknowledgement of wrong-doing was sought from the state on the behalf of the plaintiff, Joy Williams, who had been "stolen" from her parents as a baby, but the case was lost.[60]

Murakami asserts that the pain and suffering endured by Cathy Freeman's grandmother as a result of her forced separation from her mother affected Cathy's entire family, and this same pain resides deep in Cathy's heart.[61] The source of this information is an interview that Cathy Freeman gave to an English newspaper earlier in the year. So Murakami views Cathy's tears at the 400 meters awards ceremony (noting that she hardly expressed any emotion prior to this) as emblematic of reconciliation: "Cathy carrying off the gold medal in the 400 meters race, the lap of honor she made in the stadium waving both the Australian and Aboriginal flags, singing the national anthem on the victory dais with tears in her eyes: it is only natural that this was read as a symbol of reconciliation.[62] The majority of Australian spectators sang the national anthem with tears streaming down their cheeks."[63] Murakami interprets the tears in the eyes of the Australians in the stadium watching the ceremony as a sharing of her pain. Cathy Freeman, he writes, is a kind of female shaman enduring catharsis for the sake of the nation. Murakami himself is deeply affected by this and weeps as well. In this sense, the Sydney Olympics is a spiritual turning point, a milestone in the history of Australia.[64]

The Traveler Unmasked

The next entry in the Sydney diary is for Friday 29 September and is entitled "Shidonii kara no tegami" (A letter from Sydney). Here Murakami reflects on what the diary and the Olympics mean to him so far. It is possible to read this letter as one more element in the construction of the author-persona and the exotic Other of Australia that is his narrative subject, but the letter also reveals something of the pressures a working author is under when undertaking an arduous project such as this, although this too can be read as another revelation of personality. As Miner says: "[D]esign argues personality, what we can understand as . . . psychological and moral character. And what is character in our understanding of [him] as [an] individual is ideological in cultural terms." In order to assess the impact of the letter, I will quote some important passages from it:

> I've been living here for eighteen days to see the Olympics. I'm staying in an unpretentious hotel in the city, every day I ride a special Olympic train crammed with people, and commute to Olympic Park. There I watch various events and fill myself up with junk food at a cafeteria, and drink lots of water. What with it being so hot, if I don't drink copious amounts of water, I'll be in danger of becoming dehydrated. In the evening I return back to my hotel, sit in front of my computer and type away filling the pages with a record of the day's events.

One day's work usually amounts to about twenty-five to thirty pages of ruled notepaper. I do this every day. This is real hard labor. If there's something that provides some respite, then I guess it's the beer. At the end of the day, I go to the Irish pub opposite the hotel and drink the dark tap beer called "Old." . . . You'll probably ask why have I come all this way just to see the Olympics? The reason is to write a book on the Olympics. Why do I want to write a book on the Olympics? Well, in fact, I'm not sure myself. If I think about it, I've never really been interested in the Olympics. Some time ago I came across a sentence in an American novel where the author wrote, "It's as boring as the Olympics." I remember reading that line and thinking that I agreed completely. That's right, the Olympics are mostly a bore, and even when they were televised live, I hardly ever watched anything (except for the marathon, of course). . . . I've got practically no interest in the Olympic Games. So that in order to see the real thing I'd come to the Southern Hemisphere (not exactly to the end, though) and spend three weeks here is scarcely believable, even to me.[65]

Murakami then goes on to speak once again of how exotic Australia is by going on a trip to the Australian Museum in Sydney where he accesses a CD-ROM containing details of indigenous reptiles and snakes, and he is astonished by the vast number of poisonous snakes—the largest in the world—found there. Even more astonishing is the number of poisonous spiders, in which, yet again, Australia is a world leader. The construction of Australia as an exotic Other is augmented by his discovery upon his return to the hotel that his laptop has been stolen. After telling of his reporting of the theft to the local police, and a comparison with other dangerous parts of the world, like Italy, where similar things happen to unwary Japanese travelers, Murakami returns to his theme of how boring the Olympics is (he is watching a field hockey match). This begs the question of why he should spend so much time watching the games, already asked but not answered earlier in the same diary entry, and leads to the following response:

There is one thing that I have to acknowledge. A kind of pure emotion is born from the very heart of the endless continuum of boredom [induced by the Olympics]; something arises from within the stupor. I must make a confession. At these Games numerous happenings have pierced me through to the core. So deep that they have come out the other side. For example, the victory of Cathy

Freeman in the 400 meters. I truly believe that unless you were there you would not understand how overwhelming and magical it was. Wonderful events like that . . . I want to talk more about this at some other time.[66]

This passage is quite significant, for the cynical pose that Murakami's narrator-persona has adopted in relation to the Olympics as a whole is dropped to reveal the starry-eyed fan who responds to the magic of the moment. However theatrical this rhetoric seems, it has the ring of conviction and truth about it and is a strong and convincing piece of writing. At such places in the text there is a definite literary turn that betrays the ambition of its author and evokes the grand tradition of travel-writing and diaries.

The only other entry in which Murakami offers a sustained analysis of Australian society is towards the end of his three-week sojourn in the country. In the entry for 2 October, he observes that Australians love a party, and as the quality of their food is superior to the United States or United Kingdom (and cheaper), why not? This leads Murakami to an analysis of Australia as a quarry to the world (with Japan as its biggest customer). The fact that, historically, Australia is a mineral treasure trove has led to the easy-going, relaxed mode of Australian life—it has given rise to the idea of the lucky country. But, writes Murakami, with the sophisticated mining technology now available, third-world countries can export mineral resources to Asia cheaper than Australia can, and thus Australia's resource-export dependent macroeconomy is in a long-term decline. This is now becoming apparent in the growing trade deficit. Murakami fears Australia's happy-go-lucky character will inevitably change—the Olympics brightened the gloom for a tiny moment.[67]

In this section the analysis of Australia takes on political and economic overtones that contemporary readers expect of the travel diary, which in the twentieth and twenty-first centuries (and also in Dr. Johnson's time) is a factual record of the society visited by the traveler, not merely a chronicle of exotica. Australia is exoticized but not to the extent that a reader of Sir John Mandeville's *Travels* would have expected. Murakami's creation of Australia does incorporate a view of the country (typical of nature documentaries) as a remarkable repository of flora and fauna unique in the world, and his description of the physical features of the landscape presents an exotic picture of the oldest continent on earth. But Murakami also takes pains to paint a portrait of Australian civilization that deals with the contemporary issues of the relationship between black and white Australians and describes the reality of urban decay and social change in Sydney. Australians themselves are described in the usual cliché as a happy-go-lucky people largely isolated from the tensions of the world at large and speaking an exotic form of English, but his occasional interludes on local history do act to season this view by narrating the realities of the Australian past that have shaped the present.

Reflections

As an Australian who has lived most of his life in Sydney, my reading of Murakami's observations is that, given that he was in the country for only three weeks, his opinions are better informed than most and better expressed than is often the case among the few Japanese intellectuals who have written on Australia. In fact, his professionalism shines through—doing so much research in just three weeks, even if it was mostly scrutinizing the daily newspapers. Perhaps his reading of Cathy Freeman as a spiritual medium, symbolizing in her victory the triumph of reconciliation is a touch too romantic but, on the other hand, Murakami might respond, you had to be there in the stadium at that moment. The poetic power of the novelist's fine prose style is revealed here to good effect; it is, after all, the account of an artist who is perhaps entitled to construct contemporary myths of nationality, in an age when ethnicity and nationality have become sites of violent contestation.

Murakami's mixed prose style, which varies tenses and register according to the entry, discloses how his diary was composed: sometimes he was actually watching the event and sometimes he wrote later. It also creates a marvelous sense of verisimilitude, which further acts to strengthen the sympathetic persona of the author—a harried, harassed journalist doing his best for his readers. It is noticeable that Murakami was accredited as a journalist for the Games and had the wide access granted to journalists. He reminds readers at the end of his book that one of his culture heroes—Ernest Hemingway—also wrote as a journalist on the Spanish Civil War; *For Whom the Bell Tolls* arose out of that experience. Will Murakami turn his novelistic skills to a similar end at some time in the future?

One point worth repeating is just how important Murakami's near-native ability in English is to his account. Not many Australians read three daily newspapers cover to cover every morning before they go to work. Murakami's easy grasp of the avalanche of information pouring out of the Olympic machine, television, newspapers, and radio made his task easier than has been for other

Japanese writers, who often compose the occasional essay after visiting Australia that is full of egregious errors, errors they could have corrected by reading the daily newspaper. Due to the Olympics, the focus on Australian identity was also given full expression in the newspapers while Murakami was resident in the country, and this undoubtedly assisted in his grasp of contemporary Australian history and culture. Generally speaking, Murakami's generation has a better command of English than some earlier generations, although not many novelists are as expert as Murakami. His facility in English was a major factor in his construction of Australia—an Australia that most citizens of that country will have no trouble recognizing and in fact may even find it a vision of Australia that they may well embrace. It can be argued that the exotic Other constructed by Murakami can be brought home even to Australian readers as another version of self. The identity between the alien and self is usually recognized as a codependent construction; in this book, in the capable hands of the most celebrated Japanese writer of his generation, this is made self-evident.

EPILOGUE

Our visit has lasted an entire winter
and we have forgotten each word's name
The sky moves that quickly through the frame
   —Michael Palmer, from "Documentation"

I'd like to retire there and do *nothing,*
or nothing much, forever, in two bare rooms:
look through binoculars, read boring books,
old, long, long books, and write down useless notes,
talk to myself, and, foggy days,
watch the droplets slipping, heavy with light.
   —Elizabeth Bishop, from "The End of March"

The subject of the exotic or the alien is a perennial one for literature. Freud's discussion of the uncanny is primarily aesthetic, based on a reading of several eighteenth- and nineteenth-century European works of literature. Gothic is a mode of writing that dates back over two hundred years, so to analyze several works of Japanese literature written in the twentieth century that utilize such themes is not to attempt something startling or new in literary discourse. Discussion of these themes is nonetheless not all that common in studies of Japanese literature. Much more common is a direct tracing of influence from foreign literatures on the works of Japanese writers. A long history of such scholarship exists within Japan, especially in parts of the academy that are associated with the discipline of comparative literature. This is only to be expected, since the same history can also be found in scholarship on modern European literature, which is equally a hybrid product of many influences no matter which national literature of Europe is the focus of attention.

Indeed, if I may paraphrase Tolstoy, all cultures are hybrid; it is just that some are more so than others. This statement reflects the reality that the cultural history of all human societies, whether in the distant past or the present, is a history of the encounter with the Other, and the subsequent adaptations and compromises that result, as aspects of the culture of the Other are added to an already existing mixture, are but one step in a long line of such encounters. It is possible to trace the influence of foreign literatures on literature written by Japanese as far back as the beginning of recorded Japanese history, where the Other was China. And many scholars have done so. This is the very staple of comparative literature, and numerous studies in Japanese examine the influence of Chinese literature on classical Japanese literature or the influence of Western literature on literature written since the arrival of Perry in Japan. The title of Donald Keene's magisterial two-volume history of twentieth-century Japanese literature, *Dawn to the West*, is entirely apposite.

In recent Western scholarship on modern Japanese literature, there has been a shift so that the emphasis focuses more on the impact of the prewar Japanese empire on the literature of the time. This is a different kind of scholarly enterprise from traditional studies of literary influence, but even comparative scholars have come under the sway of the approach known as "postcolonial" or, more succinctly, "colonial" studies. This school of literary criticism originated in scholarship on history, but under the influence of such distinguished scholars as Edward Said, over the last two or three decades it has spread to comparative literary studies as well.[1]

In this book I do not follow the older paradigm of tracing influence, nor the more recent move of conceptualizing literature as part of a larger discourse on colonialism and its consequences. Nevertheless I have learned much from work carried out under the influence of these competing or parallel discourses, as is evident from some of the secondary sources I cite. As stated earlier, discussion of the alien or the exotic as they have been internalized or incorporated into actual works of Japanese literature or into movements in Japanese literary history is not all that common in contemporary scholarship, although several distinguished exceptions exist, and I have drawn on their work. Since my analysis is based primarily upon close readings of individual works of literature, whether poetry, prose, or nonfiction (perhaps belles-lettres is a better label for the travel diary), it does not lend itself to the high level of abstraction and massive archival research appropriate to discourses dealing with whole bodies of literature rather than individual works.[2]

Literary historians in Japan are now in the process of constructing the empirical ground upon which such genre studies can proceed. Large numbers of series reproducing the vast body of literature issued in the overseas Japanese colonial territories are now being published, and no doubt in the years to come such studies will gain momentum based upon extensive reading in the primary sources. Influence-hunting from modern European to Japanese literature also depends upon a deep knowledge of the European works that were read and translated into Japanese during the course of the twentieth century, and, as is the case elsewhere, scholars who possess the requisite tools to conduct such extensive reading are few and far between.

These are some of the reasons why I have chosen the approach that I have. This does not mean, however, that close readings of individual works of literature cannot produce deep insights into the process of absorption that characterized much of the literary production in twentieth-century Japan. The focus on translation when examining the writing of Tsubouchi Shōyō provides valuable and illuminating insights into Shōyō's overall literary ambitions, which, as Nakamura Kan's incisive analysis has shown, were linked to a larger agenda for political reform. Also Shōyō's successive revisions of his translations to make them more colloquial (but not necessarily the colloquial of everyday speech) furnish an alternative, parallel history of stylistic changes in the Japanese language that differs from accounts of the *genbun itchi* movement for language reform. In recent decades, scholars like Kamei Hideo have repeatedly stressed how slight changes in linguistic usage practiced by different authors have been crucial to understanding the nature of Japanese literature and its engagement with the world from which it drew its subject matter.

One of the key inspirations for much of Kamei's work on literary language, modes of narration, and so on is the thinker Yoshimoto Takaaki, especially *What is Beauty in Respect of Language?* his classic study of the way literature is manifested as a linguistic construct.[3] I refer to Yoshimoto's work and this specific book in Chapter 3, in discussing the poetry of Yosano Akiko. The analysis in Chapter 2 of Akiko's revolution in poetry is equally a study of the poetics of language, and like much of the discussion accompanying the close readings carried out in the preceding chapters, it is informed by Yoshimoto's hermeneutics.

Through a close reading of Akiko's verse, both in *Tangled Hair* and in her writing on childbirth, it is possible to discern a much larger project. The reason later generations took up Akiko as a pioneer feminist is precisely because of the new sensibility created in her works, especially in her poetry. The sensibility

Akiko invented was that of a new kind of Japanese woman, who required a partner different from the traditional Japanese male. Her invention of a female subjectivity that did not exist in prior Japanese literature was of immense importance not only for literature and for Japanese women but also for the political and social progress of Japan as a modern state. This is not easily demonstrated on the macro scale of history or social analysis, but it was and is obvious to any reader of Akiko's verse, and it is only in an analysis of the poetry that such a realization is possible.

The discussion of the gothic in the following two chapters is equally a product of a close reading, a careful stylistic analysis of the text under discussion. As numerous critics have demonstrated—critics of the stature of Hashimoto Yōichirō, Yamamoto Masahide, Noguchi Takehiko, Senuma Shigeki, Kamei Hideo, Leslie Fielder, and especially Peter Brooks—it is at the level of language—the rhetoric of expression so to speak—in the poetics of lexical and grammatical choice that gothic and melodramatic excess come into being. The implications of gothic melodrama for criticism of the existing social order have long been taken for granted, and they still exist today, as the frequent revivals of Shakespeare's most lurid, bloody dramas—*Titus Andronicus* and *Coriolanus*—make manifest.[4] The twentieth century was by common consent the bloodiest of centuries, so it is not surprising that those who survived the century have a taste for art that is no less dramatic.

The fiction of Izumi Kyōka and Tanizaki Jun'ichirō is still read in Japan today. Just as Kyōka's plays are frequently the subject of cinematic adaptation in contemporary Japan, and translations of Tanizaki's works increase every year, so the relevance and contemporaneity of these two most gothic authors become evident. It is their language, above all, that holds their audience in thrall. Interest in Arishima Takeo has not been revived in the twenty-first century to an equivalent extent, despite the odd book and film documenting his secret romance with Yosano Akiko.[5] It may be Arishima's fate to remain a writer's writer—he has long been a favorite author of many Japanese writers from Miyamoto Yuriko to Tanizaki himself. But this does not lessen his significance as a practitioner of gothic fiction or his importance to later Japanese writers.

It is impossible to read, understand, or appreciate Ōshiro Tatsuhiro's fiction without being aware of his Okinawan identity. Okinawa penetrates the deepest levels—the levels of metaphor, idiom, and diction—of Ōshiro's writing, not to mention his subject matter. The alien nature of Okinawan dialects cannot be ignored, for without the bracketed translations into the standard Tokyo dialect that Ōshiro provides, much of his dialogue could only be understood by Okinawan readers. His language directly confronts non-Okinawan readers who know only standard Japanese; it stares them in the face, so to speak. His subject matter is no less exotic, with shamans and mantic women at the center of the novels examined in Chapters 6 and 7. The larger project that Ōshiro is engaged in—the very essence of postcolonial writing—is obvious to any reader, even in translation, but the foreign or alien aspects of his prose are apparent only if read in the original.

The last chapter first discusses the travel diary genre because of the very complexity of this variety of nonfiction. The colonial project is often seen through the lens of travel writers like V. S. Naipaul, but the representation of colonialism in such works requires careful, close reading. For a question arises: who is saying all these things? Who is observing the society under investigation? The outsider who narrates the travel diary is always a contradictory figure—a version of the author no doubt, but how much of this authorial construct is fictional? This question calls into doubt the very notion of truth itself, as I have tried to make clear in my discussion. Chapter 8 raises questions in another direction as well, since this particular reader of Murakami's *Sydney Diary* is Sydney born and bred. As such, I constitute a tiny minority of the readership of Murakami's book, and was certainly not the reader the author envisioned or, to borrow Wayne Booth's notion, was created by the text.[6] What significance does this have for a reading of Murakami's travel diary?

This question and many others arise naturally from a reading of the *Sydney Diary*, which is, in the very capable hands of Murakami Haruki, a work of considerable power and some mystery. On my reading, the ostensible subject of the diary—Australians and their society—is less mysterious, perhaps even less alien, than its author, who has constructed at the very least a double narrative. This is often the case with writers who engage in writing the Other, for the ultimate Other is oneself: a creature the greatest of authors have sought in various fictions, and in nonfiction as well, but who may be the most elusive alien of all.

NOTES

Introduction

Epigraphs: Collins, "The Blues," *The Art of Drowning,* 91; Smith, from "Portrait (2)," *The Collected Poems,* 121.

1. Sansom, *The Western World and Japan,* 172–179.

2. Figal, *Civilization and Monsters,* 33.

3. Sansom, *The Western World and Japan.*

4. Silverberg, *Erotic Grotesque Nonsense,* 122–142; see also, on the "foreign," 227–230.

5. On the process of relativizing the self in the modern Japanese novel, see Fowler, *The Rhetoric of Confession;* Hijiya-Kirschnereit, *Rituals of Self-Revelation;* and Suzuki Tomi, *Narrating the Self.*

6. Oguma Eiji is representative of this trend among historians, although Oguma prefers the description of "sociologist." For this type of analysis, see Oguma, *"Nihonjin" no kyōkai.* For literature, see Komori, *Yuragi no Nihon bungaku.*

7. The best book on ethical criticism of texts is Booth, *The Company We Keep.*

8. On this aspect of writing, see Booth, *The Rhetoric of Fiction;* and for Japanese literature, see Suzuki Tomi, *Narrating the Self.*

9. Maeda, *Text and the City;* and Kamei, *Transformations of Sensibility.* Kamei's most recent book in Japanese which pursues the same kind of analysis is *Meiji bungakushi* (2000).

10. Tsuruta, *The Walls Within.*

11. Hutchinson and Williams, *Representing the Other.*

12. Napier, *The Fantastic in Modern in Japanese Literature,* 40–45, 54–55, 130–132.

13. My reading of Yanagita is available in Morton, *Modern Japanese Culture,* 54–103.

14. See, for instance, Becker, *Gothic Forms of Feminine Fictions;* and Spooner, *Contemporary Gothic.*

15. Tanizaki, *Sasameyuki,* pp. 46–54; *The Makioka Sisters,* 69–72.

Chapter 1: Translating the Alien

Epigraphs: Mahon, "The Last of the Fire Kings," in *The Penguin Book of Contemporary British Poetry,* 75; Simic, "The Infinitely Forked Mother Tongue," in *Translations: Experiments in Reading,* 33.

1. Hirakawa, *Japan's Love-Hate Relationship with the West,* 100.

2. Mertz, *Novel Japan,* 101–118.

3. Ibid., 104.

4. Zwicker, *Practices of the Sentimental Imagination,* 166.

5. For details of the "German Shakespeare," see Steiner, *After Babel,* 381–392; and Dennis Kennedy, "Shakespeare Worldwide."

6. Brandon, "Some Shakespeare(s) in Some Asia(s)," 3.

7. Ibid.

8. Ibid., 7.

9. Ibid., 9.

10. Ibid., 12.

11. Ibid., 18–19.

12. Niranjana, *Siting Translation,* 34.

13. Ibid., p. 46. On Bhabha's notion of hybridity, see further Loomba, *Colonialism/Postcolonialism,* 176–181.

14. Bhabha, *The Location of Culture,* 327.

15. Walter Benjamin, "The Task of the Translator."

16. Kennedy, "Shakespeare Worldwide," 262.

17. Ibid.

18. Ibid., 262–263.

19. Minami, Carruthers, and Gillies, eds., *Performing Shakespeare in Japan,* 112–146 passim, 196–220.

20. Ibid., 206, 208.

21. Steiner, *After Babel,* 395–396.

22. One major English-language study of Tsubouchi Shōyō as a novelist exists, Ryan's *The Development of Realism in the Fiction of Tsubouchi Shōyō,* but this book does not deal with Shōyō's activities as a translator of Shakespeare. Henceforth, following Japanese practice, I will use the literary sobriquet "Shōyō" to refer to Tsubouchi Shōyō, whose actual given name was Yūzō.

23. Brandon, "Some Shakespeare(s) in Some Asia(s)," 7.

24. Miller, "Tsubouchi Shōyō," 240–241.

25. Honma, "Tsubouchi Shōyō," 1342. See also, Keene, *Dawn to the West,* vol. 1, 98.

26. For a representative essay on aesthetics by Shōyō, see "Bi to wa nani zo ya" (1886), translated under the title "What is Beauty" by Michele Marra in his *Modern Japanese Aesthetics,* 48–65.

27. Miller, "Tsubouchi Shōyō," 242–243.

28. Ōmura, *Tsubouchi Shōyō*, 80–141 passim; Miller, "Tsubouchi Shōyō," 244–245.

29. Shōyō also played a pivotal role as a theoretician of the novel. For details, see Ryan, *Japan's First Modern Novel*. He was also a mentor to Futabatei Shimei (1864–1909), the "father" of the modern literary style; for details on Futabatei's role in the development of the modern style, see Cockerill, *Style and Narrative in Translations*.

30. For details on Shōyō's activities as a dramatist, see Keene, *Dawn to the West*, vol. 2, 410–417; and Poulton, *Spirits of Another Sort*, 94–101.

31. Miller, "Tsubouchi Shōyō," 245.

32. Ibid., 246.

33. Milward, "Shakespeare in Japanese Translation," 190.

34. Ibid.

35. Ōmura, *Tsubouchi Shōyō*, 281–283.

36. Ibid., 283.

37. Steiner, *After Babel*, 294.

38. Ibid., 296, 298.

39. Ibid.

40. Ibid., 382.

41. Ibid., 300.

42. For details, see Loomba, "Outsiders in Shakespeare's England"; also R. S. White, "Shakespeare Criticism in the Twentieth Century."

43. Nishihara, *Tanizaki Jun'ichirō to orientarizumu*.

44. Said, *Orientalism*.

45. Steiner, *After Babel*, 392–393.

46. Heidegger, "Language," 190.

47. Gadamer, *Truth and Method*, 293–294.

48. Venuti, *The Translator's Invisibility*, 17–19.

49. Paul Ricoeur's words are particularly apposite: "In order to reach the final untranslatable, the one translation produces, it is necessary to say how translation works, because *there is translation*." Ricoeur, *On Translation*, 32. For a fine demonstration of how to translate, see Baker, *In Other Words*.

50. Venuti, *The Translator's Invisibility*, 19–20. Zhang, *Unexpected Affinities*.

51. Venuti, *The Translator's Invisibility*, 20.

52. Tsubouchi Shōyō, *Shōyō senshū*, supplementary vol. 2, 301–302.

53. See, for example, Suzuki Yukio, "Hon'yaku."

54. Tsubouchi Shōyō, *Shōyō senshū*, supplementary vol. 3, 683–688.

55. Ibid., vol.12, 654–655. Morita Shiken (1861–1897) was a well-known Meiji critic. The *Kojiki* (Record of ancient matters) is generally recognized as the oldest Japanese "book." Presented to the Japanese court in 712, it is written in a complex mixture of ancient Japanese and Chinese that is exceedingly difficult to decipher.

56. Tsubouchi Shōyō, *Shōyō senshū*, vol. 12, 657–658.

57. Ibid., 659.

58. Ibid., vol. 5, 579–80.

59. Ibid., 581–582.

60. Ibid., 583.

61. Ibid., 585–586. A recent study that discusses *genbun itchi* is Tomasi, *Rhetoric in Modern Japan*. See also his "Quest for a New Written Language," 333–361.

62. Tsubouchi Shōyō, *Shōyō senshū*, vol. 5, 586–587.

63. Ibid., 588.

64. Ibid., 590.

65. Ibid., supplementary vol. 5, 1166.

66. Ibid., 1167.

67. Kawatake, *Sakigakeru monotachi no keifu*, 52–91 passim.

68. Fujimura, ed., *Nihon bungakushi jiten*, see "Gaikoku bungaku to no kōsho," 889.

69. Okazaki, ed., *Meiji bunka shi*, vol. 7, 404.

70. Tsubouchi Shōyō, *Shōyō senshū*, supplementary vol. 5, 283. Wirgman's text is reprinted in Kawato and Sakakibara, eds., *Sheikusupia Shū* 1.

71. Kawatake, *Nihon no Hamuretto*, 47–67.

72. Robun's complete text is reprinted in Kawato and Sakakibara, eds., *Sheikusupia Shū* 1.

73. Fujimura, ed., *Nihon bungakushi jiten*, see "Gaikoku bungaku to no kōsho," 889; Milward, "Shakespeare in Japanese Translation," 189.

74. Odagiri, ed., *Nihon kindai bungaku daijiten*, see "Kawashima Keizō," 433.

75. Kawato and Sakakibara, eds., *Sheikusupia Shū* 1, 14; Kawatake, *Sakigakeru monotachi no keifu*, 82–83.

76. Kawato and Sakakibara, eds., *Sheikusupia Shū* 1, 13–14.

77. Kawatake, *Sakigakeru monotachi no keifu*, 83–84.

78. Inoue's translation is available in Yoshino, ed., *Meiji Bunka Zenshū*, vol. 14, 312–330.

79. Kawamura Jirō, *Hon'yaku no nihongo*, 256–257; Minami, Carruthers, and Gillies, eds., *Performing Shakespeare in Japan*, 21, 38. The complete text of the Kabuki play is reprinted in Kawato and Sakakibara, eds., *Sheikusupia Shū* 1.

80. Kawato and Sakakibara Takanori, eds., *Sheikusupia Shū* 1; Kawatake, *Sakigakeru monotachi*, 85.

81. Kawatake, *Sakigakeru monotachi*, 79–81.

82. Kawatake, *Nihon no Hamuretto*, 104–109.

83. In the commentary *(kaisetsu)* in Kawato and Sakakibara Takanori, eds., *Sheikusupia Shū* 1, 327.

84. Itō Sei, *Nihon bundanshi*, vol. 1, 233–235.

85. Shakespeare, *The Riverside Shakespeare*, 1118.

86. Tsubouchi Shōyō, *Shōyō senshū*, supplementary vol. 2, 363.

87. Tsubouchi Shōyō, *Shōyō senshū*, vol. 5, 86.

88. Tsubouchi Shōyō, *Shēkusupia zenshū*, 821.

89. Nakamura Kan, *Tsubouchi Shōyō ron*, 66–72.

90. Ibid., 73–77.

91. Ibid., 74.

92. Levy, *Sirens of the Western Shore*, 211.

93. Ibid., 212.

94. Ibid.

95. Kinoshita, *Gikyoku no nihongo*, 153.

96. Itō Sei, *Nihon bundanshi*, vol. 1, 184.

97. Shakespeare, *The Riverside Shakespeare*, 1160

98. Itō Sei, *Nihon bundanshi*, vol. 1, 184–185.

99. Itō Sei, *Nihon bundanshi*, vol. 1, 185. Kawatake, *Sakigakeru monotachi*, 78–80. Kawatake, *Nihon no Hamuretto*, 106–108.

100. Itō Sei, *Nihon bundanshi*, vol. 1, 185.

101. Kawatake, *Nihon no Hamuretto*, 108.

102. Itō Sei, *Nihon bundanshi*, vol. 1, 185.

103. See the annotated version of *A Collection of Poems in the New Style* available in Yasuda, *Meiji Taishō yaku shishū*, 59–103.

104. Robert Morrell, "A Selection of New Style Verse," 21.

105. Kawatake, *Nihon no Hamuretto*, 34.

106. See the exhaustive list of Shōyō's writings in Shōyō Kyōkai, ed., *Tsubouchi Shōyō jiten*, 477, 483.

107. Kawatake, *Nihon no Hamuretto*, 150–154.

108. Ibid., p. 194, 290. Kawatake, *Sakigakeru monotachi*, 115–118.

109. Tsubouchi Shōyō, *Shaō zenshū*, vol. 1, 110.

110. Tsubouchi Shōyō, trans., *Shēkusupia zenshū*, 852.

111. Shēkusupia, *Hamuretto*, 142.

112. Kinoshita, *Gikyoku no nihongo*, 161.

113. Nakamura Kan, *Tsubouchi Shōyō ron*, 215.

114. Ibid., 213–227.

115. Shakespeare, *The Riverside Shakespeare*, 1160.

116. Tsubouchi Shōyō, *Shaō zenshū*, vol. 1, 113–114.

117. Tsubouchi Shōyō, trans., *Shēkusupia zenshū*, 852.

118. Tsubouchi Shikō, *Tsubouchi Shōyō kenkyū*, 183.

119. Kinoshita, *Gikyoku no nihongo*, 157.

120. Shakespeare, *The Riverside Shakespeare*, 9.

121. Milward, "Shakespeare in Japanese Translation," 195.

122. Ibid.

123. Kawatake, *Sakigakeru monotachi*, 114–116.

124. On the political dimensions of translation, see further Schäffner, "Politics and Translation," 134–148.

125. Milward, "Shakespeare in Japanese Translation," 207.

126. Apter, *The Translation Zone*, xi. Some scholars have reservations about the impact of translations on Meiji writing; see Zwicker, *Practices of the Sentimental Imagination*, for a different perspective. Leith Morton examines the process of how *ninjōbon* (sentimental fiction), a genre of premodern Japanese literature, influenced the modern novel in "19 Seikimatsu."

127. Apter, *The Translation Zone*, xii.

Chapter 2: Naturalizing the Alien

Epigraphs: Stein, "Poetry and Grammar," in *Look at Me Now and Here I Am*, 142–143. Ashbery, *Flow Chart*, 54.

1. See Yoda, *Gender and National Literature*, for examples of the veneration of *waka*. On the spiritual nature of *waka*, see Okano, "Uta no tanjō," 166–167; and Furuhashi, *Man'yōshū*, 46–54.

2. For an analysis of this topic, see LaMarre, *Uncovering Heian Japan*, 30–41.

3. For examples of some reactions, see Morton, "The Canonization of Yosano Akiko's *Midaregami*," 237–254.

4. Eliot, "Tradition and the Individual Talent," 71.

5. Ibid., 72.

6. Ibid.

7. Translation taken from Keene, *Dawn To the West*, 14; the original can be found in Hisamatsu, ed., *Ochiai Naobumi*, 37.

8. Miyoshi Yukio, *Nihon bungaku shi jiten [Kin gendai hen]*, 178, 182–186. See also Okano Hirohiko, "Kyūha waka to waka kairyō no iyoku."

9. Quoted in Ōta Seikyū, "Shintaishi no shigeki to waka kakushin," 39–40.

10. Miyoshi, *Nihon bungaku shi jiten [Kin gendai hen]*, 182–185.

11. Ōta Seikyū, "Shintaishi no shigeki to waka kakushin," 39–40.

12. Ibid., 39.

13. Ibid.

14. For more details of this process, see Morton, *Modernism in Practice*, 11–33.

15. Quoted Yano, *Tekkan Akiko to sono jidai*, 229.

16. Yosano Tekkan, "Yosano Hiroshi Shū," 48.

17. Naka, *Yosano Tekkan*, 80–81; Sunaga, *Tekkan to Akiko*, 52–53.

18. Quoted Sunaga, *Tekkan to Akiko*, 52–54.

19. *Myōjō* 1 (Apr. 1900): 1.

20. Yasumori, "*Midaregami* no sekai," 81.

21. *Myōjō* 6 (Sept. 1900): 68.

22. Yosano Akiko, *Teihon zenshū*, vol. 1, 199–302.

23. Quoted in Itsumi, *Hyōden*, 145; cf. Beichman, "Yosano Akiko: The Early Years," 37–54; Beichman, "Yosano Akiko: Return to the Female," 204–228.

24. Numerous translations of the poetry from *Tangled Hair* exist. One older version is that translated by Shio Sakanishi and another is by Sanford Goldstein and Seishi Shinoda, each entitled *Tangled Hair*. Recent translations include that by Sam Hamill and Keiko Matsui Gibson entitled *River of Stars*; see also Morton, *Yosano Akiko no* Midaregami *wo eigo de ajiwau.*

25. Itsumi, *Midaregami zenshaku*, 27.

26. Yosano Akiko, *Tekkan Akiko zenshū*, vol. 2, 122.

27. Yosano Akiko, *Teihon zenshū*, vol. 1, 308.

28. Ibid., 309.

29. Bloom, *The Anxiety of Influence*, 7.

30. Ibid., 91.

31. Ibid.

32. Itsumi, *Hyōden*, 148; Nishio, *Ai to bungaku*, 136; Cranston, "Young Akiko," 19–43. "Kansai" refers to the Western region of Japan, where the cities of Sakai, Kobe, Kyoto, and Osaka are located.

33. Yosano Akiko, *Teihon zenshū*, vol. 9, 305.

34. Morishima, "Sono Meijiki no Shisaku," 17; Yoneda, "Akiko," 44–57; Shimazaki, *Tōson zenshū*, vol. 1, 10.

35. Shimazaki, *Tōson zenshū*, vol. 1, 10; Morita, "Shimazaki Tōson's Four Collections of Poems," 330 [modified].

36. Shimazaki, *Tōson zenshū*, vol. 1, 10–11; Morita, "Shimazaki Tōson's Four Collections of Poems," 330 [modified].

37. Morita, "Shimazaki Tōson's Four Collections of Poems," 327; cf. Morton, "The Concept of Romantic Love," 94–96.

38. Strong, "Passion and Patience," 178–179; cf. Cranston, "The Dark Path," 60–100.

39. Yosano Akiko, *Teihon zenshū*, vol. 9, 305–306.

40. Ibid., 306–308

41. McCullough, *Brocade by Night*, 456–457.

42. Bloom, *The Anxiety of Influence*, 16.

43. *Yoshinashigusa* 13 (Apr. 1899): 38.

44. Shimazaki, *Tōson zenshū*, vol. 1, 62, 266–267; cf Morita, "Shimazaki Tōson's Four Collections of Poems," 334–335, 363–364.

45. Nakanishi, *Man'yōshū*, vol. 1, 335; cf. Levy, *The Ten Thousand Leaves*, 1981, vol. 1, 317.

46. Hisamatsu, *Ochiai Naobumi*, 94.

47. Yosano Akiko, *Tekkan Akiko zenshū*, vol. 2, 104.

48. Ibid., 214.

49. Baba, *Yosano Akiko no shūka*, 36–37; Yoneda, "Akiko," 47–53.

50. For a different perspective on *kami,* see Konno, 24 *no kiiwādo de yomu Yosano Akiko,* 163–170.

51. Yosano Akiko, *Tekkan Akiko zenshū,* vol. 2, 59.

52. *Myōjō* 15 (Sept. 1901): 65–66.

53. Haga, *Midaregami no keifu,* 22–40.

54. *Yoshiashigusa* 13 (Apr. 1899): 38.

55. Itsumi, *Shin Midaregami zenshaku,* 325–326.

56. Yosano Akiko, *Tekkan Akiko zenshū,* vol. 2, 122.

57. Quoted in Yano, *Tekkan Akiko to sono jidai,* 234.

58. Noda, "Susukida Kyūkin shū kaisetsu," 30.

59. Yano, *Doi Bansui,* 105.

60. Yosano Akiko, *Tekkan Akiko zenshū,* vol. 2, 90.

61. Yano, *Doi Bansui,* 107.

62. Yosano Akiko, *Tekkan Akiko zenshū,* vol. 2, 116.

63. Yano, *Doi Bansui,* 113.

64. Yano, *Tekkan Akiko to sono jidai,* 235.

65. Yosano Akiko, *Tekkan Akiko zenshū,* vol. 2, 82.

66. Morton, "Akiko, Tomiko and Hiroshi," 35–49.

67. Eliot, "Tradition and the Individual Talent," 73.

68. Bloom, *The Anxiety of Influence,* 14–15, 139–142.

69. Ōoka, "Nihon no shiika to Yosano Akiko," 12–18.

70. On the poetry of Nakajō Fumiko, see Kawamura Hatsue and Reichhold, *Breasts of Snow;* and Hiromi Taki, "Grief at the Loss of My Breasts," 156–169. For Tawara Machi, see Strong, "Passion and Patience"; and Tawara, *Salad Anniversary.*

71. Yosano Akiko, *Tekkan Akiko zenshū,* vol. 2, 79.

72. Ibid., 3–6.

73. Tekkan quoted in Satake, *Zenshaku,* 1–4; cf. Itsumi, *Shin Midaregami zenshaku,* 4.

74. Tekkan's rewording cited by Itsumi, *Shin Midaregami zenshaku,* 4.

75. Cited by Itsumi, *Midaregami zenshaku,* 4–5.

76. Ibid., 219–220.

77. Isoda, *Rokumeikan no keifu,* p. 140; Yasukawa Yukiko, ed., *Midaregami,* 94.

78. *Myōjō* 2 (May 1900): 2; Isoda, *Rokumeikan no keifu,* 141.

79. Yosano Akiko, *Teihon zenshū,* vol. 1, 317.

80. Quoted in Isoda, *Rokumeikan no keifu,* 143; cf. Haga *Midaregami no keifu,* 24–44.

81. Isoda, *Rokumeikan no keifu,* 148.

82. Kimata, "Tōson no romanchishizumu," 109–111.

83. Seki Ryōichi, "Chūshaku *Wakanashū,*" 49–185.

84. Cranston, "Carmine-Purple," 91.

85. Isoda, *Rokumeikan no keifu,* 137–138.

86. Ōtomo, *Goji sōsakuin*, 125.

87. Ibid., 31–32, 41–42, 115.

88. Yosano Akiko, *Tekkan Akiko zenshū*, vol. 2, 79.

89. Itsumi, *Shin Midaregami zenshaku*, 7.

90. Haga, *Midaregami no keifu*, 11.

91. Ibid., 11–15.

92. Sunaga, *Tekkan to Akiko*, 97–102.

93. Satake, *Zenshaku*, 111; Teruoka and Kawashima, eds., *Buson shū Issa shū*, 195.

94. Yosano Akiko, *Tekkan Akiko zenshū*, vol. 2, 90.

95. Itsumi, *Shin Midaregami zenshaku*, 118.

96. Quoted in Satake, *Zenshaku*, 19.

97. Ehara and Shimizu, eds., *Yosano Buson shū*, 149.

98. Satake, *Zenshaku*, 19.

99. Yosano Akiko, *Tekkan Akiko zenshū*, vol. 2, 80.

100. Ibid., 81.

101. Haga, *Midaregami no keifu*, 15–33.

102. Freud, *The Interpretation of Dreams*, 193–198.

103. Shinma, *Yosano Akiko,* 126–135; Ozaki, "Akiko to koten," 40.

104. Minemura, *Shinkokinwakashū*, 68.

105. Tanaka Yutaka and Akase, eds., *Shinkokinwakashū*, 405.

106. Kubota and Hirata, eds., *Goshūiwakashū*, 405.

107. Itsumi, *Midaregami zenshaku*, 503.

108. Itsumi, "Akiko tanka to koten," 147–150; Ozaki, "Akiko to koten," 53; Matsuura, "Akiko no Izumi Shikibu," 146–192; Taketomo, "Yosano Akiko to Izumi Shikibu," 3–19.

109. Ozaki, "Akiko to koten," 42–46; Shinma, "Yosano Akiko to *Genji Monogatari*," 158–167; Ichikawa, "Reading *Genji*," 157–174.

110. Quoted in Haga, *Midaregami no keifu*, 15.

111. Shinma, *Yosano Akiko,* 122–129.

112. Nakanishi, *Man'yōshū*, vol. 3, 59.

113. Ibid., vol. 1, 111.

114. Yosano Akiko, *Tekkan Akiko zenshū*, vol. 2, 82.

115. Ibid., 109.

116. Shimazaki, *Tōson zenshū*, vol. 1, 12–13.

117. *Myōjō* 6 (Sept. 1900): 68.

118. Nagata, "Tanka kakushin no shinsenryaku," 97–112.

119. Ibid., 103.

120. Ibid., 101–103.

121. Cf. Morton, "Yosano Akiko to kindai no ren'ai," 122–132.

Chapter 3: The Demon Within

Epigraphs: Kristeva, *Tales of Love,* 254–255. Notley, *From a Work in Progress,* 23.

1. Watanabe Sumiko, in her biography of Akiko entitled *Yosano Akiko* (140), notes that for women to write about the pain of childbirth was regarded as shameful, and Yamamoto Chie, in her biography of Akiko entitled *Yama no ugoku hi* (74), writes of how men at the time regarded women as unclean because of their association with blood.

2. William LaFleur notes that "[t]he whole ideology of the period [early Meiji era] was bent on producing a sense of motherhood that would make women feel a kind of sacred, patriotic obligation to bear all the children they possibly could." LaFleur, *Liquid Life,* 128.

3. Booth, *The Company We Keep,* 239.

4. Ibid., 268.

5. Ibid., 272.

6. Iser, *The Act of Reading.*

7. Quoted in Oguma, *"Minshū" to "aikoku,"* 631.

8. Yoshimoto, *Gengo ni totte bi to wa nanika,* 257.

9. Seki Reiko, *Ichiyō igo no josei hyōgen,* 47–50. See also Bardsley, *The Bluestockings of Japan.*

10. Yosano Akiko, *Gendai nihon shijin zenshū,* 295.

11. Watanabe, *Yosano Akiko,* 120.

12. Seki Reiko, *Ichiyō igo no josei hyōgen,* 50–53.

13. Quoted in Copeland, *Lost Leaves,* 36.

14. Irie, *Yosano Akiko to sono jidai,* 67–68.

15. Janine Beichman's excellent translation of the poem is available in Rimer and Gessel, *Modern Japanese Literature,* 302–303.

16. For a detailed discussion (and translations of Akiko's poem and other antiwar poetry), see Rabson, "Yosano Akiko on War"; and Rabson, *Righteous Cause or Tragic Folly,* 107–144.

17. Seki Reiko, *Ichiyō igo no josei hyōgen,* 57.

18. Yosano Akiko, *Tekkan Akiko zenshū,* vol. 6, 3.

19. Gluck, *Japan's Modern Myths,* 57.

20. Seki Reiko, *Ichiyō igo no josei hyōgen,* 57.

21. Itsumi, *[Shinpan] Hyōden,* 734. Yamamoto Chie goes further than Itsumi and writes that *From a Nook* is the first collection of essays on women written by a Japanese woman (in the Meiji era). Yamamoto, *Yama no ugoku hi kitaru,* 71.

22. Yosano Akiko, *Tekkan Akiko zenshū,* vol. 6, 55–58.

23. Suzuki Sadami, *Nihon no bunka nashonarizumu,* 136–140. Saeki Shin'ichi, *Senjō no seishinshi,* 244–277.

24. For a detailed discussion of Akiko as national seer, and some of the essays discussed above, see Larson, "Yosano Akiko and the Re-creation of the Female Self."

25. Yosano Akiko, *Tekkan Akiko zenshū*, vol. 6, 85–87.

26. Watanabe, *Yosano Akiko*, 140–151.

27. See Beichman, *Embracing the Firebird*, for a discussion of the female voice.

28. For information on Itō, see Morton, *Modernism in Practice*, 102–112.

29. Yosano Akiko, *Tekkan Akiko zenshū*, vol. 6, 220.

30. Ibid., 57–60, 436–438.

31. Ibid., 220.

32. Ibid.

33. Notehelfer, *Kotoku Shusui*, 152–183. See also Keene, *Emperor of Japan*, 679–692.

34. Yosano Akiko, *Tekkan Akiko zenshū*, vol. 6, 437; Yamamoto, *Yama no ugoku hi kitaru*, 67–71; Irie, *Yosano Akiko to sono jidai*, 89–96.

35. Yosano Akiko, *Tekkan Akiko zenshū*, vol. 6, 220.

36. Hirako, *Yosano Akiko no uta kanshō*, 40–41.

37. Yosano Akiko, *Tekkan Akiko zenshū*, vol. 6, 221.

38. Ibid.

39. Ibid.

40. Ibid.

41. Ibid.

42. Dodane, *Yosano Akiko*, 195.

43. Baba, *Yosano Akiko no shūka*, 177.

44. Yosano Akiko, *Tekkan Akiko zenshū*, vol. 6, 221.

45. Soh, *Moeru haha* (note that "Soh" was the poet's preferred romanization); Morton, *Modernism in Practice*, 35–83. The image of the demon symbolizes the guilt that Soh experienced as a result of his mother dying in the firebombing of Tokyo in 1945.

46. Yosano Akiko, *Tekkan Akiko zenshū*, vol. 6, 221.

47. Baba, *Yosano Akiko no shūka*, 177–178.

48. Yosano Akiko, *Tekkan Akiko zenshū*, vol. 6, 221.

49. Ibid., 222.

50. Baba, *Yosano Akiko no shūka*, 179.

51. Yosano Akiko, *Tekkan Akiko zenshū*, vol. 6, 222.

52. Ibid.

53. Ibid.

54. Ibid.

55. Ibid.

56. Baba, *Yosano Akiko no shūka*, 178.

57. Yosano Akiko, *Tekkan Akiko zenshū*, vol. 6, 222.

58. Ibid.

59. Ibid., 223.

60. Ibid.

61. Ibid.

62. For other fine translations of some of these texts, see Dodane, *Yosano Akiko*, 189–207; and Beichman, "Yosano Akiko: Return to the Female," 218–226.

63. Shinma, *Yosano Akiko*, 201.

64. For a study of the romantic portrayal of the self in *Tangled Hair*, see Morton, "*Midaregami Shiroyuri* no kenkyū." For a study of the key issues, see Chanfrault-Duchet, "Textualisation of the self and gender identity in the life-story."

65. Quoted in Tsubouchi Toshinori, "Tanshikeibungaku no tenkai," 35. On Shiki and *shasei*, see Beichman, *Masaoka Shiki*, 54–73, 104–115.

66. Tsubouchi Toshinori, "Tanshikeibungaku no tenkai," 35.

67. Senuma, *Taishō bungakushi*, 147.

68. Ibid., 148. A more detailed consideration of the connection between *Araragi* and these figures can be found in Tanaka Junji, "Shoki *Araragi* shaseisetsu."

69. Quoted in Tsubouchi Toshinori, "Tanshikeibungaku no tenkai," 36–37.

70. This has been pointed out by a number of literary historians. Some representative studies of Japanese Naturalism in English are: Suzuki Tomi, *Narrating the Self*, 48–93; Hijiya-Kirschnereit, *Rituals of Self-Revelation*, 21–57; Fowler, *The Rhetoric of Confession*, 93–145; Homma, *The Literature of Naturalism*; Sibley, "Naturalism in Japanese Literature"; and Benl, "Naturalism in Japanese Literature."

71. Senuma, *Taishō bungakushi*, 149–151.

72. Quoted in Michiura Motoko, *Onnauta no hyakunen*, 83.

73. Ibid., 78.

74. Ibid., 84.

75. Ibid., 82.

76. Akitsu, *Nihon josei bungakushi*, 74.

77. Watanabe, "Shōsetsu," 56.

78. Itsumi, *[Shinpan] Hyōden*, 733.

79. Ibid., 735.

80. Ibid., 737. Yosano Akiko, *Tekkan Akiko zenshū*, vol. 6, 103.

81. Yosano Akiko, *Tekkan Akiko zenshū*, vol. 6, 6.

82. Ibid.

83. Itsumi, *[Shinpan] Hyōden*, 736.

Chapter 4: The Gothic Novel

Epigraphs: Palmer, from "Letter 7," *At Passages*, 10. Hayden, from "Runagate, Runagate, *Collected Poems*, 59.

1. Paglia, *Sexual Personae*, 265–269; Jackson, *Fantasy*, 95–122; Mussell, *Women's Gothic and Romantic Fiction*; Thompson, *The Gothic Imagination*; Sage, *The Gothick Novel*.

2. Hashimoto, *Tanizaki Jun'ichirō no bungaku,* 23–36.

3. Snyder, *Fictions of Desire.*

4. This argument has recently been put forward in several works: Nishihara, *Tanizaki Jun'ichirō to orientarizumu;* Ken Ito, *Visions of Desire,* 30–51; Komori, *Yuragi no Nihon bungaku,* 199–227.

5. Noguchi, *Shōsetsu no nihongo,* 197–219.

6. Quoted in Sage, *The Gothick Novel,* 139.

7. Inouye, "Introduction," 2–4.

8. Izumi, *Izumi Kyōka shūsei,* vol. 1, 357–373. A translation of this work by Charles Inouye is available in Izumi, *Japanese Gothic Tales,* 11–21.

9. Keene, *Dawn to the West,* vol. 2, 210.

10. Kasahara, "Kyōkateki bi no hōhō," 50–52; Yoshida Masashi, "Izumi Kyōka to kusazōshi," 172–186.

11. Matsubara, "Kyōka bungaku to minkan denshō," 203–216.

12. Katsumoto, "Kyōka no ishinzō," 4.

13. Carpenter, "Izumi Kyōka"; Poulton, "The Grotesque and the Gothic"; and Charles Inouye, "Introduction." Note also Charles Inouye, *The Similitude of Blossoms.*

14. Jackson, *Fantasy,* 56.

15. Ibid., 64.

16. Freud, *The Standard Edition,* vol. 17, 249.

17. Izumi, *Izumi Kyōka shūsei,* vol. 4, 63–135. A translation of this work by Charles Inouye is available in Izumi, *Japanese Gothic Tales,* 21–73.

18. Mishima, "Izumi Kyōka," 25.

19. Quoted Miyoshi, "Izumi Kyōka o megutte," 23.

20. Kawamura Jirō, "Dōshisareta kūkan," 137.

21. Izumi, *Izumi Kyōka shūsei,* vol. 4, 82–83.

22. Jackson, *Fantasy,* 124.

23. Quoted ibid., 68.

24. Izumi, *Izumi Kyōka shūsei,* vol. 4, 84.

25. Ibid.

26. A study that links Kyōka's use of motifs arising both from late Edo writing and Wilde is Iwasa, "Shisei," 84–86.

27. Noguchi, *Shōsetsu no nihongo,* 218.

28. Higashi Masao, "Mashō to Seisei," 407. Higashi writes that out of the 300 or so stories and novels Kyōka wrote, two-thirds were tales of the supernatural (401–402).

29. A lecture on this subject by Tanaka Reigi, a professor at Dōshisha University in Kyoto, can be found at the following Internet site: //rakurakucampus.jp/basis/hst_0312.html. See also Tanaka, "Murasaki shoji," 128–147.

30. Izumi, *Izumi Kyōka shū,* 163.

31. Cornyetz, *Dangerous Women, Deadly Words,* 37.

32. Izumi, *Izumi Kyōka shū*, 88.

33. For information on Kyōka's relationship with the Naturalist movement, see Muramatsu, *Izumi Kyōka*, 212–251.

34. For a lengthy quotation from Kyōka's essay, entitled "Romanchikku to shizenshugi" (The Romantic and Naturalism), see Muramatsu, *Izumi Kyōka*, 217–218. Gerald Figel discusses this and one or two other essays that Kyōka wrote on Naturalism in *Civilization and Monsters*, 158–166.

35. Izumi, *Izumi Kyōka shū*, 148–149.

36. Ibid., 157–158.

37. Charles Inouye, *The Similitude of Blossoms*, 288. Muramatsu makes a similar comment, but notes that this is because of the dominance of the Naturalist mode of fiction; see his *Izumi Kyōka*, 247.

38. Izumi, *Izumi Kyōka shū*, 96.

39. Ibid., 103–104.

40. Ibid., 135–136.

41. Ibid., 140.

42. Ibid., 150.

43. Ibid., 163.

44. See Jackson, *Fantasy*, 121, for a discussion of the politics of gothic fiction, and also various essays on the gothic and politics in Punter, *A Companion to the Gothic*.

45. For the connections between Tanizaki and Wilde, see Yoshida, *Tanbi-ha sakka ron*, 176–177.

46. Ibid., 176–177; Muramatsu, "Tanizaki Jun'ichirō to Izumi Kyōka," 469. A translation Ivan Morris made of "The Tattooer" is available in Morris, *Modern Japanese Stories*, 90–101; another by Howard Hibbett is available in Tanizaki, *Seven Japanese Tales*, 160–170.

47. Itō Sei, *Tanizaki Jun'ichirō no bungaku*, 34–36.

48. Itō Sei, *Daigyaku jiken zengo*, 199. See also Yoshida Seiichi's account of how Tanizaki admired Kafū (Yoshida, *Nagai Kafū*, 96). Mitsuko Iriye has translated *American Tales* into English; see Nagai, *American Stories*.

49. Nishihara, *Tanizaki Jun'ichirō to orientarizumu*, 81–87.

50. Ibid., 87.

51. Muramatsu, "Tanizaki Jun'ichirō to Izumi Kyōka," 461–462.

52. Charles Inouye, *The Similitude of Blossoms*, 290.

53. Ibid.

54. Ito, *Visions of Desire*, 55.

55. Nishihara, *Tanizaki Jun'ichirō to orientarizumu*, 87.

56. Ibid., 91.

57. Ibid., 90.

58. Tanizaki, *Zenshū*, vol. 1, 63.

59. Ibid., 64–65.

60. Ibid., 68.

61. For reflections on feminism, the gothic, and confinement, see Becker, *Gothic Forms of Feminine Fictions,* 36–39.

62. Tanizaki, *Zenshū,* vol. 1, 69.

63. Ibid., 71–72.

64. *Chijin no ai* has been translated into English under the title of *Naomi* by Anthony Chambers.

65. Matsumura, "Tanizaki Jun'ichirō no seikimatsu," 42. See also Inoue, "Tanizaki Jun'ichirō no seikimatsu," 15, who also describes the work as autobiographical.

66. Tanizaki, *Zenshū,* vol. 2, 405–406.

67. Inoue, "Tanizaki Jun'ichirō no seikimatsu," 15.

68. Matsumura, "Tanizaki Jun'ichirō no seikimatsu to 'mazohizumu,'" 42–43; Chambers, *The Secret Window,* 51–55.

69. Nozaki, *Tanizaki Jun'ichirō to ikoku no gengo.*

70. Thomas LaMarre has recently translated the story under the title "The Tumor with a Human Face" in his book *Shadows on the Screen,* 86–101.

71. Tanizaki, *Zenshū,* vol. 5, 287–288.

72. Ibid., 288–289.

73. Ibid., 291.

74. Tanizaki's story was turned into an actual film in 1982, directed by Takeshi Tetsuji, and was released under the title of *Oiran* (Courtesan).

75. Tanizaki intended to produce a film script of this story so it could be made into a feature film, but that did not eventuate, possibly due to the risk of censorship. It was announced in the film journal *Kinema junpō* in May 1920, and repeated in the next issue, that Tanizaki had been contracted to write the scenario. For details, see Akesaki, "Jinmenso no sasayaki," 2–3.

76. See Keene, *Dawn to the West,* vol. 1, 747–748, for these details and more information on the subject.

77. Nozaki, *Tanizaki Jun'ichirō to ikoku no gengo,* 130–135.

78. Ibid., 137–138. For another discussion of the story, see also Golley, *When Our Eyes No Longer See,* 97–101.

79. Nozaki, *Tanizaki Jun'ichirō to ikoku no gengo,* 145–151; Plato, *Phaedo,* 230.

80. Tanizaki, *Zenshū, v*ol. 5, 301.

81. It is also interesting to note that stage and film versions of Stevenson's novel were common in the decades preceding the publication of Tanizaki's tale.

82. Nozaki, *Tanizaki Jun'ichirō to ikoku no gengo,* 136.

83. Ibid., 142–143. For information on the impact of Freud and Ellis on Japanese literature, see Morton, *Divided Self,* 124, 152–153, 170–173.

84. Nozaki, *Tanizaki Jun'ichirō to ikoku no gengo,* 142–143.

85. Becker, *Gothic Forms of Feminine Fictions,* 56–65.

86. Ibid., 58.

87. Ibid., 59.

88. In *Visions of Desire*, 73, Ken Ito discusses Tanizaki's new ideal of the West and translates a quotation from Tanizaki extolling the new type of female beauty that he espoused at this time.

89. See also on this point Yoshida, *Tanbi-ha sakka ron*, 175–180; and Ōhashi, "Tanizaki to Pō," 434–435. It should be noted here that Arishima was one of Tanizaki's favorite authors and is mentioned in Tanizaki's novel *Naomi*.

Chapter 5: Gothic Stylistics

Epigraphs: Ashbery, *Flow Chart*, 8; Smith, *Collected Poems*, 186.

1. Figel, *Civilization and Monsters*, 218.

2. Ibid.

3. Yamamoto Masahide, *Kindai buntai hassei*, 53–56 passim. Cf. Twine, *Language and the Modern State*, 155–162. All quotations from Arishima are from the *Arishima Takeo zenshū*, hereafter *Works*.

4. Yamamoto, *Kindai buntai hassei*, 53–56 passim. For more information on this school, see Morton, *Divided Self*, 96–99, 135–138; Kohl et al., *The White Birch School;* and Mortimer, *Meeting the Sensei*.

5. Yamamoto, *Kindai buntai hassei*, 53–56 passim.

6. Ibid., 56.

7. Murō Saisei described Arishima's style as *bata-kusai* ("stinking of butter," that is, Western), as quoted in the *Itō Sei zenshū*, vol.19, 225.

8. Quoted in Yasukawa Sadao, *Arishima Takeo ron*, 1–2. Also see Arishima, *A Certain Woman*, 24, n. 43.

9. Nakamura Akira, "Arishima Takeo no buntai," 68–77.

10. Ibid., 69–72.

11. Ibid., 74.

12. Ibid., 68–69, 74–75.

13. Tanizaki, *Bunshō tokuhon*, 50–69. For Arishima's translation-like style, see Uesugi Yoshikazu's comments on the novel *Umareizuru nayami* (The agony brought by birth, 1918) in his *Arishima Takeo*, 228–229.

14. Noguchi, *Shōsetsu no nihongo*, 197–210.

15. Ibid., 199.

16. Ibid., 202–203.

17. Ibid., 207–210. For a study examining Arishima and Hōmei, see Ikari, "Arishima Takeo no kinōteki bungakuron."

18. Ibid., 214–217.

19. Quoted by Niwa, *Arishima Takeo ron*, 121.

20. Ibid., 131.

21. Brooks, *The Melodramatic Imagination*, 16–17. For more conventional treatments of the gothic, see Punter, ed., *A Companion to the Gothic;* and Sage, ed., *The Gothick Novel.*

22. Brooks quoted by Brewster, "Gothic and the Madness of Interpretation," 283.

23. Brooks, *The Melodramatic Imagination*, 19–20.

24. Ibid., ix.

25. Ibid., xiii.

26. Ibid., 9–10.

27. Ibid., 36. For an early expression of the problem of excess in Arishima, see Morton, *Divided Self,* x; on the stories, see Morton, *Divided Self,* 148–156, 127–134. Japanese critics have long been conscious of Arishima's "gothic" or "melodramatic" excesses; see, for example, Nakamura Kogetsu's criticisms of *The Laboratory* (as too sentimental), also Nanbu Shūtarō's and Kanō Sakujirō's criticism of *The Weed Crushed by the Stone* in the *bekkan* (supplementary volume) of Arishima, *Works,* 464, 484–487.

28. Brooks, *The Melodramatic Imagination*, 36.

29. For the details and the original manuscript, see Kindai bungaku kenkyū shiryō sōsho (4), eds. *Arishima Takeo mikan genkō,* especially 81–85.

30. Quoted in Arishima, *Works (bekkan),* 435. For a detailed study of the work and possible connections to Gorky, see Morton "An Introduction to Arishima Takeo," 42–69.

31. Quoted in Arishima, *Works (bekkan),* 456.

32. Morton, "An Introduction to Arishima Takeo."

33. Nishigaki, *Arishima Takeo ron,* 170–172. Uesugi, *Arishima Takeo,* 110–115.

34. Matsumoto, "Kankan mushi ni tsuite," 15.

35. Senuma, "Takeo no buntai nado," 73.

36. Ibid.

37. Nishigaki, *Arishima Takeo ron,* 168. Kikuchi, *Arishima Takeo,* also hints at this possibility (55); Okuda, "Arishima Takeo," 44, 47, 50.

38. Teramoto and Matsuura, *Kindai shōsetsu,* 105. Note that in his discussion Matsuura is referring specifically to the first draft of *Rust-chippers* (set in Yokohama), but in this respect this argument applies to the later version equally well.

39. Ibid., 106, 112.

40. Brooks, *The Melodramatic Imagination*, 171.

41. Arishima, *Works,* vol. 2, 47 (first quote) and 48 (second quote).

42. Ibid., 52 (Chopin) and 60 (Napoleon).

43. Compare Morton, "An Introduction to Arishima Takeo," 58–64, esp. 58.

44. Arishima, *Works,* vol. 2, 61.

45. Brooks, *The Melodramatic Imagination*, 145.

46. Ibid., 144

47. Cody Poulton points out that Kyōka's use of melodrama involved "quasi-realistic social critiques," and in this he resembles Arishima; see Poulton, *Spirits of Another Sort,* 54.

48. An early exploration of some of these ideas can be found in Morton, *Divided Self,* 127–134 *(The Laboratory)* and 148–156 *(The Weed Crushed by the Stone).* Cf. Anderer, *Other Worlds,* 127–128 (for *Jikkenshitsu*).

49. Brooks, *The Melodramatic Imagination,* 19.

50. Arishima, *Works,* vol. 2, 601.

51. Brooks, *The Melodramatic Imagination,* 40.

52. Quoted in Sage, ed., *The Gothick Novel,* 100–108.

53. Arishima, *Works,* vol. 12, 122. Yasuko died just two months later.

54. Ibid., vol. 2., 481.

55. Ibid., 481–482.

56. Ibid., 483.

57. Ibid.

58. Ibid., 484.

59. Ibid.

60. Mizutani, "Umareizuru Nayami ron oboegaki," 52.

61. Nakamura Miharu, "Arishima Takeo," 2, 6–7.

62. Brooks, *The Melodramatic Imagination,* 126.

63. Nakamura Miharu, "'Kain no matsuei,'" 92.

64. Komori, *Kōzō to shite no katari.*

65. De Man, *The Rhetoric of Romanticism,* 9–10.

66. See further Nakamura Miharu, "Kotoba o kaku nowa dare ka," 1–10.

67. Arishima, *Works,* vol. 8, 49. From *Zatsushin issoku* (1921).

Chapter 6: Female Shamans

Epigraphs: Milton, *English Minor Poems,* 25; Blake, *The Norton Anthology,* 504.

1. A pioneering anthology of Okinawan literature was published in 2000, see Molasky and Rabson, *Southern Exposure.*

2. Keene, *Emperor of Japan,* 302.

3. According to Molasky and Rabson, *Southern Exposure,* 20, approximately one-quarter of the prewar population of Okinawa perished in the fighting.

4. The famous Okinawan poet Yamanokuchi Baku commented on this issue in his 1962 essay, "Yoriai setai no shima" (Multicultural islands), 189–191.

5. A recent volume detailing these differences is the Okinawan poet Takara Ben's *Okinawa seikatsushi* (Records of Okinawan life).

6. This novel was translated into English by Steve Rabson in *Okinawa,* 31–79.

7. This essay is found in Ōshiro, *Gushō kara no koe,* 272–276. For further infor-

mation on the nature of *yuta,* see Morton, "*Yuta* as the Postcolonial Other in Ōshiro Tatsuhiro's Fiction," 257–259.

8. Quoted in Okamoto, *Okinawa bungaku no chihei,* 100.

9. Ibid.

10. Ibid.

11. Okinawa Bungaku Zenshū Henshū Iinkai, ed., *Okinawa bungaku zenshū,* vol. 18, 36–38.

12. Frye, "The Archetypes of Literature," 18.

13. Ōshiro, *Gushō kara no koe,* 147–207.

14. Ibid., 148.

15. Ibid., 150.

16. Ibid., 270.

17. Ibid., 184.

18. Ibid.

19. Ibid., 203.

20. Ōshiro, "Kindai Okinawa bungaku to hōgen," 199–209.

21. Ōshiro, *Kōgen wo motomete.*

22. Ibid., 292–293.

23. Ibid., 293.

24. Ibid.

25. Ibid.

26. Frye, "The Archetypes of Literature," 18.

27. Ōshiro, *Gushō kara no koe,* 197.

28. Ibid.

29. Ibid., 205–206.

30. Ibid., 207.

31. Frye, "The Imaginative and the Imaginary," 152.

32. Booth, *The Company We Keep,* 341.

33. Ōshiro, *Kōgen wo motomete,* 302.

34. Ōshiro, *Gushō kara no koe,* 149.

35. Kawahashi, "Seven Hindrances of Women?" 86.

36. Cited in ibid., 91.

37. Ōshiro, *Kōgen wo motomete,* 286.

Chapter 7: History/Fiction/Identity

Epigraphs: Eliot, *The Norton Anthology,* 1017; Bishop, *The Norton Anthology,* 1138.

1. The sole anthology of Okinawan literature available in English is Molasky and Rabson, eds. *Southern Exposure.*

2. Keene, *Emperor of Japan,* 220.

3. Ibid., 302.

4. Nelson, "Japan in the Life of Early Ryukyu," 385.

5. Smits, *Visions of Ryukyu*, 42.

6. Oguma, *"Nihonjin" no kyōkai.* On Shimao Toshio, see Gabriel, *Mad Wives and Island Dreams;* on "Yaponesia," see Gabriel, 164–165.

7. Yanagita Kunio, *Yanagita Kunio zenshū,* vol.1.

8. Ōe Kenzaburō, *Okinawa nōto,* 16.

9. Morton, *Modern Japanese Culture,* 43–44; Clarke, "Japonesia," 7–21; Sparling, *"The Sting of Death."*

10. Okamoto, *Gendai bungaku ni miru Okinawa no jigazō.*

11. A translation of Ōshiro's *Cocktail Party* is available in Rabson, ed., *Okinawa;* another translation of an Ōshiro story is in Molasky and Rabson, eds., *Southern Exposure,* 113–156.

12. Okamoto, *Okinawa bungaku no chihei,* 101–102; Molasky, *The American Occupation of Japan,* 3.

13. Okamoto, *Gendai bungaku ni miru Okinawa no jigazō,* 64–67.

14. Ibid., 205. On Ōshiro's fiction, see also Morton, "Posutokoroniaru no tasha to shite no Yuta," 11–30; and Morton, *"Yuta* as the Postcolonial Other in Ōshiro Tatsuhiro's Fiction."

15. Bloom, *Omens of Millennium,* 144.

16. Ibid., 144.

17. Freud, *The Standard Edition,* vol. 17, 230.

18. Kerr, *Okinawa,* 97.

19. Ibid.

20. Ibid., 99.

21. Ibid., 100–101.

22. Ibid., 102–103.

23. Ibid., 98.

24. Ōshiro, *Ōshiro Tatsuhiro zenshū,* vol. 12, 309–312.

25. Ibid., 330–331.

26. Ōshiro, *Kōgen o motomete,* 296–297.

27. Ibid., 299–300.

28. Blacker, *The Catalpa Bow,* 113.

29. Okaya, *Minami no seishinshi,* 90.

30. Ibid., 90.

31. Ibid., 90–92.

32. Ōshiro, *Kōgen o motomete,* 300–302.

33. Ibid., 303.

34. Ōshiro, *Hāfutaimu Okinawa,* 11–13.

35. Hall, cited by Loomba, *Colonialism/Postcolonialism,* 181.

36. Cited by Loomba, 182–183.

37. Bhabha, *The Location of Culture,* 13.

38. Ōshiro, *Ōshiro Tatsuhiro zenshū,* vol. 4, 95.

39. Ibid., 98.

40. Ibid., 5–6.

41. Hokama Shuzen, ed., *Omoro sōshi,* vol. 1, 14.

42. Ibid., 449.

43. Ōshiro, *Ōshiro Tatsuhiro zenshū,* vol. 4, 36–37.

44. Ibid., 17.

45. Ibid., 23.

46. Ibid.

47. Ibid., 79.

48. Matayoshi, "Shinwa to seiji ga orinasu sasupensu," 346–347.

49. For a more detailed exploration of the notion of hybridity as it applies to Ōshiro's fiction, see Morton, "Ōshiro Tatsuhiro bungaku ni okeru posutokoroniaru."

Chapter 8: The Alien Without

Epigraphs: Forbes, *Damaged Glamour,* 17; Slessor, *Collected Poems,* 323.

1. A very early version of Chapter 8 appeared in Broinowski, *Double Vision,* published by Pandanus Books (Australia) in 2004. Keene, *Seeds in the Heart,* 359–361.

2. Fujimura, ed. *qv* "Kikō bungaku." *Nihon bungakushi jiten,* 89. Studies of Japanese travel diaries from classical times are also available in English, for example, Plutschow and Fukuda, *Four Japanese Travel Diaries of the Middle Ages.*

3. Miner, *Naming Properties,* 11.

4. Ibid., 215.

5. Booth, *The Company We Keep,* 268.

6. Miner, *Naming Properties,* 270–271.

7. Ibid., 279.

8. Mori, *Doitsu nikki,* 7–223.

9. Keene, *Modern Japanese Diaries,* 202.

10. Ibid., 2.

11. Ibid., 119–132, 224–246.

12. Yosano Akiko, *Travels in Manchuria and Mongolia.* For an example of an academic study, see Fogel, *The Literature of Travel.*

13. Sakaki, *Obsessions,* 82–102.

14. For details of this work, see Morton, *Modern Japanese Culture,* 54–102.

15. Okuji, "Nogami Yaeko 'Unzen,'" 219. For a short-listing of some examples of modern Japanese travel writings, see Gabriel "Back to the Familiar," 151–152.

16. Ackroyd, *Albion,* 269–270.

17. For details about Australian authors who have written on Japan, see Broinowski, *The Yellow Lady.*

18. Perram, "The Transfiguration and Mythologization," 92–93.

19. In addition to those examined in this chapter, Murakami wrote other travel narratives not treated here, such as *Tsukaimichi no nai fūkei* and *Tokyo surume kurabu.*

20. A number of English-language book-length studies of Murakami exist: Rubin, *Haruki Murakami and the Music of Words;* Strecher's *Dances with Sheep;* Suter, *The Japanization of Modernity;* and Seats, *Murakami Haruki.* But for a short introduction to Murakami's writing, see Morton, *Modern Japanese Culture,* 178–185.

21. Gabriel, "Back to the Familiar," 152.

22. Ibid.

23. Ibid. The sales figures are cited in Seats, *Murakami Haruki,* 26. Despite having been translated into English soon after publication, in 2000 a new, different English translation of this novel appeared; see Murakami, *Norwegian Wood.*

24. Gabriel, "Back to the Familiar," 153.

25. Ibid., 154.

26. Ibid., 155.

27. Ibid., 156.

28. Murakami, *Henkyō kinkyō,* 11.

29. Ibid., 17.

30. Ibid.

31. Gabriel, "Back to the Familiar," 164–165.

32. Murakami, *Henkyō kinkyō,* 299.

33. Ibid., 300.

34. Murakami, *Zensakuhin 1979–1989,* vol. 3, 179.

35. Murakami, *The Scrap.*

36. Murakami, *Sydney!*

37. Ibid., 407.

38. Ibid., 83.

39. Ibid., 88, 95.

40. Ibid., 90.

41. Ibid., 101–102.

42. Ibid., 273, 292–294.

43. Ibid., 93.

44. Ibid., 101–102.

45. Ibid., 102; also see 287–288.

46. Ibid., 410.

47. Ibid., 50.

48. Ibid., 51.

49. Murakami, *Sydney,* 62. This arises from the fact that the rail line taking him to Parramatta travels through older inner suburbs that have shifted over time from industrial workers' cottages to slums (although at the time he arrived in Sydney they were in the process of gentrification).

50. Ibid., 60–73.

51. Ibid., 95–101.

52. Ibid., 108.

53. Ibid.

54. Ibid., 102.

55. Ibid., 107–108.

56. Ibid., 146–177.

57. Ibid., 228.

58. Ibid., 274–275.

59. Ibid., 273–281.

60. Ibid., 283.

61. Ibid., 281–284.

62. In this connection, it should be noted that on 13 February 2008, the prime minister of Australia, Mr. Kevin Rudd, moved a motion of apology in the federal Parliament to the "stolen generation," which was passed without opposition.

63. Murakami, *Sydney!* 284.

64. Ibid.

65. Ibid., 286–288.

66. Ibid., 299.

67. Ibid., 331–345.

Epilogue

Epigraphs: Palmer, *Notes for Echo Lake,* 36; Bishop, *Geography 111,* 43.

1. See, for example, Said, *Culture and Imperialism.*

2. Napier, *The Fantastic in Modern Japanese Literature,* is a brave attempt to construct this kind of scholarship in English for a specific genre of Japanese literature.

3. See the discussion of *What is Beauty in Respect of Language* in Morton, *Modern Japanese Culture,* 113–124.

4. For criticism of the existing social order, see Becker, *Gothic Forms of Feminine Fictions;* and Spooner, *Contemporary Gothic.*

5. Nagahata Michiko has argued that Arishima had an affair with Akiko. For details, see Nagahata, *Yume no kakehashi* and *Hana no ran.* Arishima specialists have generally accepted these arguments.

6. Booth, in *The Company We Keep,* discusses the process of "reader making" at several points.

BIBLIOGRAPHY

Ackroyd, Peter. *Albion: The Origins of the English Imagination*. London: Chatto & Windus, 2002.

Akesaki Chiaki. "Jinmenso no sasayaki: Tanizaki Jun'ichirō ga tsukurenakatta eiga." *Shōwa bungaku* 53 (Sept. 2006): 1–13.

Akitsu Ei. "Tanka." In *[Hajimete manabu] Nihon josei bungakushi: Kingendai hen*, eds. Iwabuchi Hiroko and Kidate Sachie, 69–78. Tokyo: Minerva Shobō, 2005.

Anderer, Paul. *Other Worlds: Arishima Takeo and the Bounds of Modern Japanese Fiction*. New York: Columbia University Press, 1984.

Apter, Emily. *The Translation Zone: A New Comparative Literature*. Princeton: Princeton University Press, 2006.

Arishima Takeo. *Arishima Takeo zenshū*. Ed. Senuma Shigeki et al. 15 vols. Tokyo: Chikuma Shobō, 1980–1986.

———. *A Certain Woman*. Trans. Kenneth Strong. Tokyo: University of Tokyo Press, 1978.

Ashbery, John. *Flow Chart*. New York: Alfred A. Knopf, 1992.

Baba Akiko. *Yosano Akiko no shūka [gendai tanka kanshō shiriizu]*. Tokyo: Tanka Shinbunsha, 1984.

Baker, Mona. *In Other Words: A Coursebook on Translation*. London: Routledge, 1992, rpt. 2007.

Bardsley, Jan. *The Bluestockings of Japan: New Woman Essays and Fiction from Seito. 1911–1916*. Ann Arbor: Center for Japanese Studies, The University of Michigan, 2007.

Becker, Susanne. *Gothic Forms of Feminine Fictions*. Manchester: Manchester University Press, 1999.

Beichman, Janine. *Embracing the Firebird: Yosano Akiko and the Birth of the Female*

Voice in Modern Japanese Poetry. Honolulu: University of Hawai'i Press, 2002.

———. *Masaoka Shiki.* Tokyo, New York: Kodansha International, 1986.

———. "Yosano Akiko: The Early Years." *Japan Quarterly* 37, no. 1 (Jan.–Mar. 1990): 37–54.

———. "Yosano Akiko: Return to the Female." *Japan Quarterly* 37, no. 2 (Apr.–June 1990): 204–228.

Benjamin, Walter. "The Task of the Translator." In *The Translation Studies Reader,* ed. Lawrence Venuti, 75–85. 2nd ed. New York: Routledge, 1995.

Benl, Oscar. "Naturalism in Japanese Literature." *Monumenta* Nipponica 9, nos. 1–2 (1953): 1–33.

Bhabha, Homi. *The Location of Culture.* London: Routledge, 1994, rpt. 2007.

Bishop, Elizabeth. "At the Fishhouses." In *The Norton Anthology of Poetry,* 1138. 3rd ed. New York: W. W. Norton & Company, 1970.

———. *Geography 111.* London: Chatto & Windus, 1977.

Blacker, Carmen. *The Catalpa Bow: A Study of Shamanistic Practices in Japan.* London: George Allen & Unwin Ltd., 1975.

Blake, William. "A Divine Image." In *The Norton Anthology of Poetry,* 504. 3rd ed. New York: W. W. Norton & Company, 1970.

Bloom, Harold. *The Anxiety of Influence: A Theory of Poetry.* Oxford: Oxford University Press, 1973.

———. *Omens of Millennium: The Gnosis of Angels, Dreams and Resurrection.* London: Fourth Estate, 1996.

Booth, Wayne. *The Company We Keep: An Ethics of Fiction.* Berkeley: University of California Press, 1988.

———. *The Rhetoric of Fiction.* 2nd ed. Chicago: University of Chicago Press, 1983.

Brandon, James R. "Some Shakespeare(s) in Some Asia(s)." *Asian Studies Review* 20, no. 3 (Apr. 1997): 1–26.

Brewster, Scott. "Gothic and the Madness of Interpretation." In *A Companion to the Gothic,* ed. David Punter, 281–292. Oxford: Blackwell Publishers, 2001.

Broinowski, Alison. *Double Vision: Asian Accounts of Australia.* Canberra: Pandanus Books, 2004.

———. *The Yellow Lady: Australian Impressions of Asia.* Melbourne: Oxford University Press, 1992.

Brooks, Peter. *The Melodramatic Imagination: Balzac, Henry James, Melodrama and the Mode of Excess.* New York: Columbia University Press, 1985.

Carpenter, Juliet. "Izumi Kyōka: Meiji-era Gothic." *Japan Quarterly* 31, no. 2 (Apr.-June 1984): 154–158.

Chambers, Anthony Hood. *The Secret Window: Ideal Worlds in Tanizaki's Fiction.* Cambridge, MA: Council on East Asian Studies, Harvard University, 1994.

Chanfrault-Duchet, Marie-Françoise. "Textualisation of the self and gender identity in the life-story." In *Feminism and Autobiography: Texts, Theories, Methods,* eds. Tess Cosslet, Celia Lury, and Penny Summerfield, 61–76. London: Routledge, 2000.

Clarke, Hugh. "Japonesia, the Black Current and the Origins of the Japanese." *The Journal of the Oriental Society of Australia* 17 (1985): 7–21.

Cockerill, Hiroko. *Style and Narrative in Translations: The Contribution of Futabatei Shimei.* Manchester: St. Jerome Publishing, 2006.

Collins, Billy. *The Art of Drowning.* Pittsburgh, PA: University of Pittsburgh Press, 1995.

Copeland, Rebecca. *Lost Leaves: Women Writers of Meiji Japan.* Honolulu: University of Hawai'i Press, 2000.

Cornyetz, Nina. *Dangerous Women, Deadly Words: Phallic Fantasy and Modernity in Three Japanese Writers.* Stanford, CA: Stanford University Press, 1999.

Cranston, Edwin A. "Carmine-Purple: A Translation of 'Enji-Murasaki,' the First Ninety-eight Poems of Yosano Akiko's *Midaregami.*" *Journal of the Association of Teachers of Japanese* 25, no. 1 (Apr. 1991): 91–111.

———. "The Dark Path: Images of Longing in Japanese Love Poetry." *Harvard Journal of Asiatic Studies* 35 (1975): 60–100.

———. "Young Akiko: The Literary Debut of Yosano Akiko (1878–1942)." *Literature East and West* 18, no. 1 (Mar. 1974): 19–43.

De Man, Paul. *The Rhetoric of Romanticism.* New York: Columbia University Press, 1984.

Dodane, Claire. *Yosano Akiko: Poète de la passion et figure de proue du féminisme japonais.* Paris: Publications Orientalistes de France, 2000.

Ehara Taizō, and Shimizu Takayuki, eds. *Yosano Buson shū.* Tokyo: Asahi Shinbunsha (Nihon koten zenshū), 1975.

Eliot, T. S. "The Dry Salvages." In *The Norton Anthology of Poetry,* 1017. 3rd ed. New York: W. W. Norton & Company, 1970.

———. "Tradition and the Individual Talent." In *20th Century Literary Criticism: A Reader,* ed. David Lodge, 71–77. London: Longman, 1972.

Figel, Gerald. *Civilization and Monsters: Spirits of Modernity in Meiji Japan.* Durham, NC: Duke University Press, 1999.

Fogel, Joshua A. *The Literature of Travel in the Japanese Rediscovery of China, 1862–1945.* Stanford, CA: Stanford University Press, 1996.

Forbes, John. *Damaged Glamour.* Rose Bay, NSW: Brandl & Schlesinger Book Publishing, 1998.

Fowler, Edward. *The Rhetoric of Confession: Shishōsetsu in Early Twentieth-century Japanese Fiction.* Berkeley: University of California Press, 1988.

Freud, Sigmund. *The Interpretation of Dreams.* Trans. A. A. Brill. Chicago: Encyclopaedia Britannica, 1989.

———. *The Standard Edition of the Complete Psychological Works of Sigmund Freud.* Trans. James Strachey and Anna Freud. Vol. 17. London: The Hogarth Press and the Institute of Psycho-Analysis, 1955, rpt. 1995.

Frye, Northrop. "The Archetypes of Literature." In his *Fables of Identity: Studies in Poetic Mythology,* 7–21. New York: Harcourt, Brace & World Inc., 1963.

———. "The Imaginative and the Imaginary." In his *Fables of Identity: Studies in Poetic Mythology,* 151–168. New York: Harcourt, Brace & World Inc., 1963.

Fujimura Saku, ed. *Nihon bungakushi jiten.* Tokyo: Nihon Hyōronshinsha, 1954.

Furuhashi Nobuyoshi. *Man'yōshū: Uta no hajimari.* Tokyo: Chikuma Shinsho, 1994.

Gabriel, Philip. "Back to the Familiar: The Travel Writings of Murakami Haruki." *Japanese Language and Literature* 36, no. 2 (Oct. 2002): 151–169.

———. *Mad Wives and Island Dreams: Shimao Toshio and the Margins of Japanese Literature.* Honolulu: University of Hawai'i Press, 1999.

Gadamer, Hans-Georg. *Truth and Method.* Trans. Joel Weinsheimer and P. G. Marshall. 2nd rev. ed. New York: Continuum, 1994.

Gessel, Van C., ed. *Japanese Fiction Writers 1868–1945.* Detroit, MI: Gale Research, 1997.

Gluck, Carol. *Japan's Modern Myths: Ideology in the Late Meiji Period.* Princeton, NJ: Princeton University Press, 1985.

Golley, Gregory. *When Our Eyes No Longer See: Realism, Science and Ecology in Japanese Literary Modernism.* Cambridge, MA: Harvard University Asia Center, 2008.

Haga Tōru. *Midaregami no keifu.* Tokyo: Bijitsu Kōronsha, 1981.

Hashimoto Yoshiichirō. *Tanizaki Jun'ichirō no bungaku.* Rev. ed. Tokyo: Ōfūsha, 1976.

Hayden, Robert. *Collected Poems.* Ed. Frederick Glaysher. New York: Liveright Publishing Corporation, 1985.

Heidegger, Martin. "Language." In *Poetry, Language, Thought,* trans. and intro. Albert Hofstadter, 187–211. New York: Harper and Row, 1971.

Higashi Masao. "Mashō to Seisei." In *Izumi Kyōka shū: Kurokabe,* ed. Higashi Masao, 401–407. Tokyo: Chikuma Bunko, 2006.

Hijiya-Kirschnereit, Irmela. *Rituals of Self-Revelation: Shishōsetsu as Literary Genre and Social-cultural Phenomenon.* Cambridge, MA: Council on East Asian Studies, Harvard University, 1996.

Hirakawa Sukehiro. *Japan's Love-hate Relationship with the West.* Folkestone, Kent: Global Oriental, 2005.

Hirako Kyōko. *Yosano Akiko no uta kanshō.* Tokyo: Tanka Shinbunsha, 2003.

Hisamatsu Sen'ichi, ed. *Ochiai Naobumi, Ueda Kazutoshi, Haga Yaichi, Fujioka Sakutarō.* Tokyo: Chikuma Shobō, 1977.

Hokama Shuzen, ed. *Omoro sōshi.* Vol. 1. Tokyo: Iwanami Bunko, 2000.

Homma Kenshiro. *The Literature of Naturalism: An East-West Comparative Study.* Kyoto: Yamaguchi Publishing House, 1983.

Honma Hisao. "Tsubouchi Shōyō: Shēkusupia to no renkan ni oite." In *Shēkusupia zenshū,* ed. and trans. Tsubouchi Shōyō, 1342–1346. Tokyo: Shinjusha, 1957.

Hutchinson, Rachael, and Mark Williams, eds. *Representing the Other in Modern Japanese Literature.* London: Routledge, 2007.

Ichikawa Chihiro. "Reading Genji: Yosano Akiko and the Tale of Genji: Ukifune and Midaregami." *Journal of the Association of Teachers of Japanese* 28, no. 2 (Nov. 1994): 157–174.

Ikari Akira. "Arishima Takeo no kinōteki bungakuron: Hōmei to no ronsō o megutte." *Kokugo to Kokubungaku* (Sept. 1962).

Inoue, Ken. "Tanizaki Jun'ichirō no seikimatsu." In *Tanizaki Jun'ichirō to seikimatsu,* ed. Muramatsu Masaie, 7–29. Kyoto: Shibunkaku Shuppan, 2002.

Inouye, Charles Shirō. "Introduction." In *Izumi Kyōka, Japanese Gothic Tales.* Honolulu: University of Hawaiʻi Press, 1996.

———. *The Similitude of Blossoms: A Critical Biography of Izumi Kyōka (1873–1939), Japanese Novelist and Playwright.* Cambridge, MA: Harvard University Asia Center, 1998.

Irie Haruyuki. *Yosano Akiko to sono jidai: Josei kaihō to kajin no jinsei.* Tokyo: Shin Nihon Shuppansha, 2003.

Iser, Wolfgang. *The Act of Reading: A Theory of Aesthetic Response.* Baltimore, MD: The John Hopkins University, 1978.

Isoda Kōichi. *Rokumeikan no keifu.* Tokyo: Kōdansha Bungei Bunko, 1991.

Ito, Ken K. *Visions of Desire: Tanizaki's Fictional Worlds.* Stanford, CA: Stanford University Press, 1991.

Itō Sei. *Itō Sei zenshū.* 24 vols. Tokyo: Shinchōsha, 1973.

———. *Nihon bundanshi: Daigyaku jiken zengo.* Vol. 16. Tokyo: Kōdansha Bungei Bunko, 1994.

———. *Nihon bundanshi: Kaikaki no hitobito.* Vol. 1. Tokyo: Kōdansha Bungei Bunko, 1994.

———. *Tanizaki Jun'ichirō no bungaku.* Tokyo: Chūō Kōronsha, 1970.

Itsumi Kumi. "Akiko tanka to koten." In *Yosano Akiko [Shin Bungei tokuhon],* eds. Taguchi Keiko et al., 147–158. Tokyo: Kawade Shobō Shinsha, 1991.

———. *Hyōden: Yosano Tekkan Akiko.* Tokyo: Yagi Shoten, 1975.

———. *Midaregami zenshaku.* Tokyo: Ōfūsha, 1978.

———. *Shin Midaregami zenshaku.* Tokyo: Yagi Shoten, 1996.

———. *[Shinpan] Hyōden Yosano Hiroshi Akiko: Meiji hen.* Tokyo: Yagi Shoten, 2007.

Iwabuchi Hiroko, and Kidata Sachie. eds. *[Hajimete manabu] Nihon josei bungakushi: Kingendai hen.* Tokyo: Minerva Shobō, 2005.

Iwasa Sōshirō. "Shisei: Femme Fatale no Tanjō." In *Tanizaki Jun'ichirō: Monogatari no hōhō,* ed. Chiba Shunji, 73–89. Tokyo: Yūseidō Shuppan, 1990.

Izumi Kyōka. *[Bungō kaidan kessaku sen] Izumi Kyōka shū: Kurokabe.* Ed. Higashi Masao. Tokyo: Chikuma Bunko, 2006.

———. *Izumi Kyōka shūsei.* Vol. 1. Tokyo: Chikuma Bunko, 1996.

———. *Izumi Kyōka shūsei.* Vol. 4. Tokyo: Chikuma Bunko, 1995.

———. *Japanese Gothic Tales.* Trans. Charles Shirō Inouye. Honolulu: University of Hawai'i Press, 1996

———. *Ronshū Taishōki no Izumi Kyōka,* Ed. Izumi Kyōka Kenkyūkai. Tokyo: Ōfūsha, 1999.

Jackson, Rosemary. *Fantasy: The Literature of Subversion.* London: Methuen, 1981.

Kamei Hideo. *Meiji bungakushi.* Tokyo: Iwanami Shoten, 2000.

———. *Transformations of Sensibility: The Phenomenology of Meiji Literature.* Trans. and ed. with an introduction by Michael Bourdaghs. Ann Arbor: Center for Japanese Studies, University of Michigan, 2002.

Kasahara Nobuo. "Kyōkateki bi no hōhō." In *[Nihon bungaku kenkyū shiryō sōsho] Izumi Kyōka,* ed. Nihon bungaku kenkyū shiryō kankōkai, 44–54. Tokyo: Yuseidō, 1980.

Katsumoto Seiichirō. "Kyōka no ishinzō." In *[Nihon bungaku kenkyū shiryō sōsho]*

Izumi Kyōka, ed. Nihon bungaku kenkyū shiryō kankōkai, 1–7. Tokyo: Yuse-idō, 1980.

Kawahashi, Noriko. "Seven Hindrances of Women? A Popular Discourse on Okinawan Women and Religion." *Japanese Journal of Religious Studies* 27, nos. 1–2 (2000): 85–98.

Kawamura Hatsue, and Jane Reichhold. *Breasts of Snow: Fumiko Nakajo: Her Tanka and Her Life.* Tokyo: The Japan Times Ltd., 2004.

Kawamura Jirō. "Dōshisareta kūkan: 'Shunchū.'" In *Gunzō Nihon no sakka 5: Izumi Kyōka*, ed. Tsushima Yūko, 132–139. Tokyo: Shogakukan, 1992.

———. *Honyaku no nihongo.* Tokyo: Chūō Kōronsha, 1981.

Kawatake Toshio. *Nihon no Hamuretto.* Tokyo: Nansōsha, 1972.

———. *Sakigakeru monotachi no keifu.* Tokyo: Tōseisha, 1985.

Kawato Michiaki, and Sakakibara Takanori, eds. *Meiji hon'yaku bungaku zenshū: Sheikusupia shū 1.* Vol. 1. Tokyo: Ōzorasha, 1996.

Keene, Donald. *Dawn to the West: Japanese Literature in the Modern Era—Fiction.* Vol. 1. New York: Holt, Rinehart and Winston, 1984.

———. *Dawn to the West: Japanese Literature in the Modern Era—Poetry, Drama, Criticism.* Vol. 2. New York: Holt, Rinehart and Winston, 1984.

———. *Emperor of Japan: Meiji and His World, 1852–1912.* New York: Columbia University Press, 2002.

———. *Modern Japanese Diaries: The Japanese at Home and Abroad as Revealed through Their Diaries.* New York: Henry Holt and Company, 1995.

———. *Seeds in the Heart: Japanese Literature from Earliest Times to the Late Sixteenth Century.* New York: Henry Holt and Company, 1993.

Kennedy, Dennis. "Shakespeare Worldwide." In *The Cambridge Companion to Shakespeare,* eds. Margreta de Grazia and Stanley Wells, 253–257. Cambridge: Cambridge University Press, 2001.

Kerr, George H. *Okinawa: The History of an Island People.* Rev. ed. With an afterword by Mitsugu Sakihara. Boston, MA: Tuttle Publishing, 2000.

Kikuchi Hiroshi. *Arishima Takeo.* Tokyo: Shinbisha, 1986.

Kimata Satoshi. "Tōson no romanchishizumu." In *Nihon bungaku kōza 10,* ed. Nihon bungaku kyōkai, 103–119. Tokyo: Taishūkan Shoten, 1988.

Kindai Bungaku Kenkyū Shiryō Sōsho (4), ed. *Arishima Takeo mikan genkō: Kankan mushi hoka nihen.* Tokyo: Kindai Bungakukan, 1973.

Kinoshita Junji. *Gikyoku no nihongo.* Tokyo: Chūō Kōronsha, 1982.

Kohl, Stephen W., et al. *The White Birch School (Shirakabaha) of Japanese Literature: Some Sketches and Commentary.* Eugene: University of Oregon, 1975.

Komori Yōichi. *Kōzō to shite no katari.* Tokyo: Shin'yōsha, 1988, rpt. 1992.

———. *Yuragi no Nihon bungaku.* Tokyo: NHK Bukkusu, 1998, rpt. 2001.

Konno Sumi. *24 no kiiwādo de yomu Yosano Akiko.* Tokyo: Honami Shoten, 2005.

Kristeva, Julia. *Tales of Love.* Trans. Leon S. Roudiez. New York: Columbia University Press, 1987.

Kubota Jun, and Hirata Yoshinobu, eds. *Goshūiwakashū [Shin Nihon koten bungaku taikei].* Vol. 8. Tokyo: Iwanami Shoten, 1994.

Kuhiwczak, Piotr, and Karen Littau, eds. *A Companion to Translation Studies.* Toronto: Multilingual Matters Ltd, 2007.

LaFleur, William R. *Liquid Life: Abortion and Buddhism in Japan.* Princeton, NJ: Princeton University Press, 1992.

LaMarre, Thomas. *Shadows on the Screen: Tanizaki Jun'ichirō on Cinema and "Oriental Aesthetics."* Ann Arbor: Center for Japanese Studies, The University of Michigan, 2005.

———. *Uncovering Heian Japan: An Archaeology of Sensation and Inscription.* Durham, NC: Duke University Press, 2000.

Larson, Phyllis Hyland. "Yosano Akiko and the Re-creation of the Female Self: An Autogynography." *Journal of the Association of Teachers of Japanese* 25, no. 1 (1991): 11–27.

Levy, Ian Hideo, trans. *The Ten Thousand Leaves: A Translation of Man'yōshū, Japan's Premier Anthology of Classical Poetry.* Vol. 1. Princeton, NJ: Princeton University Press, 1981.

Levy, Indra. *Sirens of the Western Shore: The Westernesque Femme Fatale, Translation and Vernacular Style in Modern Japanese Literature.* New York: Columbia University Press, 2006.

Loomba, Ania. *Colonialism/Postcolonialism.* London: Routledge, 1998.

———. "Outsiders in Shakespeare"s England." In *The Cambridge Companion to Shakespeare,* eds. Grazia de Margreta and Stanley Wells, 147–166. Cambridge: Cambridge University Press, 2001.

Maeda Ai. *Text and the City: Essays on Japanese Modernity.* Ed. with an introduction by James A. Fujii. Durham, NC: Duke University Press, 2004.

Mahon, Derek. "The Last of the Fire Kings." In *The Penguin Book of Contemporary British Poetry,* eds. Blake Morrison and Andrew Motion, 75. Harmondsworth: Penguin, 1982.

Margreta, Grazia de, and Stanley Wells, eds. *The Cambridge Companion to Shakespeare.* Cambridge: Cambridge University Press, 2001.

Marra, Michele, ed. *Modern Japanese Aesthetics: A Reader.* Honolulu: University of Hawai'i Press, 1999.

Matayoshi Eiki. "Shinwa to seiji ga orinasu sasupensu." In *Ōshiro Tatsuhiro zenshū,* vol. 4: 345–355. Tokyo: Bensei Shuppan, 2002.

Matsubara Junichi. "Kyōka bungaku to minkan denshō to." In *Izumi Kyōka,* ed. Nihon bungaku kenkyū shiryō kankōkai, 62–84. Tokyo: Yūseidō, 1980.

Matsumoto Chūji. "Kankan Mushi ni Tsuite." In *Sakuhinron: Arishima Takeo,* eds. Uesugi Yoshikazu and Yasukawa Sadao, 9–27. Tokyo: Sōbunsha Shuppan, 1981.

Matsumura Masaie. "Tanizaki Jun'ichirō no seikimatsu to 'mazohizumu.'" In *Tanizaki Jun'ichirō to seikimatsu,* 29–48. Kyoto: Shibunkaku Shuppan, 2002.

———, ed. *Tanizaki Jun'ichirō to seikimatsu.* Kyoto: Shibunkaku Shuppan, 2002.

Matsuura Ayumi. "Akiko no Izumi Shikibu." In *Yosano Akiko wo manabu hito no tame ni,* eds. Ueda Hiroshi and Tomimura Shunzō, 146–162. Kyoto: Sekai Shisōsha, 1995.

McCullough, Helen Craig. *Brocade by Night: "Kokin Wakashū" and the Court Style in Japanese Classical Poetry.* Stanford, CA: Stanford University Press, 1985.

Mertz, John Pierre. *Novel Japan: Spaces of Nationhood in Early Meiji Narrative, 1870-88.* Ann Arbor: Center for Japanese Studies, University of Michigan, 2003.

Michiura Motoko. *Onnauta no hyakunen.* Tokyo: Iwanami Shinsho, 2002.

Miller, J. Scott. "Tsubouchi Shōyō (1859–1935)." In *Japanese Fiction Writers 1868-1945,* ed. Van C. Gessel, 240–241. Detroit, MI: Gale Research, 1997.

Milton, John. *English Minor Poems/Paradise Lost/Samson Agonistes/Areopagitica.* Chicago: Encyclopedia Britannica Inc., 1989.

Milward, Peter. "Shakespeare in Japanese Translation." In *Studies in Japanese Culture: Tradition and Experiment,* ed. Joseph Roggendorf, 187–207. Tokyo: Sophia University, 1963.

Minami Ryūta, Ian Carruthers, and John Gillies, eds. *Performing Shakespeare in Japan.* Cambridge: Cambridge University Press, 2001.

Minemura Fumito, ed. *Shinkokinwakashū.* Tokyo: Shōgakukan, 1974.

Miner, Earl. *Naming Properties: Nominal Reference in Travel Writings by Bashō and Sora, Johnson and Boswell.* Ann Arbor: University of Michigan Press, 1996.

Mishima Yukio. "Izumi Kyōka." In *Gunzō Nihon no sakka 5: Izumi Kyōka,* ed. Tsushima Yūko, 23–29. Tokyo: Shōgakukan, 1992.

Miyoshi Yukio. "Izumi Kyōka o megutte: Zoku 'kyokō' no imi." In *Izumi Kyōka,* ed. Nihon bungaku kenkyū shiryō kankōkai. Tokyo: Yūseidō, 1980.

——, Yamamoto, Kenkichi, and Yoshida Seiichi, eds. *Nihon bungaku shi jiten: Kin-gendai hen.* Tokyo: Kadokawa Shoten, 1987.

Mizutani Akio. "Umareizuru Nayami ron oboegaki." In *Kindai Nihon bungei to kirisutokyō [Ton Tokushū gō],* eds. Mizutani Akio and Yonekura Mitsuru, 52–59. Nishinomiya: Kwansei Gakuin daigaku shūkyō katsudō iinkai bungaku kenkyū gurūpu, 1978.

Molasky, Michael S. *The American Occupation of Japan: Literature and Memory.* London: Routledge, 2001.

——, and Steve Rabson, eds. *Southern Exposure: Modern Japanese Literature from Okinawa.* Honolulu: University of Hawai'i Press, 2000.

Mori, Ōgai. *Doitsu nikki/Kokura nikki. Mori Ōgai zenshū,* vol. 18. Tokyo: Chikuma Bunko, 1996.

Morishima Yukie. "Yosano Akiko: Sono Meijiki no Shisaku." *Nihon Bungaku* 55 (1980): 16–32.

Morita, James. "Shimazaki Tōson's Four Collections of Poems." *Monumenta Nipponica* 25, no. 3 (1970): 325–369.

Morrell, Robert "A Selection of New Style Verse (Shintaishishō, 1882)." In *Literature East & West* 19, nos. 1–4 (Jan.–Dec. 1975).

Morris, Ivan, ed. *Modern Japanese Stories.* Tokyo: Charles E. Tuttle Co. Inc., 1962.

Mortimer, Maya. *Meeting the Sensei: The Role of the Master in Shirakaba Writers.* Leiden: Brill, 2000.

Morton, Leith. "19 Seikimatsu ni okeru Ren'ai Bungaku no Hensei: Ninjōbon kara Shōsetsu e." [Nichibunken] *Nihon kenkyū* 37 (2008): 259–291.

——. "Akiko, Tomiko and Hiroshi: Tanka as Conversation in Fin-de-siècle Japan." *Japanese Studies: Bulletin of the Japanese Studies Association of Australia* 14, no. 3 (1994): 35–50.

——. "The Canonization of Yosano Akiko's *Midaregami.*" *Japanese Studies* 20: 3 (2000): 237–254.

——. "The Clash of Traditions: New Style Poetry (Shintaishi) and the Waka Tradition in Yosano Akiko's *Midaregami.*" In *The Renewal of Song: Renovation in Lyric Conception and Practice,* eds. Earl Miner and Amiya Dev, 104–144. Calcutta: Seagull Books, 2000.

——. "The Concept of Romantic Love in the *Taiyō* Magazine 1895–1905." *Nichibunken Japan Review* 83 (1997): 79–103.

——. *Divided Self: A Biography of Arishima Takeo.* Sydney: Allen & Unwin, 1988.

———. "An Introduction to Arishima Takeo: A Comparative Study of Kankan mushi and Kain no matsuei." *Journal of the Oriental Society of Australia* 12 (1977): 42–69.

———. "*Midaregami Shiroyuri* no kenkyū": Seikimatsu no tekusuto kōsaku no ichirei to shite." *Gengo bunka ronsō [Word and Act]* 13 (2008): 39–56.

———. *Modern Japanese Culture: The Insider View.* Melbourne: Oxford University Press, 2003.

———. *Modernism in Practice: An Introduction to Postwar Japanese Poetry.* Honolulu: University of Hawai'i Press, 2004.

———. "Ōshiro Tatsuhiro bungaku ni okeru posutokoroniaru: Haiburiddo to shite no yuta/noro." In *Ryūkyū ko: Kasanariau rekishi ninshiki,* ed. Yoshinari Naoki, 239–261. Tokyo: Shinwasha, 2007.

———. "Posutokoroniaru no tasha to shite no yuta: Aidentitii no keisei to iji." *Okinawagaku: Okinawagaku kenkyūsho kiyō* 8 (Aug. 2005): 11–30.

———. *Yosano Akiko no* Midaregami *wo eigo de ajiwau.* Tokyo: Chūkei Shuppan, 2007.

———. "Yosano Akiko to kindai no ren'ai." *Mugendai* (Aug. 1993): 122–132.

———. "Yosano Akiko's *Midaregami* (1901), Modernity and Kansai Culture." *Journal of the Oriental Society of Australia* 34 (2002): 64–81.

———. "*Yuta* as the Postcolonial Other in Ōshiro Tatsuhiro's Fiction." In *Representing the Other in Modern Japanese Literature,* eds. Rachael Hutchinson and Mark Williams, 253–255. London: Routledge, 2007.

Murakami Haruki. *Henkyō kinkyō.* Tokyo: Shincho Bunko, 2000.

———. *Murakami Haruki zensakuhin 1979–1989.* Vol. 3. Tokyo: Kōdansha, 1990.

———. *Norwegian Wood.* Trans. Jay Rubin. New York: Vintage International, 2000.

———. *The Scrap: Natsukashi no 1980 nendai.* Tokyo: Bungei Shunjū, 1987.

———. *Sydney! [Shidonii].* Tokyo: Bungei Shunjū, 2001.

———. *Tanizaki Jun'ichirō to seikimatsu.* Kyoto: Shibunkaku Shuppan, 2002.

Muramatsu Sadataka. *Izumi Kyōka: Kotoba no renkinjutsushi.* Tokyo: Shakaishisōsha, 1973, rpt. 1993.

———. "Tanizaki Jun'ichirō to Izumi Kyōka." In *Tanizaki Jun'ichirō: Kindai bungaku kenkyū sōsho,* ed. Ara Masato. Tokyo: Yagi Shoten, 1972.

Mussell, Kay. *Women's Gothic and Romantic Fiction: A Reference Guide.* Westport, CT: Greenwood Press, 1981.

Myōjō. Ed. Yosano Tekkan et al. Tokyo: Tokyo shinshisha, 1900.

Nagahata Michiko. *Hana no ran.* Tokyo: Shinhyōron, 1987.

———. *Yume no kakehashi: Akiko to Takeo yūjō.* Tokyo: Shinhyōron, 1985.

Nagai Kafū. *American Stories.* Trans. with an introduction by Mitsuko Iriye. New York: Columbia University Press, 2000.

Nagata Kazuhiro. "Tanka kakushin no shinsenryaku: *Midaregami* no atarashisa." In *Yosano Akiko wo manabu hito no tame ni,* 97–112. Kyoto: Sekai Shisōsha, 1995.

Naka Akira. *Yosano Tekkan.* Tokyo: Ōfūsha, 1988.

Nakamura Akira. "Arishima Takeo no buntai—Aru onna no hiyū—hyōgen kara—." *Kokubungaku: kaishaku to kanshō [Shibundō]: Tokushū: Arishima Takeo no sekai* 54, no. 2 (1989): 68–79.

Nakamura Kan. *Tsubouchi Shōyō ron: Kindai nihon no monogatari kūkan.* Tokyo: Yūseidō Shuppan, 1986.

Nakamura Miharu. "Arishima Takeo 'Aru Seryō Kanja' to 'Hyōgenshugi' e no sekkin." *Nihon bungei ronsō* 4 (1985):1–7.

———. "'Kain no Matsuei': Chinmoku to hiyu." *Kokubungaku: Kaishaku to kanshō (Tokushū: Arishima Takeo no sekai)* 54, no. 2 (1989): 90–95.

———. "Kotoba o kaku nowa dare ka Gendai shokantai yōshiki no saikisei." *Shōwa bungaku kenkyū [Tokushū: hōhō to shite no shokan to nikki]* 24 (1992): 1–10.

Nakanishi Susumu, ed. *Man'yōshū.* Vol. 1. Tokyo: Kōdansha Bunko, 1987.

Naniwa seinen bungakkai, ed. *Yoshiashigusa/kansai bungaku.* Tokyo: Kansai seinen bungakkai, 1897–1900.

Napier, Susan. *The Fantastic in Modern Japanese Literature: The Subversion of Modernity.* London: Routledge, 1996.

Nelson, Thomas. "Japan in the Life of Early Ryukyu." *The Journal of Japanese Studies* 32, no. 2 (Summer 2006): 367–392.

Nihon bungaku kenkyū shiryō kankōkai, ed. *[Nihon bungaku kenkyū shiryō sōsho]* *Izumi Kyōka.* Tokyo: Yuseidō, 1980.

Niranjana, Tejaswini. *Siting Translation: History, Post-Structuralism, and the Colonial Context.* Berkeley: University of California Press, 1992.

Nishigaki Tsutomu. *Arishima Takeo ron.* Tokyo: Yūseidō, 1971.

Nishihara Daisuke. *Tanizaki Jun'ichirō to orientarizumu.* Tokyo: Chūō Kōron Shinsha, 2003.

Nishio Norihito. *Akiko Tomiko Meiji no atarashii onna: Ai to bungaku.* Tokyo: Yūhikaku, 1986.

Niwa Kazuhiko. *Arishima Takeo ron: Kankei no totte "dōjō" to wa nanika?* Nagoya: Fūrindō, 1987.

Noda Utarō. "Susukida Kyūkin shū kaisetsu." In *Doi Bansui, Susukida Kyūkin, Kambara Ariake shū,* eds. Noda Utarō et al., 22–36. Tokyo: Kadokawa Shoten, 1972.

Noguchi Takehiko. *Shōsetsu no nihongo.* Tokyo: Chūō Kōronsha, 1980.

Notehelfer, F. G. *Kotoku Shusui: Portrait of a Japanese Radical.* Cambridge: Cambridge University Press, 1971.

Notley, Alice. *From a Work in Progress.* New York: Dia Art Foundation, 1988.

Nozaki Kan. *Tanizaki Jun'ichirō to ikoku no gengo.* Kyoto: Jinbun Shoin, 2003.

Odagiri Susumu, ed. *Nihon kindai bungaku daijiten: Takujō han.* Tokyo: Kōdansha, 1984.

Ōe Kenzaburō. *Okinawa nōto.* Tokyo: Iwanami Shinsho, 1970.

Oguma Eiji. *"Minshū" to "aikoku": Sengo Nihon no nashonarizumu to kōkyōsei.* Tokyo: Shin'yōsha, 2002.

———. *"Nihonjin" no kyōkai: Okinawa, Ainu, Taiwan, Chōsen shokuminchi shihai kara fukki undō made.* Tokyo: Shinyōsha, 1998, 2000.

Ōhashi Kenzaburō. "Tanizaki to Pō." In *Tanizaki Jun'ichirō: Kindai bungaku kenkyū sōsho,* ed. Ara Masato, 434–445. Tokyo: Yagi Shoten, 1972.

Okamoto Keitoku. *Gendai bungaku ni miru Okinawa no jigazō.* Tokyo: Kōbunkan, 1996.

———. *Okinawa bungaku no chihei.* Tokyo: Sanichi Shobō, 1981.

Okano Hirohiko. "Kyūha waka to waka kairyō no iyoku." In *Meiji tanka no bungaku choryū,* ed. Meiji Jingu, 7–38. Tokyo: Tanka Shinbunsha, 1996.

———. "Uta no tanjō." In *Nihon bungaku no rekishi: Kami to kami wo matsuru mono,* eds. Kobayashi Yukio et al., 166–188. Tokyo: Kadokawa Shoten, 1967.

Okaya Kōji. *Minami no seishinshi.* Tokyo: Shinchōsha, 2000.

Okazaki Yoshie, ed. *Meiji bunka shi [shinsōhan].* Vol. 7 *[bungei].* Tokyo: Hara Shobō, 1980.

Okinawa Bungaku Zenshū Henshū Iinkai, ed. *Okinawa bungaku zenshū.* Vol. 18. Tokyo: Kokusho Kankōkai, 1992.

Okuda Kōji. "Arishima Takeo 'Kankan mushi' ni tsuite: Kōtoku Shūsui 'Chokusetsu kōdōron' to no ruisei." *Nihon Bungaku* 41, no. 9 (1992).

Okuji Nobumasa. "Nogami Yaeko 'Unzen,'" *Kokubungaku: Kaishaku to kanshō* 72, no. 4 (April 2007): 219–222.

Ōmura Hiroyoshi. *Tsubouchi Shōyō.* Tokyo: Yoshikawa Kōbunkan, 1958, rpt. 1987.

Ōoka Makoto. "Nihon no shiika to Yosano Akiko." *Sakai no Akiko kara sekai no Akiko e,* 12–18. Sakai: Yosano Akiko Botsugo 50 Shū Nen Kinen Kokusai Shiika Kaigi Jikkō Iinkai, 1992.

Ōshiro Tatsuhiro. *Gushō kara no koe.* Tokyo: Bungei Shunjū, 1992.

———. *Hāfutaimu Okinawa.* Naha: Niraisha, 1994.

———. "Kindai Okinawa bungaku to hōgen." In *Sekai ni tsunagu Okinawa kenkyū,* ed. Okinawa Kenkyū Kokusai Shinpojiumu Jikkō Iinkai, 199–209. Naha: Okinawa Bunka Kyōkai, 2001.

———. *Kōgen wo motomete: Sengo gojūnen to watashi.* Naha: Okinawa Taimuzu Sha, 1997.

———. *Ōshiro Tatsuhiro zenshū.* Vol. 4. Tokyo: Bensei Shuppan, 2002.

———. *Ōshiro Tatsuhiro zenshū.* Vol. 12. Tokyo: Bensei Shuppan, 2002.

Ōta Seikyū, "Shintaishi no shigeki to waka kakushin." In *Meiji tanka no bungaku choryū,* ed. Meiji Jingu, 3–65. Tokyo: Tanka Shinbunsha, 1996.

Ōtomo Hideto. *Yosano Akiko* Midaregami *goji sōsakuin.* Tokyo: Kasama Sakuin Sōsho, 1977.

Ozaki Saeko. "Akiko to koten." In *Yosano Akiko wo manabu hito no tame ni,* eds. Ueda Hiroshi and Tomimura Shunzō, 38–55. Kyoto: Sekai Shisōsha, 1995.

Paglia, Camille. *Sexual Personae: Art and Decadence from Nefertiti to Emily Dickenson.* Harmondsworth: Penguin Books, 1992.

Palmer, Michael. *At Passages.* New York: New Directions, 1995.

———. "Notes for Echo Lake." San Francisco: North Point Press, 1981.

Perram, Garvin. "The Transfiguration and Mythologization of the Natural Landscape in Selected Works by Peter Matthiessen." *Gengo bunka ronsō [Word and Act]* 11 (2007): 87–103.

Plato. *The Dialogues of Plato: Phaedo.* Trans. Benjamin Jowett. Chicago: Encyclopaedia Britannica Inc, 1989.

Plutschow, Herbert, and Fukuda Hideichi, trans. *Four Japanese Travel Diaries of the Middle Ages.* Ithaca, NY: Cornell University East Asia Papers, 1981.

Poulton, Cody. M. "The Grotesque and the Gothic: Izumi Kyōka's Japan." *Japan Quarterly* 41, no. 3 (July-September 1994).

———. *Spirits of Another Sort: The Plays of Izumi Kyōka.* Ann Arbor: Center for Japanese Studies, University of Michigan, 2001.

Punter, David, ed. *A Companion to the Gothic.* Oxford: Blackwell Publishers, 2001.

Rabson, Steve, ed. *Okinawa: Two Postwar Novellas by Ōshiro Tatsuhiro and Higashi Mineo.* Berkeley: Institute of East Asian Studies, University of California, 1989.

———. *Righteous Cause or Tragic Folly: Changing Views of War in Modern Japa-*

nese Poetry. Ann Arbor: Center for Japanese Studies, University of Michigan, 1998.

————. "Yosano Akiko on War: To Give One's Life or Not—A Question of Which War." *Journal of the Association of Teachers of Japanese* 25, no. 1 (1991): 45–74.

Ricoeur, Paul. *On Translation.* Trans. Eileen Brennan. London: Routledge, 2006.

Rimer, J. Thomas, and Van C. Gessel, eds. *The Columbia Anthology of Modern Japanese Literature.* Vol. 1: *From Restoration to Occupation 1868–1945.* New York: Columbia University Press, 2005.

Roggendorf, Joseph, ed. *Studies in Japanese Culture: Tradition and Experiment.* Tokyo: Sophia University, 1963.

Rowley, G. G. *Yosano Akiko and* The Tale of Genji. Ann Arbor: Center for Japanese Studies, University of Michigan, 2000.

Rubin, Jay. *Haruki Murakami and the Music of Words.* London: Harvill Press, 2002.

Ryan, Marleigh. *The Development of Realism in the Fiction of Tsubouchi Shōyō.* Seattle: University of Washington Press, 1975.

————. *Japan's First Modern Novel: Ukigumo of Futabatei Shimei.* New York: Columbia University Press, 1967.

Saeki Shin'ichi. *Senjō no seishinshi: Bushidō to iu gen'ei.* Tokyo: NHK Books, 2004.

Sage, Victor, ed. *The Gothick Novel.* Hampshire: Macmillan, 1990.

Said, Edward. *Culture and Imperialism.* New York: Vintage, 1994.

————. *Orientalism.* New York: Pantheon Books, 1978.

Sakaki, Atsuko. *Obsessions with the Sino-Japanese Polarity in Japanese Literature.* Honolulu: University of Hawai'i Press, 2006.

Sansom, G. B. *The Western World and Japan: A Study in the Interaction of European and Asiatic Cultures.* New York: Alfred A. Knopf, 1973.

Satake Kazuhiko. *Zenshaku Midaregami kenkyū.* Tokyo: Yūhōdō, 1957.

Schäffner, Christina. "Politics and Translation." In *A Companion to Translation Studies,* eds. Piotr Kuhiwczak and Karen Littau, 134–148. Toronto: Multilingual Matters Ltd, 2007.

Seats, Michael. *Murakami Haruki: The Simulacrum in Contemporary Japanese Culture.* Plymouth, UK: Lexington Books, 2006.

Seki Reiko. *Ichiyō igo no josei hyōgen sutairu media jendā.* Tokyo: Kanrin Shobō, 2003.

Seki Ryōichi. "Chūshaku Wakanashū." In *[Nihon kindai bungaku taikei vol. 14] Tōson shishū,* eds. Itō Sei et al., 49–187. Tokyo: Kadokawa Shoten, 1971.

Senuma Shigeki. *Taishō bungakushi.* Tokyo: Kōdansha, 1985.

———. "Takeo no buntai nado." *Hoppō Bungei* 1, no. 1 (Jan. 1968).

Shakespeare, William. *The Riverside Shakespeare.* Ed. G. Blakemore Evans. Boston: Houghton Mifflin Co., 1974.

Shēkusupia. *Hamuretto.* Trans. Nojima Hidekatsu. Tokyo: Iwanami Bunko, 2001.

Shimazaki Tōson. *Tōson zenshū.* 17 vols. Tokyo: Chikuma Shobō, 1966, rpt. 1976.

Shinma Shin'ichi. *Yosano Akiko.* Tokyo: Ōfūsha, 1981.

———. "Yosano Akiko to Genji monogatari." In *Shin Bungei Tokuhon: Yosano Akiko,* eds. Taguchi Keiko et al., 158–171. Tokyo: Kawade Shobō Shinsha, 1991.

Shōyō Kyōkai, ed. *Tsubouchi Shōyō jiten.* Tokyo: Heibonsha, 1985.

Sibley, William F. "Naturalism in Japanese Literature." *Harvard Journal of Asiatic Studies* 28 (1968): 157–169.

Silverberg, Miriam. *Erotic Grotesque Nonsense: The Mass Culture of Japanese Modern Times.* Berkeley: University of California Press, 2006.

Simic, Charles. "The Infinitely Forked Mother Tongue." In *Translations: Experiments in Reading,* ed. Don Wellman, 33. Cambridge, MA: O.ARS 3, 1983.

Slessor, Kenneth. *Collected Poems.* Eds. Dennis Haskell and Geoffrey Dutton. Sydney: Angus & Robertson, 1994.

Smith, Stevie. *The Collected Poems of Stevie Smith.* London: Penguin Books, 1985.

Smits, Gregory. *Visions of Ryukyu: Identity and Ideology in Early-Modern Thought and Politics.* Honolulu: University of Hawai'i Press, 1999.

Snyder, Stephen. *Fictions of Desire: Narrative Form in the Novels of Nagai Kafū.* Honolulu: University of Hawai'i Press, 2000.

Soh Sakon. *Moeru haha.* Tokyo: Yayoi Shobō, 1968.

Sparling, Kathryn. *"The Sting of Death" and Other Stories by Shimao Toshio.* Ann Arbor: Center for Japanese Studies, University of Michigan, 1985.

Spooner, Catherine. *Contemporary Gothic.* London: Reaktion Books, 2006.

Stein, Gertrude. "Poetry and Grammar." In *Look at Me Now and Here I Am: Writings and Lectures 1911–45,* ed. Patricia Meyerowitz, 125–148. Harmondsworth: Penguin Books, 1971.

Steiner, George. *After Babel: Aspects of Language and Translation.* New York: Oxford University Press, 1975.

Strecher, Matthew Carl. *Dances with Sheep: The Quest for Identity in the Fiction of Murakami Haruki.* Ann Arbor: Center for Japanese Studies, University of Michigan, 2002.

Strong, Sarah. "Passion and Patience: Aspects of Feminine Poetic Heritage in Yosano Akiko's *Midaregami* and Tawara Machi's *Sarada Kinenbi.*" *Journal of the Association of Teachers of Japanese* 25, no. 2 (1991): 177–194.

Sunaga Akihiko. *Tekkan to Akiko.* Tokyo: Kinokuniya Shoten, 1971.

Suter, Rebecca. *The Japanization of Modernity: Murakami Haruki between Japan and the United States.* Cambridge, MA: Harvard University Asia Center, 2008.

Suzuki Sadami. *Nihon no bunka nashonarizumu.* Tokyo: Heibonsha Shinsho, 2005.

Suzuki Tomi. *Narrating the Self: Fictions of Japanese Modernity.* Stanford: Stanford University Press, 1996.

Suzuki Yukio. "Hon'yaku." In *Tsubouchi Shōyō jiten,* ed. Shōyō Kyōkai, 342–343. Tokyo: Heibonsha, 1985.

Taguchi Keiko et al., eds. *Yosano Akiko: [Shin Bungei Tokuhon].* Tokyo: Kawade Shobō Shinsha, 1991.

Takara, Ben. *Okinawa seikatsushi.* Tokyo: Iwanami Shinsho, 2005.

Taketomo Takako. "Yosano Akiko to Izumi Shikibu." *Yosano Akiko kenkyū* 86 (March 1990): 3–19.

Taki, Hiromi. "Grief at the Loss of My Breasts: On the Tanka of Nakajō Fumiko (1922–1954)." *Journal of the Oriental Society of Australia* 22–23, no. 1 (1990–1991): 156–169.

Tanaka Junji. "Shoki *Araragi* shaseisetsu." In *Ronshū Myōjō to Araragi,* ed. Waka bungaku kai, 121–139. Tokyo: Kasama Shoin, 1983.

Tanaka Reigi. "'Murasaki shōji' no seiritsu katei." In *Ronshū Taishōki no Izumi Kyōka,* ed. Izumi Kyōka Kenkyūkai, 128–148. Tokyo: Ōfūsha, 1999.

Tanaka Yutaka, and Akase Shingo, eds. *Shinkokinwakashū.* In *Shin Nihon koten bungaku taikei.* Vol. 11. Tokyo: Iwanami Shoten, 1992.

Tanizaki, Jun'ichirō. *Bunshō tokuhon.* Tokyo: Ōbunsha Bunko, 1970, rpt. 1980.

———. *The Makioka Sisters.* Trans. Edward G. Seidensticker. Tokyo: Charles E. Tuttle, 1973.

———. *Naomi.* Trans. Anthony H. Chambers. New York: Alfred A. Knopf, 1985.

———. *Sasameyuki.* In *Gendai Nihon Bungaku Taikei.* Vol. 31. Tokyo: Chikuma Shobō, 1970.

———. *Seven Japanese Tales.* Trans. Howard Hibbett. New York: Vintage Books, 1991.

———. *Tanizaki Jun'ichirō zenshū.* 28 vols. Tokyo: Chūō Kōronsha, 1966–1967.

Tawara Machi. *Salad Anniversary.* Trans. Jack Stamm. Tokyo: Kawade Shobō shinsha, 1988.

Teramoto Yoshinori, and Matsuura Takeshi, eds. *Kindai shōsetsu no hyōgen* 3. Tokyo: Kyōiku Shuppan Sentā, 1989.

Teruoka Yasutaka, and Kawashima Tsuyu, eds. *Buson shū Issa shū*. Tokyo: Iwanami Shoten, 1959.

Thompson, G. R. *The Gothic Imagination: Essays in Dark Romanticism*. Pullman, WA: Washington State University Press, 1974.

Tōgo Katsumi, ed. *Izumi Kyōka: Bi to gensō*. Vol. 12. Tokyo: Yuseidō, 1991.

Tomasi, Massimiliano. "Quest for a New Written Language: Western Rhetoric and the Genbun Itchi Movement." *Monumenta Nipponica* 54, no. 3 (1999): 333–361.

———. *Rhetoric in Modern Japan: Western Influences on the Development of Narrative and Oratorical Style*. Honolulu: University of Hawai'i Press, 2004.

Tsubouchi Shikō. *Tsubouchi Shōyō kenkyū*. Tokyo: Nihon Tosho Sentā, 1992.

Tsubouchi Shōyō, trans. *Shaō zenshū: Shōyō yaku Shēkusubiya zenshū*. Vol. 5. Tokyo: Meicho Fukyūkai, 1989.

———, trans. *Shēkusupia zenshū*. Tokyo: Shinjusha, 1957.

———. *Shōyō senshū*. Ed. Shōyō Kyōkai. 15 vols. Tokyo: Daiichishobō, 1977–1978.

Tsubouchi Toshinori. "Tanshikeibungaku no tenkai." In *Nihon bungakushi: 20 seiki no bungaku 2*, ed. Kubota Jun et al., 25–49. Vol. 13. Tokyo: Iwanami shoten, 1996.

Tsuruta Kinya. *The Walls Within: Images of Westerners in Japan and Images of the Japanese Abroad*. Vancouver: The Institute of Asian Research, University of British Columbia, 1989.

Twine, Nanette. *Language and the Modern State: The Reform of Written Japanese*. London: Routledge, 1991.

Ueda Hiroshi, and Tomimura Shunzō, eds. *Yosano Akiko wo manabu hito no tame ni*. Kyoto: Sekai Shisōsha, 1995.

Uesugi Yoshikazu. *Arishima Takeo: Hito to sono shōsetsu sekai*. Tokyo: Meiji Shoin, 1985.

Venuti, Lawrence, ed. *The Translation Studies Reader*. 2d. ed. London: Routledge, 2004.

———. *The Translator's Invisibility: A History of Translation*. London: Routledge, 1995.

Watanabe Sumiko. "Shōsetsu." In *[Hajimete manabu] Nihon josei bungakushi: Kingendai hen*, eds. Iwabuchi Hiroko and Kidate Sachie, 53–68. Tokyo: Minerva Shobō, 2005.

————. *Yosano Akiko*. Tokyo: Shintensha, 1998.

Warner, Marina. *No Go the Bogeyman: Scaring, Lulling and Making Mock*. London: Vintage, 2000.

White, R. S. "Shakespeare Criticism in the Twentieth Century." In *The Cambridge Companion to Shakespeare,* eds. Grazia de Margreta and Stanley Wells, 290–291. Cambridge: Cambridge University Press, 2001.

Wilkinson, Robert, ed. *New Essays in Comparative Aesthetics*. Newcastle: Cambridge Scholars Publishing, 2007.

Yamamoto Chie. *Yama no ugoku hi kitaru: Hyōden Yosano Akiko*. Tokyo: Ōtsuki Shoten, 1986.

Yamamoto Masahide. *Kindai buntai hassei no shiteki kenkyū*. Tokyo: Iwanami Shoten, 1965.

Yamanokuchi, Baku. "Yoriai setai no shima." In *Yamanokuchi Baku Okinawa zuihitsu shū,* 189–199. Tokyo: Heibonsha Library, 2004.

Yanagita Kunio. *Yanagita Kunio zenshū*. Vol. 1. Tokyo: Chikuma Shobō [Bunko], 1994.

Yano Hōjin. *Tekka Akiko to sono jidai* (shinsōhan). Tokyo: Yayoi Shobō, 1988.

————, ed. *Doi Bansui, Kambara Ariake, Susukida Kyūkin shū*. Tokyo: Chikuma Shobō, 1977.

Yasuda, Yasuo, ed. *Meiji Taishō yaku shishū*. Tokyo: Kadokawa Shoten, 1971.

Yasukawa Sadao. *Arishima Takeo ron*. Tokyo: Meiji Shoin, 1967.

Yasukawa Yukiko, ed. *Midaregami* [Yosano Akiko]. Tokyo: Kadokawa Bunko, 1956, rpt. 1993.

Yasumori Toshitaka. "*Midaregami* no sekai." In *Yosano Akiko wo manabu hito no tame ni,* eds. Ueda Hiroshi and Tomimura Shunzō, 78–96. Kyoto: Sekai Shisōsha, 1995.

Yoda Tomiko. *Gender and National Literature: Heian Texts in the Construction of Japanese Modernity*. Durham, NC: Duke University Press, 2004.

Yoneda Toshiaki. "Akiko: Kotoba ga kōkyō wo kaeru." *Nihon Bungaku* 30, no. 1 (1981): 44–57.

Yosano Akiko. *Gendai nihon shijin zenshū [Zenshishū taisei]*. Jōkan. Tokyo: Sōgensha, 1954.

————. *River of Stars: Selected Poems of Yosano Akiko*. Trans. Sam Hamill and Keiko Matsui Gibson. Boston: Shambhala, 1996.

————. *Tangled Hair*. Trans. Sanford Goldstein and Seishi Shinoda. Lafayette: Purdue University Press, 1971.

————. *Tangled Hair*. Trans. Shio Sakanishi. Boston: Marshall Jones, 1935.

————. *Teihon Yosano Akiko zenshū*. 20 vols. Ed. Kimata Osamu. Tokyo: Kōdansha, 1979–1981.

————. *Tekkan Akiko zenshū*. Vol. 2. Ed. Itsumi Kumi. Tokyo: Bensei Shuppan, 2002.

————. *Tekkan Akiko zenshū*. Vol. 6. Ed. Itsumi Kumi. Tokyo: Bensei Shuppan, 2002.

————. *Travels in Manchuria and Mongolia: A Feminist Poet from Japan Encounters Prewar China*. Trans. Joshua A. Fogel. New York: Columbia University Press, 2001.

Yosano Tekkan. "Yosano Hiroshi shū." In *Kindai tanka shū,* eds. Shinma Shin'ichi et al., 46–79. Tokyo: Kadokawa Shoten, 1973.

Yoshida Masashi. "Izumi Kyōka to kusazōshi." In *[Nihon bungaku kenkyū sōsho shinshū] Izumi Kyōka: Bi to gensō,* vol. 12, ed. Tōgo Katsumi, 172–186. Tokyo: Yuseidō, 1991.

Yoshida Seiichi. *Nagai Kafū.* Tokyo: Shinchōsha, 1971.

————. *Yoshida Seiichi chosakushū: Tanbi-ha sakka ron.* Vol. 10. Tokyo: Ōfūsha, 1981.

Yoshimoto Takaaki. *[Teihon] Gengo ni totte bi to wa nanika.* Vol. 1. Tokyo: Kadokawa Shoten, 1990.

————. *Yoshimoto Takaaki zen chosakushū.* Vol. 1. Tokyo: Keisei Shobō, 1982.

Yoshino Sakuzō, ed. *Meiji bunka zenshū.* Vol. 14. Tokyo: Nihon Hyōronsha, 1927.

Zhang Longxi. *Unexpected Affinities: Reading across Cultures.* Toronto: University of Toronto Press, 2007.

Zwicker, Jonathon E. *Practices of the Sentimental Imagination: Melodrama, the Novel and the Social Imaginary in Nineteenth Century Japan.* Cambridge, MA: Harvard University Asia Center, 2006.

INDEX

Aborigines, 191–192, 195
Ackroyd, Peter, 183–184
aesthetics: of Arishima Takeo, 134; decadence in Japanese literature and, 98–99; the interpretation of literature and, 74–75, 181; Japanese Naturalism and, 92, 96; Orientalism and, 114; of Sigmund Freud, 201; of Tanizaki Jun'ichirō, 119; Tsubouchi Shōyō on, 15, 32; Yosano Akiko's poetry and, 49, 84
Akiko, Baba, 56, 88–90
alien (the): Arishima Takeo and, 126–128; Izumi Kyōka and, 112; as literary subject, 201–202; meaning of, 1–9; motherhood and, 73–74; Okinawa as, 140–141, 157, 177; Ōshiro Tatsuhirō and, 204–205; Shakespeare as, 11–12, 19; Tanizaki Jun'ichirō and, 119, 124–125; translation and, 16–20, 27, 32–33, 42; Yosano Akiko's naturalization of, 44, 60, 72; in Yosano Akiko's poetry, 84, 92, 94–96
alterity, 12, 18, 20
Amaterasu Ōmikami, 151, 172
America, 119; Murakami Haruki and, 184–186, 188, 194, 197; Okinawa and, 7, 141–142, 149, 158, 162; Ōshiro Tatsuhiro and, 142, 149
anti-Naturalist, 107, 127
Apter, Emily, 42
Araragi, 93–94
Arishima Takeo: *Aru onna* (A certain woman), 128, 131; "Gasu" (Fog), 136–138; *Ishi ni hishigareta zassō* (The weed crushed by the stone), 131, 136; *Jikkenshitsu* (The laboratory), 131, 136, 223n.27; *Kain no matsuei* (Descendant of Cain), 128, 138; *Kankan mushi* (Rust-chippers), 132–134, 136; "Un-Japanese style" and, 127–129. *See also* aesthetics; alien (the); death; demons; exotic (the); gothic; melodrama; realism; Romanticism; self (the)
Art Nouveau, 56, 67–68
Aston, W. G., 47
Atlanta, 179, 188
Atsuko Sakaki, 4, 182
Australia, 8, 179, 184, 187, 189–200, 205. *See also* Murakami Haruki
Ayame Dayū, 119–125

bakemono. See monsters
Benjamin, Walter, 13

ABOUT THE AUTHOR

Leith Morton received a Ph.D. in Japanese from the University of Sydney in 1983. Over the past thirty years he has been a visiting researcher and lecturer at universities in Australia, Japan, the United States, Poland, Germany, Britain, and Canada. He was formerly senior lecturer in Japanese at the University of Sydney and foundation professor of Japanese at the University of Newcastle. He is now a professor at the Tokyo Institute of Technology.

Morton is the author of six books of poetry, including *a day at the races* (2003), *At the Hotel Zudabollo* (2004), and *Tokyo: A Poem in Four Chapters* (2006). His primary research interests are modern Japanese literature and culture, and he has published numerous books and translations, including *Modern Japanese Culture: The Insider View* (2003) and *Modernism in Practice: An Introduction to Postwar Japanese Poetry* (2004).

Production Notes for **Morton / The Alien Within**

Designed by the University of Hawai'i Press Production Department
with Minion text and display in Agenda

Composition by Josie Herr

Printed on 55# Glat. Offset B18, 360 ppi